DISCARD

The
CHURCH

Born in Indiana and educated at Elmhurst College in Illinois and at Eden Theological Seminary in Missouri, CARL J. SCHERZER has served several pastorates in the Midwest. Since 1944 he has been chaplain of the Protestant Deaconess Hospital in Evansville, Indiana, where he is also an instructor in the School of Nursing.

In addition to his work as chaplain and instructor, Mr. Scherzer is secretary of the Chaplains' Association of the American Protestant Hospital Association; secretary of the Commission on Benevolent Institutions of the Evangelical and Reformed Church; and a member of the Department of Pastoral Services of the Federal Council of the Churches of Christ in America.

The
CHURCH
and HEALING

CARL J. SCHERZER

Chaplain of the Protestant Deaconess Hospital
Evansville, Indiana

Philadelphia
THE WESTMINSTER PRESS

Lovingly dedicated
to
Virginia
and our
Joy and Gretchen

PREFACE

This is a book that has long needed to be written. Carl Scherzer has done an excellent job in collecting and presenting his material. In this book we gain a perspective of the vital subject of the Church and healing which should help us to take significant steps forward in reclaiming that part of the gospel upon which the contemporary Church has defaulted. This study was necessary before we could gain the perspective we needed, for the field of health and healing is a complicated one, and it is no easy task to think one's way through the confusion.

According to New Testament scholars, Jesus gave approximately one third of his time during the period of his preaching and teaching to a ministry to individuals. When the healing miracles are examined carefully, the reader discovers that each miracle illustrates or illumines some principle, some understanding of life and of God, over and beyond the miracle itself. Some scholars emphasize this fact a great deal in their study of the miracles. Regardless of whether Jesus or his disciples made miracles point beyond themselves as a considered practice or not, the fact remains that Jesus gave a great amount of attention to the healing of both body and mind. He not only considered health important, but he demonstrated both healing and health. Instances are related of his being tired and discouraged and sad and even angry, and all these conditions underlie and contribute to illness; but there is no instance reported in the Gospels of his ever being sick. Repeatedly modern psychiatry has made a great

7

point of an insight only to discover that Jesus had both taught and demonstrated it while his followers had lost sight of its implications for health. This fact has led one psychiatrist of my acquaintance to observe that " the Bible is the greatest textbook upon psychiatry in the world."

As Carl Scherzer has so ably pointed out in the following chapters, the Church has followed the example of our Lord in its concern with healing. Naturally this interest and the resulting contributions have fluctuated, at times being quite strong, at times having little significance at all. The modern and contemporary scene, naturally, interests us most of all. In fact, the reason for this book is to answer partially the questions, *What is the role of healing in the contemporary Church?* and *What is the contribution of the contemporary Church to healing?* These questions could not be answered without the support of a perspective from a historic point of view.

After reading this book, we should have no doubt in our minds about the tradition of healing in which we stand, nor concerning the contribution that the Church can and may make to health and healing. Only the question of *how* remains. The fact also remains that the Church *has not* and *is not* making its legitimate contribution to health and healing at present. For the past few years I have been saying that the Church has defaulted upon a third of the gospel. The figure does not run so high as that at present, because of the growing consciousness of and the interest now being shown toward the whole subject of health, but we are only upon the edge of the attention that must be given to it if it is to have the place our Lord seems to have intended that it should have.

More attention now is being given this subject by the clergy of the old established branches of the Church in any one month than was given during a ten-year period earlier in the century. When I graduated from a leading theological seminary in 1933, I had received only a two-hour lecture upon the specific task of ministry to the sick, and I could not refer to a single book or article upon the subject. More material, both articles and books, was published in any month during 1949 than was published during the last fifty years of the nineteenth century and the first twenty-five of the twentieth. Yet those were the years when medicine was moving into the scientific period, when the doctor was beginning to study and treat disease and moving toward the great discoveries in medicine that were to add twenty to thirty years to the length of every person's life in the United States. These also were the years that marked the rise of the healing sects in America. The doctor on the one side had become interested in disease and increasingly had overlooked the person whom the disease had. On the other hand the established Protestant Churches, beyond their interest in conversion, gave little or no attention to the individual — seemingly with the single exception of the work of Elwood Worcester, which was rejected (see chapter on " The Emmanuel Movement "). We had emphasized the doctrine of " the priesthood of all believers " so strongly that we overlooked the fact that many cannot be priests and that all sooner or later need to be ministered unto.

We have made considerable progress since World War I, as Mr. Scherzer points out, but we have only begun. The Church is not carrying its load; and with the possibility of some kind of socialized medicine upon the horizon, under which the medical profession would become even more mechanized in its care of the patient, and with a variety of healers running hither and yon making all kinds of ridiculous claims and following all kinds of bizarre practices, it is time that the established Churches take the responsibility of health and healing seriously. It is not enough to build great hospitals and turn them over to the medical profession to run as it sees fit. And I would be the first to argue that the doctor is a religious person; he may not always be a Christian by doctrinal standards, but he is religious. He knows

and trusts *the Force that makes for health,* which most call
nature, but which some call God.

What is the Churches' contribution to health and healing?
Mr. Scherzer is careful in his closing chapter not to commit
himself as a prophet. He is a wise man. I do not write as a
prophet, but as an optimist. I do not know whether we shall
be wise enough, nor whether we shall be able to command
the devotion, talent, and courage that can meet the challenge the Church faces. There are many signs that we shall.
The needs are present in our people; it has been said that a
third of the nation's population is sick in one way or another. There is a receptivity on the part of our people; the
purchase of the " peace of mind " books is an indication of
the need. Also, there is a receptivity and eagerness on the
part of the leaders of the Church; and, further, there is an
attitude of friendliness on the part of large numbers of the
allied professions.

Specifically, as I review the story that Mr. Scherzer has
told, I believe the contribution of the Church lies in the following areas:

First, the Church can work in the field of prevention. This
is both at the point of instruction of children and with parents concerning children. It is in the area of prevention that
mental hygiene and psychiatry have been most active, but at
the same time they have shown an amazing naïveté concerning the fact that they are teaching the Church its own lesson,
namely, *love.*

Secondly, the Church can teach people about themselves,
and how the strong destructive emotions of anger, hostility,
fear, anxiety, resentment, and frustration help to bring about
illness. It can describe the replacement of these feelings with
the more positive emotions of confidence, hope, friendliness,
affection, love — emotions that can best be understood in
terms of religion.

Thirdly — and this is more difficult to describe because
here we have been afraid and have either done nothing or

have lost our perspective — the Church can carry on treatment. It is when we talk about treatment that the physician and many clergymen become alarmed. Likewise they become alarmed when we talk about faith healing. If what we must do can be understood only in terms of " treatment " and " faith healing," then we must use them; and we should recognize in the light of this book that we are hardly being original. To say that the medical profession is now doing all that needs to be done is simply not to understand how health is gained; it is doing a part of what the Church has done in the past, but it is not doing and cannot do what the Church can do. Although many doctors have real religious sensibilities, medical science, as such, has no philosophy concerning the ultimate meaning of life. If the medical profession ever claims ability to do what the Church can do, the forces of religion should become alarmed, because the doctor in his medical training receives less instruction concerning spiritual aspects of life than I received in ministry to the sick during my seminary training — a total of two hours!

By the Church carrying on faith healing, I mean that special formal services should be held for the purpose of releasing the great healing emotions. These services can be both preventive and curative. I have said repeatedly that the disease of this generation is emotional tension. Unless negative emotional feelings can be relieved they lead inevitably to either mental or physical illness and often to both. The general practitioner tells us that between fifty and seventy-five per cent of all the people who come to him have no organic disease. That is another way of saying that at the time these people seek the doctor's help they have only emotional troubles; but if these tensions are not relieved, and the average doctor has neither the time, the equipment, nor the ritual to help such people, they eventually become sick with specific diseases. Much of the elaborate equipment and technique of modern medicine deals with diagnosis, for sound treatment rests upon diagnosis; but equipment and technique cannot meet the emotional and spiritual needs of people.

I have referred to the healing emotions. These are needed in instances of both physical and mental illnesses. The person facing a surgical operation needs the strength that comes from confidence; the person who has an ulcer of the gastro-intestinal tract needs hope and an optimistic attitude; and so on. These are attitudes with which the Church deals. In fact, it seems difficult if not impossible to achieve them outside the Church.

Finally, the Church can make a unique contribution through the practice of pastoral care, of which counseling is a part. This is the art of helping a person to understand himself through talking to another, one who stands free from the confusion, the pain, the frustration. It is here that the Church and the medical profession, particularly psychiatry, join hands; but as yet only limited progress has been made in co-operation between psychiatry and the ministry. Psychiatry has been so busy carrying on its research and establishing itself as a specialty within its own profession that it has given little attention to others who work with individuals. But sooner or later lines of co-operation must be established. The Church needs psychiatry; and if psychiatry is to get out of the mental hospital and make its legitimate contribution in the open areas of culture, it must have the support of the Church and the co-operation of the clergy.

The clergyman, in my opinion, is the most influential single individual in the community in shaping culture and human behavior. The fact that he is often shortsighted and fails in his task does not invalidate this statement. He has the words of eternal life and hope: " Lord, to whom else can we go? "

RUSSELL L. DICKS

Duke University, 1950

CONTENTS

Preface 7

Foreword 15

Part I

OUR TRADITION

I The Background of Healing 21
II The Period of the Ancient Church 31
III The Medieval Period 48

Part II

THE REFORMATION AND POST-REFORMATION PERIODS

IV The Reformation 63
V The Counter Reformation 77
VI Religion and Healing in England 87
VII Healing and Compassion 101

Part III

THE MODERN PERIOD

VIII Nursing Orders and Church Hospitals 115
IX Healing by Faith and by Medicine 135
X Christian Science 147
XI New Thought and Unity 160
XII The Emmanuel Movement 169

XIII	Medical Missions	185
XIV	Some Modern Healers	196
XV	Healing Sects and Individuals	206

Part IV

LOOKING AHEAD

XVI	The Commission on Religion and Health	219
XVII	Chaplaincy Programs in Hospitals	229
XVIII	Looking Ahead	249
	Bibliography	257
	Notes	266
	Index	270

FOREWORD

One day, after a class in psychology, a few of the student nurses stayed to talk a little more about the discussion we had in the class a few moments previously. One of them, out of the clear sky, asked, " Chaplain, why does the Church have hospitals? " I tried to answer the question briefly by saying, "Because Jesus was interested in healing people." While this served as a brief answer, it certainly did not tell the whole story. After I had given considerable thought to Jesus' concern for healing, a letter came from Dr. Russell L. Dicks in which he wrote, " We need a study of the Church and healing." With my previous interest in the spiritual welfare of the sick, this stimulus was sufficient to motivate me to undertake this study.

When I began writing, I little realized the tremendous amount of research that would be necessary to visualize and to understand the healing mission of the Church. Through the centuries since the time of Christ many attempts have been and are being made to recapture the healing power of the Lord. There is a tremendous amount of literature extant on the subject, so much that the problem was not in finding it but rather in choosing what is important enough to be included in this story.

The Church and individuals who profess to follow Christ outside the Church have made a great contribution to the alleviation of suffering. Those who are intimately associated with many sick people are keenly aware of the fact that the healing spirit of Jesus is manifested today by consecrated people who have dedicated their lives to the healing ministry

15

both in medical and Church vocations. There is a growing understanding of how God works in and through individuals to accomplish his healing purposes. As the years pass and Christ becomes better understood, his eternal spiritual principles will be increasingly applied.

Many instances of healing are presented here as they were reported in their time. The attempt is made to report such cases in an unbiased manner and permit the reader to evaluate them as he wishes. In other instances, especially when dealing with current spiritual healing, the attempt is made to analyze and evaluate.

Words of appreciation are to be expressed first of all to Dr. Russell L. Dicks, who read this manuscript and offered invaluable guidance and counsel from his rich experience and deep insight, and to Dr. Ray Petry, Professor of Church History at the Divinity School of Duke University, for valuable suggestions.

Miss Evah Ostrander, librarian of the Hammond Library of the Chicago Theological Seminary, and her assistant, Mrs. Alice S. Boyack, were tremendously helpful, sometimes in finding the almost unfindable. Appreciation is also expressed to the librarians at Evansville libraries and the Evansville College Library and the Reverend Dr. Armin Haeussler.

A number of Roman Catholic priests and Sisters lent books and pamphlets and were helpful in interpreting the story of the Roman Catholic Church in its ministry of healing; their kindness is deeply appreciated.

Local physicians and pharmacists gave access to their libraries, especially Dr. Herman Baker and Mr. Edward Wolfgang, to whom appreciation is expressed. Dr. Albert G. Hahn, the Executive Director of the American Protestant Hospital Association, Mrs. Hahn, and Mrs. Karl Weber supplied many facts, and Sister Lina Appel and Sister Sophia Bartelt supplied books and pamphlets about the diaconate that were informative. Dr. E. M. McKown, Dean of Evansville College, was kind enough to go over portions of the manuscript with me and to offer suggestions that were helpful.

For a story as inclusive as this it was necessary to use information compiled by many scholars now living and by those of the past. An attempt is made to give due credit in each instance of direct reference, and other credit is given through the bibliography.

The purpose of this book is to present a readable, comprehensive study of the influence of our Lord's Spirit as it expressed itself in a ministry of healing through his Church, and to show that his spirit of compassion for the sick and suffering is living in the world today.

— CARL J. SCHERZER

Protestant Deaconess Hospital
Evansville, Indiana

Part 1

◆

OUR TRADITION

I. THE BACKGROUND OF HEALING

A woman became very ill on a train; when it arrived at the depot she was placed in an ambulance and rushed to a hospital. Attendants were on duty in the emergency room to receive her upon arrival. A house physician made an examination and ordered her to bed. She requested a private room; and since there was one available, she was soon there. The house doctor summoned the surgeon who was on call, and, after a thorough examination, he decided that an operation was necessary. It was an emergency.

This woman was in a strange city and among people she did not know, placing her life in the hands of people whom she had never seen before. The hospital accepted her upon arrival, although the attendants had never heard of her and knew nothing about her personal life or responsibility. That made no difference. She was placed in a room, given nursing care, the best medical and surgical attention available, and the use of the surgery, the laboratory, and the X-ray departments. All this and much more, including food, laundry, light, and heat, were placed at the disposal of the woman whose life was in jeopardy.

The house doctor informed the chaplain of her presence while he was waiting for the surgeon to arrive, so the chaplain visited with her before she went to the operating room and tried to assure her that she was with people who were friendly and capable. She asked him to call a friend in a distant city and tell him what had happened. This the chaplain promised to do, and did as soon as the surgeon had made his examination and decided to operate. She had no relatives; at least she did not ask the chaplain to inform any. After her medical preparation and a prayer she went to surgery. The next day some beautiful flowers came from her friend, but there were no visits other than those of the chaplain. In conversations held almost every day she told him the story of her life, which had known its share of loneliness and disappointments.

After she had recovered sufficiently to return home, the hospital attendants bade her adieu and wished her well. She said that she really hated to leave; and soon after arriving at her destination she sent the chaplain a letter of appreciation in which she wrote: "I was indeed sorry to leave the hospital, but with me go the best thoughts of the hospital and more and greater respect for the ministerial and medical professions. Medicine and religion go hand in hand, there is no doubt."

It was thoughtful on her part to write that letter. It is interesting also to report that later she wrote again to say she was attending a church and had become acquainted with the minister. All this happened because a woman became seriously ill on a train and was taken to a Church-related hospital. The physician, the surgeon, the nurses, and the personnel of the institution came to her aid because one time, years ago, some Christian people decided to have a Church-related hospital in that city. When she left the institution, she had received spiritual help as well as physical aid.

PRE-CHRISTIAN INFLUENCES

Medicine and religion have gone " hand in hand " more or less since the dawn of history. The story of medicine really had its origin with primitive man. Beliefs always play an important role in scientific development, and they played an important part in the progress of the healing arts also. In some respects beliefs hindered the advancement of medicine and surgery, and then again other beliefs encouraged certain people to take progressive steps. For instance, in ancient days the medicine man treated disease by dealing with spirits and ghosts; and then with the advent of Christianity some who were activated by the spirit of Jesus reached out beyond these sham battles with disease and ventured into the field of humanitarian relief of suffering. While certain beliefs retarded, others promoted the healing arts.

Healing and religion were conceived as identical by the ancient Greeks and Romans. Their temples were used as places where sacrifices could be brought to assuage the anger of a god or gain his favor so that health might be restored. Apollo was supposed to have passed on to the son of Cronus, the centaur Chiron, his knowledge of healing. He, in turn, educated Hercules, Achilles, and especially Aesculapius, who became the great healing god of Greece. Legends attribute most of the latter's cures to magic, and say that he even threatened to depopulate Hades and bring the residents back to earth. One of the best-known of his children was the daughter Hygieia, whose name is used in medicine today. She became the Greek goddess of health. Panakeia was the goddess of the healing powers found in herbs. A panacea is still defined as a remedy for almost any disease.

But there were some conditions, such as wounds or cuts, that were so real and obvious that they could hardly be treated by magic alone. So they were treated in a more practical, although unsanitary, way. Even though they were regarded as the result of malign influences of a god, still they could be treated with wine or oil or a concoction made of herbs. The pagan temples were the places of healing. They were not hospitals where patients stayed, but were places where people simply went to be treated and healed. The crowd usually waited until toward the close of the day to see a written list of the cures the god had accomplished that day; of course, nothing was said about those who were not cured.

The ancient priests used an interesting psychological approach to the patient. A priest of Aesculapius would rate as an excellent showman today. As the people waited for the treatment, he assured them they would be healed and showed them evidence to prove his contention. They were conducted or carried individually or in small groups on a tour of the temple, and the priest in charge told about the marvelous cures and explained the meaning of the tablets and symbols that covered the walls. He impressed the holiness of the place upon them through his manner of speaking and his attitude of reverence. All this convinced the patient that he certainly would be healed. As a matter of fact, just his presence in this holy place made him feel better. Then a list of the cures effected that day were read to him, and he was ready to be healed.

Toward the close of the day the patient was dressed in a white robe and directed to a couch in the temple. He was told that he could rest there through the night, and he could sleep reassured that his worries were about over. Then the priests offered solemn prayers to the gods and the lights were extinguished. There was silence and he could lie there quietly thinking about Aesculapius and his healing daughter Hygieia. Soon he was asleep, and the god and goddess appeared to him in his dreams and helped him.

It seemed like only a moment when he awoke and the dim light of dawn came into the temple. A priest was there by his couch, and the priest fondled a snake while a dog wagged its tail in a friendly manner. The snake crawled over the bed, the dog licked his hand as he patted its head. The priest spoke to him reassuringly and told him what medicines to take and the patient arose. He was cured!

He could walk now. How good is the god Aesculapius and his healing daughter! He was overcome with joy and told the priest to report his cure that day. In gratitude he would leave an offering, perhaps money or perhaps a little statue of metal or clay on which the priest could mark where the pain had been before the cure. This would help to convince others. How he talked about his experience once he arrived at his home again! And his friends told others. The temple of Aesculapius was verily a wonderful place for healing.

This is a description of the way healing was done. As time went on, a code of ethics was evolved, and the young man who wanted to be a physician promised to be honorable, not to use poisons except to cure, and not to divulge any confidences. He also promised to pass on to his colleagues any new treatment he might find and not keep it secret for purposes of exploitation.

The Greeks excelled in the healing arts in the Western civilization. The physician was a thinker as well as a healer. Hippocrates developed the method of examining a sick person to determine the cause of his illness. He accumulated facts about these causes. During their conquests the Greeks also assimilated what scientific knowledge they could get from conquered peoples. They learned something about anatomy and discovered nerves in the body. Then they in turn were dominated by the Romans politically, but in that position they brought their culture to Rome. At about the time Jesus was born there was already a " hospital " on an island in the Tiber River near Rome. It was used as a place to expose ill and overworked slaves. If the slave recovered, he did not have to return to his master. The island was soon used by many poor people. However, other hospitals were built, primarily for the use of Roman soldiers. There were no charity hospitals, because the Romans did not feel themselves obligated to take care of anyone who could not pay his way. It was after the influence of the spirit of Jesus spread in Western civilization and became a motivating force in many lives that a deep concern for the physical and spiritual welfare of the poor and the sick became evident.

HEALING IN THE GOSPELS

Luke, one of the early converts to Christianity, is called a physician in the Scripture (Col. 4:14). His name indicates his Greek origin. Undoubtedly he was versed in the customs and practices of his profession. According to tradition, he practiced in Antioch and knew the Roman medical practices as well as the Greek customs. Luke was attracted to the Christian faith, and with other early followers of Jesus he manifested a great interest in sick people. He became a companion of Paul and later wrote one of the Gospels and The Acts of the Apostles. In The Acts he tells about the miracles that were wrought by the Holy Spirit and by the apostles and other disciples. As a physician he was also especially interested in our Lord's miracles of healing.

Jesus was very much concerned about the health of people. We know that to be true because he performed more miracles of healing than of any other category. In his healing ministry Jesus accepted the scientific knowledge that was prevalent in his day. He did not teach demonology, but he did seem to accept it, and he is believed to have worked on that basis. At Capernaum Jesus found a man who had a spirit of an unclean devil (Luke 4:33-37), and healed the man by causing the spirit to come out of him. Luke records the miracle; the belief in unclean spirits was acceptable to the physician. It was also believed that saliva had curative powers and physicians of that day used it as a medicine on wounds. Even the saliva of the dog had some curative powers and that accounts for the observation by Luke (Luke 16:21) that dogs licked the sores of Lazarus. When Jesus healed the blind man (Mark 8:22-26), he used saliva on his eyes in the healing process.

While Jesus accepted the scientific knowledge available in his time, he did not stop there. He recognized the importance of psychological and spiritual factors in sickness and health. He knew there was an interrelationship between all the factors of a total personality and in some instances psychological or spiritual factors contributed to or were the cause of the physical disorder. When the man who had palsy was let down through the roof because of the crowd into the presence of Jesus (Luke 5:18–26), our Lord recognized his spiritual state, that he had difficulty with a guilt anxiety, and said to him, "Man, thy sins are forgiven thee." In this approach Jesus was ahead of his day, and the intellectuals who were there to watch him criticized him for this approach.

On another occasion, when Jesus came near the pool of Bethesda (John 5:1–18) where sick people came or were brought to be healed by its waters, his attention was drawn to a man in whom he recognized two spiritual stresses. In the first place, he strengthened the man's desire to be healed, and when he was assured that the man really believed that he could get well again, the Lord healed him. It is worth noting, in the second place, that when Jesus met this healed man in the Temple later, he said to him, "Behold, thou art made whole: sin no more, lest a worse thing come unto thee."

A study of the life of Jesus reveals that he healed many people. A number of specific instances of healing are recorded in the Gospels, but in addition to these Luke relates that he healed many more (Luke 6:17). It is not necessary here to review all those instances. Many books have been written that analyze and study our Lord's healing ministry. It can be said that any Biblical scholar will agree that Jesus set the example for his followers in his concern for the sick. As a matter of fact, before he ascended into heaven he left three divine imperatives for his disciples to follow, namely: preach (Matt. 10:7), teach (Matt. 28:19, 20), heal (Matt. 10:1). He emphasized these imperatives by his own life to such an extent that there was no doubt in the disciples' minds that these were to constitute their mission.

Another attitude of Jesus that influenced his followers was his spirit of compassion. Love, mercy, and kindness all were a way of his life. These virtues influenced the Christians' attitude toward people who were poor, or oppressed, or underprivileged; and they also caused them to be concerned about the sick. Luke (Luke 10:17) is the first to mention that when the Seventy returned after their first venture in evangelism they reported to Jesus, " even the devils are subject unto us through thy name." Individual miracles of healing are recorded by Luke in The Acts. The stories of the lame man healed by Peter (Acts 3:1–11) at the gate of the Temple and the man named Æneas who was cured of the palsy also by Peter (Acts 9:32–35) are notable examples. Paul is credited with healing powers when the father of Publius and many other sick persons were cured (Acts 28:7–9). However, the Scripture does not imply that Peter or Paul used this power to heal in Jesus' name all the sick who were brought to them. As a matter of fact, Paul left Trophimus at Miletum while he was sick (II Tim. 4:20). On another occasion he wrote about Epaphroditus (Phil. 2:26, 27), who was recovering from a serious illness, but Paul does not say that he attempted to heal this friend.

While the ability to heal miraculously seems to have been confined to only a few of the early followers of Jesus, nevertheless it can safely be assumed that nearly all these Christians were interested in the care and cure of the sick, and such service became one of the functions of the diaconate. Those who did not possess the ability to heal miraculously could use their time and talents to cure otherwise and to care for the sick. In other words, all of them were motivated by compassion.

The diaconate in the very early Church had its origin in the ministry of help. Perhaps it should be explained what is meant by the " diaconate." The word comes from the Greek verb that means to serve, or to minister, or to help. The word " deacon " comes from it. Sometimes it is said in good humor, " We need deacons who deac." Etymologically, that isn't a bad expression; it means, " We need helpers or ministers who help or minister." This office originated at Jerusalem (Acts 6:2, 3) to give assistance to the apostles in rendering aid to the members of the congregation. The first helpers were men only. At this early state of development the preachers, teachers, and helpers were all men (I Cor. 12:28).

But it was not long until there were deaconesses also (Rom. 16: 1, 2). The first one mentioned as such is Phebe who was the deaconess of the church at Cenchrea. But even though she is the first one definitely called a deaconess, it may be said that the office was in existence when Jesus was living. Women disciples followed Jesus also and " ministered unto him of their substance " (Luke 8:3). These were deaconesses, if not in office, certainly in practice. Among them were Mary Magdalene, Joanna, Susanna, and Mary the mother of James, and Salome. Partaking of the spirit of Jesus, they were the originators of the office of the deaconess.

After the diaconate was established in the growing Church, it was not long until these holy women were recognized officially. There were also voluntary helpers such as Tryphena, Tryphosa, and Persis (Rom. 16:12). In the household of Stephanas (I Cor. 1:16; 16:15) also there were those women who voluntarily ministered to the needs of the saints. Another group of deaconesses is mentioned in the First Letter to Timothy (ch. 5:3-16). Pliny mentioned them in his letter to Trajan about A.D. 110 when he referred to " young women who are called ministrae," that is, " deaconesses." As the Church grew in numbers the orders of " helpers " made an ever greater contribution in the ministry to the sick which will be considered later.

This chapter covers the earliest years of the existence of the Christian Church. Since the primary interest of this book is in the Church and healing, any other phase of the development of Church organization, polity, or doctrine is purposely neglected. That course will be followed through the rest of this book except where any of these matters influence the healing mission of the Church. Suffice it to say now, the Church received its interest in the healing arts from Jesus. He not only healed the sick, but, more important, taught love, kindness, consideration, and other virtues which may be summed up in the word " compassion." This compassion in the lives of his followers impelled them to be interested in the sick and the suffering. Just as their Lord did what he could to relieve the sick, they too would help all in trouble.

II. THE PERIOD OF THE ANCIENT CHURCH

ANCIENT HEALING PRACTICES

Before taking up the study of the Early Church and heal-ing, we should become better acquainted with the means and practices of healing that were in vogue during the first four centuries of the Christian Era. In the section on " Pre-Christian Influences," we spoke of the myth of Aesculapius and the healing customs that grew out of it. Some of these customs influenced Christian practices.

In the fifth century before Christ, a Greek was born who influenced the development of the healing arts for many centuries. That man was Hippocrates, who is regarded as the father of the modern era in medicine. He is credited with dividing the sciences of philosophy and medicine so that in later centuries each should pursue its own course unham-pered by the other. He said that disease is due to natural causes, and sought to determine the causes so as to prevent the disease. From the philosophers he borrowed the idea that there are four elements in the universe: earth, air, fire, and water. From these there are four states of being: heat, mois-ture, dryness, and coldness. There are four fluid substances in the body: blood, phlegm, yellow bile, and black bile. When these four humors are in proper proportions, a person is in health; when they get out of proportion and a person has more than he needs of one or more, he is sick. The way to cure the sick person was to help him to restore the proper balance. Hippocrates was really the first physician who ac-tually examined the patient and tried to determine how a sick man was different from a healthy one.

Far more popular, however, among the masses of the people, were the physicians who used the old methods of their forefathers. They went to the shops of the rhizopodist or "root-cutter" for their herbs. A "root-cutter" was a man who gathered roots and herbs for medicinal purposes. The most popular remedy was the mandrake because, with a stretch of the imagination, a person can think it resembles a human body. It was supposed to scream when it was pulled from the ground, and it had to be pulled by a dog. A heavy string was tied around the mandrake and fastened to the dog. Then the master held his ears shut and called the dog; he was not supposed to hear the shriek. Even Shakespeare mentions the shriek of the mandrake (*Romeo and Juliet,* Act IV).

Another great influence in medical science of that day was Dioscorides, who was a surgeon in the army of Nero. He founded what is called *Materia Medica,* the materials of medicine, in which he classified some six hundred plants, herbs, roots, and plant products. About ninety of them are still in use in the practice of medicine.

The man of that period who influenced the Church in its relation to healing more than any other was the Roman writer Pliny, who lived at the time of the apostles; his works were acceptable to the Christians even though he was not a Christian himself. He believed that every plant and herb had some special medicinal value. For every disease there was a plant to cure it, and it was the physician's business to find the right plant. The Christians believed that everything on earth has a value or a purpose, so they accepted Pliny's philosophy and his works were in great favor among them. Later it will be seen how monks cultivated various plants and herbs for their medicinal values.

The last physician to be mentioned in this connection is Galen, who was born in Asia Minor about A.D. 130; after some experience there, he went to Alexandria in Egypt. This city was a great center of learning, but even there it was hard to find a human body for dissection. He must have seen human skeletons, and he did dissect hogs and apes and from this experience gained information about the internal organs. Some of his opinions, gained from that experience, were unfortunate, but, aside from that, he gained the reputation of being a great physician and surgeon. Galen became the authority on anatomy for more than a thousand years; and even sixteen hundred years later when Dr. William Harvey discovered how blood flows through the veins, many of Dr. Harvey's colleagues said that he was wrong because he contradicted Galen!

Galen's specific contribution to medicine is in the fact that he tried to bring system into medical knowledge. He wrote down and organized for future study what knowledge had been gained in the six hundred years since Hippocrates in understanding and treating disease. He also believed the humor theories and sought to prescribe the proper herbs to balance the humors. Thus if a person suffered a fever, he should be treated with a cold medicine, such as cucumber seeds. In fact, Galen classified the herbs and plants into the four classes — hot, cold, wet, and dry — and these were to be properly prescribed according to the ailment.

The foregoing gives a fleeting glimpse of the healing knowledge and practices of the apostolic and postapostolic years. These were the things experienced by Christians who saw the practices of pagan physicians and were treated by them. The Christians in their own way also used outward signs or materials which were believed to have healing power when administered by a bishop or his representatives or by any of the elders of the church. Just as our Lord accepted the scientific knowledge of his day, so did his followers, who worked with it also in his name.

CHRISTIAN HEALING PRACTICES

In the postapostolic period the ancient Church's attitude toward healing depended on the direction of the thought and the customs of the believers. The suspicion and hostility of the Roman authorities and pagan neighbors made life for the Christians very uncertain. It is easy to understand why some of them became very otherworldly. They thought of heaven as a place where uncertainty and suffering would end, and thus it became a place devoutly to be desired. While they were in the world, they were not of the world, and this apartness from the pagan society developed a communal loyalty and personal affection in which they found a measure of security. The Christian community was regarded as an approximation of the City of God which they anticipated.

Naturally, some went to ascetic extremes. Since they believed that the end of the world was near at hand or that the heavenly Jerusalem would soon come upon the earth, they felt that the physical needs of the individual could very well be denied. Strenuous asceticism also became a method of protest against what they considered to be a growing worldliness in the Church, especially after Christianity became legally recognized. Celibacy was regarded as a virtue by these Christians who fasted, abstained from meat, and found many other ways to deny the natural demands of the flesh. They felt that they must withdraw from active participation in the Church of which they were a minority group.

This trend in Christian thought and life contributed little to the healing arts. In certain histories of medicine these Christians are cited as an example of the manner in which the Church stood in the way of medical progress. But in any fair appraisal it will be found that this group was a small minority of the Christians in the ancient Church. There were other trends of thought and custom that did contribute to the healing arts beyond the credit they are usually given in medical histories.

One of these trends is found among those who continued the practices of our Lord and the early disciples, as well as the example of Paul and Peter. They continued to practice the observation of Mark (Mark 6:13), "And they cast out many devils, and anointed with oil many that were sick, and healed them." Luke also reports (Luke 9:6), "And they departed, and went through the towns, preaching the gospel, and healing every where." James (James 5:14, 15), the brother of the Lord, gives the specific directions: "Is any sick among you? let him call for the elders of the church; and let them pray over him, anointing him with oil in the name of the Lord: and the prayer of faith shall save the sick, and the Lord shall raise him up; and if he have committed sins, they shall be forgiven him."

The Acts of the Apostles (Acts 5: 15, 16) gives examples of the healing work of the disciples and tells how the people brought the sick to them, as they did to Jesus: "and them that were vexed with unclean spirits: and they were healed every one."

These practices carried over into the postapostolic period. The Early Church Fathers, such as Irenaeus (Irenaeus, *Against Heresies,* Book II, Chapter XXI), Justin Martyr, Tertullian, and Origen, refer to the Church as having the power to heal and to raise from the dead. Justin Martyr mentions among the gifts conferred upon the Christians that of healing, and says that it was practiced by many Christians. Origen (Origen, *Against Celsus,* Book III, Chapter XXIV), in writing about the healing power of Jesus' name, says that more cures were effected in that way than through the teachings of Aesculapius. Quadratus, who lived and wrote during the time of Hadrian, attests that the works of the Saviour were still in evidence. Those who were healed and raised from the dead were seen by many for a long time afterward; the cured lived out their normal life spans.

The most common healing practice of the Early Church was the use of oil. The Lord taught his disciples to use oil; Mark wrote, "And anointed with oil many that were sick, and healed them." James (James 5:13–15), the brother of the Lord, states the practice clearly and gives it as a command to the followers of Jesus. He specifically states that the patient should be anointed by the elders of the church and, as prayer is offered, the sick one will be saved and raised up. These instructions of Jesus and James led to a widespread use of oil in the healing among the Christians and the laying on of hands in the Early Church; later it became one of the Sacraments of the Church.

The use of oil was not at first restricted to the officials of the Church. The first mention that is found of its use after the passage in James is by the writer Tertullian in A.D. 211 (*Ad Scapulam* 4, Ante-Nicene Christian Library Translation). He used the healing arts of the Christians as an argument with the proconsul Scapula in influencing him to stop persecuting them. Tertullian named individuals who were cured by anointing.

A later writer, Saint Martin of Tours, about 395, tells of an incident that occurred when the consecrated oil was drunk by a patient. A dumb girl was brought to him by her father. The bishop after blessing a little oil and repeating a special formula, held the girl's tongue with his fingers, and poured the consecrated oil in her mouth. Then he asked her the name of her father, and she spoke it. At this, the father, who had watched the proceedings, cried out with joy and fell upon his knees before Martin and witnessed that this was the first time he had heard the voice of his daughter.

Oil was not the only medicament used by Christians in healing; water and bread were also consecrated for that purpose. Some of the extant consecrating prayers are attributed to Serapion, the bishop of Thmuis, who lived in Lower Egypt about the year 350. The Apostolic Constitutions contain a prayer of consecration that was widely used: " O Lord of hosts, the God of powers, the creator of the waters, and the supplier of oil, who art compassionate, and a lover of mankind, who hast given water for drink and for cleansing, and oil to give man a cheerful and joyful countenance; do Thou now also sanctify this water and this oil through Thy

Christ, in the name of him or her that has offered them, and grant them a power to restore health, to drive away diseases, to banish demons, and to disperse all snares through Christ our hope, with whom glory, honour and worship be to Thee, and to the Holy Ghost, for ever. Amen." (The Apostolic Constitutions, Book VIII, Section IV, Paragraph XXIX.)

Father Fuller, in his book, *Anointing of the Sick,* tells about the drinking of water that was blessed. The incident occurred in Upper Egypt, where Saint Theodore was the abbot. The father of a girl who was dying came to the monastery and begged the abbot to come to his house and pray over her. The abbot could not go at that time but offered to pray for the child. He explained to the father that God is everywhere and He would hear his prayers even if he were not with the child. This did not satisfy the father, and to reassure him the abbot gave him a silver cup which the man filled with water and asked the holy man to bless. This the abbot did, looking up to heaven and praying with tears in his eyes and then made the sign of the cross over the cup of water. The father hastened home with the water and opened the child's mouth far enough for her to swallow some of it. The girl immediately improved and completely recovered.

Many such stories of healing are extant from the post-apostolic days. In many instances medical and spiritual treatment were combined. Oil and water were used internally as well as externally. In fact, it seems that nearly all medicaments were used by Christians, with prayer, for the healing of the sick. There was no conflict with the physicians of that day. Sometimes, in cases of paralysis, the oil was used in massage, being first blessed, and while it was applied, prayer was offered for the sufferer much as the modern clergyman prays with a patient today.

Holy Communion also was used for healing purposes. The apostle Paul (I Cor. 11:29, 30) writes that those who receive the Lord's Supper unworthily are guilty of the body and blood of the Lord. Here Paul refers to irreverence or the excesses of the Corinthian church which he condemned. Because of this irreverence and excess the apostle says, " For this cause many are weak and sickly among you, and many sleep." From this it can be deducted that when the sacrament is received in faith and reverence it should have the effect of raising the vitality and strengthening the body and thus aid the process of healing. The sacrament of Communion is administered to the sick by the clergy today, primarily because of its spiritual value, but enough is known about spiritual things today to be certain that spiritual well-being has its influence on the physical body.

Surgery, as well as medicine, was used with prayer in the healing arts. Wax from the sanctuary lamps, dried figs, myrtle in wine, a piece of lemon, honey, salted quail, lentils, wine, green leaves, and other medicines were used also by the Church in its healing practices. Any recognized medicines could be used with prayer after they had been properly blessed.

The use of relics in healing also goes back to these early years of the Christian Church. As a matter of fact it goes back beyond that period. The Old Testament (II Kings 13:21) reports how a dead man was raised to life by contact with the bones of Elisha. But there was no widespread use of relics until New Testament times. The apostle Paul (Acts 19:12) permitted the use of his handkerchiefs and other pieces of his clothes to be carried away and used for healing purposes. The garment of Jesus was touched by a sick person, who was healed thereby.

There are precedents for the use of relics in the Scriptures, although the references to it are quite meager. The use of relics in the Early Church grew out of the idea that anything associated with a holy place, such as a church, or with a holy person becomes imbued with the same holy spirit. The first relics used by the Church in healing seem to have been oil or other materials from the places of worship. The saints were buried in the catacombs of Rome, where the Christians worshiped. Since the saints possessed the power to heal when they were alive, it was reasoned that their gift remained with them after death. For many centuries the bones of the buried saints were not moved, but the place where one rested was considered to be a holy place. A handkerchief that was used to touch the tomb became especially sacred, or even a piece of the earth near the burial place. Sometimes altars were built over the burial places of saints. It was not until later years that the bones of the saints were touched or moved in any way. The material possessions of the bishops and others who were especially holy were also regarded as having healing values. The practice of using them in healing was developed in a later period.

In this early period Christians became conscious of holy places or shrines. If the burial place of a saint was especially holy, it seemed reasonable to believe that it might also have a special blessing for the one who prayed there. There is no doubt that God can be worshiped anywhere, but worshipers have the feeling that he is worshiped more effectively in a church that is dedicated to him. This same feeling of reverence for holy things led the early Christians to believe that hallowed places were especially efficacious in healing. In later years the sick were brought to churches in order that they might have the benefit of sleeping in a sacred place. (Some Christians do that today: who can say that there is no healing value in a cat nap taken while the minister preaches!)

During the first three centuries Christianity was regarded with suspicion and hatred by the Roman authorities. Until the year 250, beginning with the reign of Nero, there were fierce sporadic, local persecutions. The suppression of Christianity was left largely to local authorities, and at certain times in various places the followers of Christ suffered greatly for their convictions; life for the Christian was uncertain, to say the least. It seems that this uncertainty challenged courageous people to join their ranks, and the number of the Christians continued to increase. Then Decius ascended the throne in A.D. 249 and the next year issued an edict that required all Christians without exception to perform the rites of the Roman religion. It was Decius' purpose to re-establish the glory of Rome, and to do it he felt that he had to stamp out the religion he regarded as an enemy of the State. Years of terrible persecution followed, but the Church finally emerged victoriously from the struggle with heathenism. In A.D. 312 Constantine, in the Edict of Milan, gave religious liberty to the Romans and decreed that henceforth everyone in the Empire would be at liberty to profess whatever religion he wished. Thereafter Christians could practice their religion with its ministries of compassion without fear or apology.

EARLY NURSING ORDERS

One of the trends in Christian thought and practice that made a great contribution in the field of healing was a continued interest in the diaconate. A good number of Christians felt an impelling compassion for the sick and suffering, and placed the emphasis upon helping and nursing the sick. Information about the diaconate is to be found in the Apostolic Constitutions.

The Apostolic Constitutions are a collection of laws and precepts of the Early Church. There is a difference of opinion among authorities as to the exact date of their origin; some favor the latter half of the third century and others place it a century later. The Constitutions contain the rules and precepts supposedly originating with the apostles themselves. Be that as it may, these writings are ancient and are important in this connection because they bring information about the orders of deaconesses and widows.

In Book III, Section II, according to the translation by Dr. Whiston, edited by Dr. James Donaldson, the bishop was instructed to ordain deaconesses: " Let not therefore either a bishop, or a presbyter, or a deacon, or any one else of the sacerdotal catalogue, defile his tongue with calumny, lest he inherit a curse instead of a blessing; and also let it be the bishop's business and care that no lay person utter any curse — for he ought to take care of all, — of the clergy, of the virgins, of the widows, of the laity. For which reason, O Bishop, do thou ordain thy fellow-workers, the laborers for life and for righteousness, such deacons as are pleasing to God, such whom thou provest to be worthy among the people, and such as shall be ready for the necessities of their ministration. Ordain also a deaconess who is faithful and holy, for the ministrations toward women. For sometimes he cannot send a deacon, who is a man, to the women, on account of unbelievers."

As to the duties of the deacons, Clement in his Epistle to James in Chapter XII said, " And let them learn who are suffering under bodily disease, and let them bring them to the notice of the multitude who do not know of them that they may visit them, and supply their wants according to the judgment of the president."

The deaconess was set aside for her office with an ordination service: " Concerning a deaconess, I, Bartholomew, make this Constitution: O Bishop, thou shalt lay thy hands upon her in the presence of the presbytery, and of the deacons and deaconesses, and shalt say: O Eternal God, the Father of our Lord Jesus Christ, the creator of man and of woman, who didst replenish with the Spirit Miriam and Deborah, and Anna, and Huldah; who didst not distain that Thy only begotten Son should be born of a woman; who also in the tabernacle of the testimony, and in the temple, didst ordain women to be keepers of Thy holy gates, do Thou now also look down upon this Thy servant, who is to be ordained to the office of deaconess, and grant her Thy Holy Spirit, and ' cleanse her from all filthiness of flesh and spirit ' that she may worthily discharge the work which is committed to her to Thy glory, and the praise of Thy Christ, with whom glory and adoration be to Thee and the Holy

Spirit forever. Amen " (Book VIII, Section III, of the Constitutions).

Deaconesses had charge of the ministry to the needs of the women and were assisted by an Order of Widows. The Constitutions stated the qualifications of a member of this order as follows: " But true widows are those which have had only one husband, having a good report among the generality for good works; widows indeed, sober, chaste, faithful, pious, who have brought up their children well, and have entertained strangers unblameably, which are to be supported as devoted to God " (Book III, Section L, Article III).

The earliest leaders of Christianity, Paul, Peter, and other missionaries, often found sanctuary in Christian homes. The Order of Widows is believed to have grown out of this practice and seems to have been divided into two groups, ecclesiastical widows and widows. A member did not necessarily have to be a real widow. It was a designation for those who offered themselves and their homes for the performance of all manner of Christian service, especially the care of the sick poor people.

Widows held a position inferior to the deaconesses and were directed by them in the ministrations to the poor and those afflicted with disease. There was a time also when the age of a widow was important; before she could enter the office she had to be sixty years old or older. The age limit however was changed from time to time.

Along with the deaconesses and widows there was a third order of women in the diaconate known as the virgins. The Order of Virgins is not mentioned in the Constitutions, but other writers of the postapostolic period mention them often. Basil in 379 recognized them as an order of the Church. In his letter to Amphilochius, he wrote that an ecclesiastical virgin was a woman who voluntarily devoted herself to the Lord, renounced marriage, and embraced a life of holiness. She must have attained the age of sixteen or seventeen, be in full possession of her faculties, and could be ranked among the virgins only after she had submitted to a strict examination to determine her sincerity.

When Christians started to regard virginity as a symbol of purity, the Order of Virgins came into being. In this again the Roman influence is apparent, because the ancient Roman temples also had an order of virgins. The Christian virgins dedicated themselves to a life of virtue and service. Women of all three orders lived ascetic lives and were accorded respect next to the clergy. Their lives were regarded as a living sacrifice unto the Lord.

It is interesting to note that the nursing profession traces its origin to these early Christian orders.[1] The deacons and the deaconesses carried the Church into the home. They did the best they could in caring for the sick and the poor, by using the remedies current in their day and resorting to prayer and the laying on of hands. The Order of Deaconesses also had other work to do in the Church, such as preparing women and girls for baptism and watching over the common meals of the congregation. It is thought by some that they also prepared the elements of Holy Communion. At one time their office was so important that they were permitted to baptize, but that was only for a short time. The administration of the sacraments, with this exception, has always been restricted to the clergy, except in emergencies. So it is seen that the deaconesses had other work to do, and during the passing of centuries there were periods when the order almost disappeared, only to be revived again in subsequent years. Today the order still functions in many Protestant denominations and is replaced by other orders in the Roman Catholic Church.

It was one of the deaconesses, Fabiola, who founded the first charity hospital at Rome about A.D. 300. She was a member of a patrician family and was greatly influenced by Marcella, a Roman matron who was a Christian and very much interested in the care of the sick poor. Fabiola must have been quite wealthy, because her home was so large that a portion of it could be used as a charity hospital. These noble ladies did not hesitate to do the most menial tasks in their care of the sick.

After the death of Fabiola, Jerome wrote a letter about her addressed to Oceanus.[2] He lauded her virtues as a Christian widow and wrote that she sold her property — it was a large one and suitable to her rank — and turned it into money that she used for the benefit of the poor. The first thing she did after her conversion was to found an infirmary and gather into it sufferers from the streets, giving their poor bodies, worn with sickness and hunger, all a nurse's care. He also described her care of the sick, how she washed away the purulent matter from wounds, gave food with her own hands, and moistened the lips of the dying with drops of water.

Probably the best-known of all the deaconesses was Paula, who was a friend of Fabiola. Paula was a woman of a distinguished Roman family and very wealthy. When she was quite young, she married a Roman senator named Toxotius and became the mother of four daughters. When the Roman Synod met in 382, she entertained some of the bishops in her home. These men made a favorable impression upon her, and through them she met Jerome, who later influenced her life greatly. She lost her husband in death two years prior to that Synod meeting. Then a daughter died in 384 and still another in 386. During these years she gave herself to religious service and established a number of hospitals in Rome. It is said of her that she served the sick quite humbly and gave them food, rubbed their feet, and boiled water with which to bathe them. Unstintingly she gave herself to this Christian service, and because she loved to do it, she was afraid it would not have merit as a Christian work.

After the death of her second daughter, Paula sailed for the East and joined Jerome at Antioch. From there she traveled to Egypt and finally returned and settled in Bethlehem. Being well versed in Greek and Latin, she pursued her studies of the Bible with Jerome, but she never lost her interest in charitable work. Paula founded a hospital at Bethlehem also, then a monastery, and later a convent. She impoverished herself with her charities and laid a weight of debt upon her daughter. Even Jerome could not dissuade her from her excess of charity and work. As a matter of fact, it is said that her personal sacrifices of physical strength in many services caused her death. She was buried in the Cave of the Nativity at Bethlehem, and at her funeral there was an imposing demonstration of the esteem in which she was held.

There were many others who devoted themselves to the care of the sick. These Christian women developed what was known as the xenodochium, an institution that became the center of relief and the forerunner of the modern hospital. The homeless, the stranger — in fact, all who needed help — were welcome. Rooms were set aside for the sick. The nursing was done by the Orders of Deaconesses, Widows, and Virgins. Priests who were physicians were stationed in these institutions and later became their directors. Money was donated by wealthy converts and secured by beggary. Reliable accounts from that day tell of the daily bread lines and the medical and nursing relief that was offered.

CLERICAL MINISTRIES OF HEALING

Thus far only the development of nursing care by women in the ancient Church has been considered. It is understood that in those warring days there were more women than men. For those who might have been dependent and lonely, this service was a healthful outlet and offered a measure of independence and esteem.

But the Church reached into the field of nursing through bishops and monks also. For instance, Saint Basil, a Greek bishop of Caesarea who was a brother of Macrina, is credited with setting up a system of visiting the sick and a system of nursing care. Saint Basil was also interested in healing, and became instrumental in founding a number of xenodochia. He planned the institutions carefully, and they were built at the edges of towns or cities. As far as possible, each institution included an inn for travelers; facilities for ambulatory patients; a hospital for bed care; homes for the aged, cripples, orphans, and foundlings. A building for lepers was usually included also, and there were living quarters for the personnel. There were " ductores," or guides, who went out and found patients and brought them to the hospital.

The clergy were taking an increasingly active part in the ministry of healing. This trend was quite the opposite of the philosophy mentioned previously that negated the physical and made a lack of emphasis on physical things a virtue. But on occasion, especially during an epidemic, even some of the hermits appeared on the scene to lend a helping hand and organize an emergency hospital. There was such an instance at Edessa, in Asia Minor, in the middle of the fourth century. When an epidemic spread through the terror-stricken city, a Christian deacon named Saint Ephraem came from his seclusion in a nearby desert, gathered money and public support, with which he bought three hundred beds and placed them in a public portico. He acted as a doctor and nurse until the emergency was over and then seems to have retired to seclusion again.

But the greater influence of the Church on healing is to be found in men such as Saint Basil and others who had a sustaining interest in that field of Christian service. It should be mentioned here that the care of the sick was not regarded with esteem by the pagan Romans. In fact, most of their physicians were Greek slaves. The average Roman placed his confidence in magic and quackery. The medical and surgical physicians, it seems, were most highly regarded when they served the gladiators and the army. There was not much glamour attached to caring for or healing the ordinary or the poor sick, and it was in this medical field among the poor that the Church made its most significant contribution in the postapostolic period. Healing was for all people, not only for certain groups or classes of society.

There was little compassion toward the poor in the pagan world. A few of the very rich offered spectacles occasionally to amuse them and divert their thoughts from their condition. The attitude of the authorities was to keep the masses of the poor in subjection and use them to their advantage. There were many guilds formed by people of the lower classes who had common interests or trades. They found it necessary to co-operate with one another to better their condition. But there was nothing in the guilds that approximated actual charity.

Christ taught the importance of the individual and the dignity of man. His followers were interested in the welfare of all people, including the poor. Healing, heretofore, was the prerogative of those who could afford what was offered or were wealthy enough to have educated slaves, or of those who served in the Roman legions and the gladiators. The Christians, rich and poor alike, were imbued with the compassion of their Lord; and this compassion expressed itself in their deep concern for the welfare of the poor and underprivileged. The most obvious need was the care of the neglected poor sick and it is in this field that they excelled. In this they set the precedent for future generations in our Western Christian civilization.

III. THE MEDIEVAL PERIOD

MEDIEVAL MEDICAL PRACTICE

As the postapostolic period blended into the medieval age of our Western civilization, the Church was the primary medium through which the healing arts were promoted. During this period, until the time of the crusaders, there were only a few schools in Europe where anatomy could be studied other than in the monasteries. The chief textbook was by Galen, which was studied in hand-copied versions. The school at Salerno used also an " Anatomy of a Pig " as a text. But there were some medical students who managed to study the human body and made valuable contributions to medicine and surgery.

Countless mountebanks claimed to know something about medicine and surgery; but they resorted mostly to showmanship, magic, and herb cures and had little professional training in the healing arts. Another factor that militated against secular healing was the fact that the physician often had to leave a community for his own safety if a patient died who happened to be a prominent person. Gutram, king of Burgundy, killed two surgeons in the year 580 when they could not save the life of his queen. John of Burgundy had a surgeon thrown in the river Oder because he could not cure John's blindness. As the Church grew in power and influence, its clergy could not be molested or even tried in secular courts. So the monks and priests could carry on their healing work without fear of death or torture as a consequence of failure.

Roots and herbs were cultivated by the monks in monastery gardens, and members of the orders read what literature was available on healing and studied the works of Galen. They even performed surgery to some extent until an edict of the Church quite inadvertently brought surgery into disrepute. The thought occurred to the Holy Fathers that a monk might accidentally kill a person while performing an operation. In order to prevent such a possibility, the Church passed a law in 1163 forbidding the shedding of blood. After a while it became a common belief that the Church forbade all surgery because it entailed the shedding of blood.

Then about the year 1300, in connection with the Crusades, Pope Boniface VIII decreed that a human body could not be cut up. This decree was the outgrowth of a practice that originated in the Crusades. When a crusader lost his life, far from home, in a holy cause, it was a much simpler matter to return only his bones to his family for burial. In such instances the body was cut up and the flesh boiled from the bones. The Church frowned upon this practice and finally issued a decree forbidding it. While the edict was not intended to forbid dissection of a human body for medical study, that was one of the results.

Surgery thus came into disrespect and the medical physician regarded the surgeon with disdain. After the passing of years, surgery, with some exceptions, was taken over by the barbers.

Through the entire period monks were engaged in the work of healing. Almost every monastery had its rooms for the sick. Hospitals were built in connection with cathedrals also. As the Orders of Deaconesses, Widows, and Virgins declined, male nursing orders were founded, such as the Knights Hospitalers and the Teutonic Knights which will be considered later in this chapter. Some of these monks became better known for their healing success than others, and people came from far and near to be helped by their powers. Saint John of Beverly (about A.D. 700) was one of these.

There are extant accounts of the healing that he did, rang-
ing all the way from co-operation with the physician to miraculous cures at the point of death. Saint John came to the
monastery called Inderwood, near a burying place dedicated
to Saint Michael the Archangel. Since it was about the beginning of Lent when he arrived, he asked some of the
monks to bring a poor person for whom he might provide
care as an alms, a custom he always followed.

They brought in a dumb young man who had never
spoken a word. Besides that he had scabs on his scalp, so
badly that there was no hair left except in a circle around his
head. When the first week of Lent was over, Saint John sent
for the young man and asked to see his tongue. Then he
held his chin in one hand, made the sign of the cross on his
tongue with the finger of his other hand, and told the youth
to draw back his tongue and say " Yea." The boy's tongue
was immediately loosed and he spoke. Then the bishop had
him speak the letters of the alphabet, make syllables, and
finally speak sentences, which he did.

After this cure was effected, the bishop ordered the physician to take over and heal the scabs on his head. This the
physician did, and with the bishop's prayers a good head of
hair grew as his scalp healed. The young man made such a
nice appearance and was so intelligent that the bishop offered to keep him with his group, but the young man preferred to return home.[3]

Saint John also used holy water as a healing medium. The
abbot of that same monastery related that Saint John was
invited by an earl to consecrate a chapel on his estate about
two miles from the monastery. The earl's wife had been seriously ill for forty days, and for three weeks she was so critical that she could not be carried from her room. The bishop
consecrated some water upon the altar and sent it to the
house. After the dedication, the earl begged Saint John to
dine in his home, but the bishop was eager to get back to the
monastery. When the earl promised to give alms to the poor

and entreated him to come and give his blessing, the bishop finally consented.

When they arrived, the earl's wife was already healed. The brothers who brought the holy water had been instructed to give her some to drink and to wash with it the place of pain on her body. The healing took place immediately, she arose, was strong enough to serve the meal, and returned the cup to Saint John as a token that she had been completely healed.

There are many such instances of healing reported during this period. Some of the better known of the Christians who are credited with these miracles were Saint John of Beverly, who has been mentioned; Saint Bernard; Saint Francis of Assisi; and Saint Catherine of Siena.

The practice of using relics in healing grew widely in this period also. Mementos carried away from the graves of saints or from sanctuaries, parts of the clothing of saints, sacred bones, and other relics were used extensively by bishops and others. In fact, relics of the saints became so highly regarded that each cathedral or chapel was hardly considered sacred unless it had a relic of some kind or other. When the Lombard queen, Theodelinda, in the time of Gregory the Great (A.D. 590–604), sent an abbot after relics for her cathedral, he came back with over seventy vials of oil, each with the name of a saint from whose tomb it was taken.

Incubation, or sleeping in holy places, soon became another practice of healing. The church that held a sacred relic, as well as the consecrated Host, was believed to have healing powers. Naturally, if a sick person were permitted to sleep in such a holy place, this patient would be under the healing influences for a longer period of time. These churches, famous for their cures, were equipped with mattresses and couches, as well as having priests and attendants constantly on duty for the comfort of the patient. After sincere devotions and prayers for healing, the patient was permitted to sleep. In any case he thought or dreamed about the saint touching or operating upon him or he received instructions in his vision about medicines to take for a cure. Many said they were healed, and writers of that period attest the genuineness of some of the cures.

Among the diseases of which patients were relieved were paralysis, dumbness, blindness, barrenness, scrofula, dyspepsia, a broken leg, deformities, lameness, gout, cataract, ulcer, and dropsy. The case is related of a man who evidently was carried to a church that was equipped with a bath. For three days he prayed, and then the saint of that church appeared to him in the form of a monk. It was a waking vision. The monk told him to arise and go into the warm water. The patient said that he could not, but when the saint insisted, he tried, sliding like a snake into the bath while the saint stood by him. When he made an effort to arise, he found that he was healed.

Some churches became better known than others for their healing qualities; these became shrines to which many pilgrims came for help. In fact there were shrines all over Europe in the Middle Ages. Pilgrims traveled great distances to visit and worship at a favorite or well-known shrine. It was the great desire of almost every devout Christian not only to visit a shrine, but if at all possible, some day actually to visit the Holy Land where Jesus had lived.

THE CRUSADES AND THE HOSPITAL ORDERS

The closing centuries of the first thousand years of our Christian Era saw vast shifting of populations. In 1066, William conquered England; a few years later, in 1076, the Turks took Jerusalem. The Holy Land was in the hands of infidels who desecrated the holy places. A Christian pilgrim could no longer visit the land of his Lord and worship at the shrines, the most sacred of which was the Holy Sepulcher from which Jesus arose. There was a growing indignation among Christians all over Europe because of this situation, and this feeling grew into a righteous zeal to conquer the Holy Land in the name of the Lord.

In those days a monk, Peter the Hermit, rode through Germany and France telling in every village about the tortures endured by Christian pilgrims to the Holy Land. During the years he preached, 1094 and 1095, there was a famine and an epidemic in Germany. The people became excited, and many felt that these scourges were the result of their inertia — a punishment because they let the infidels control the Holy Land and torture and kill the pilgrims. In great bands, without adequate provisions and arms, they set out for the Holy Land. Many were slaughtered in Hungary; others under the personal leadership of Peter reached Asia Minor and were massacred by the Turks.

This was only the beginning of the crusades and for many years thereafter Christian knights and Moslems fought back and forth for the shrines of the Holy Land. There was even a children's crusade, composed of thousands of children from Germany and France. Great numbers perished on the way, and others were lured aboard ships and sold into slavery in Egypt.

The best-known of all the crusaders was King Louis IX of France, known as Saint Louis, who personally led his troops in two crusades. He died a martyr to the cause in Tunis in 1270, when he succumbed to a fever that broke out in his army. Sire de Joinville, personal historian of the king, tells about the virtues of this ruler and his concern for the welfare of the people. He obtained sacred relics in Constantinople which included what was believed to be the Saviour's crown of thorns and a part of the original cross. The king walked barefooted in the procession when these relics were presented to the clergy of Paris.

His biographer characterized him in this manner: " This holy man loved God with all his heart, and imitated His works: which was evident in this, that as God died for the love which He bore His people, so he (Louis) put his body in peril several times for the love which he bore his people. The great love which he had for his people appeared in what he said to his eldest son, Louis, when very sick at Fontainebleau: 'Fair son,' said he, 'I beg thee to make thyself loved by the people of thy kingdom; for indeed I should prefer that a Scot from Scotland came and ruled the people of the kingdom well and faithfully, rather than thou shouldst rule them ill in the sight of all.' " [4]

Although the crusades did not accomplish their primary purpose, they did influence the Church in its relation to healing. One disease in particular, leprosy, was brought back to Europe from the Orient; as it spread, the Church tried to meet the needs of those who became ill. Hospitals were built by monks to care for them. These institutions were called lazarettos, after Lazarus, the leper of the New Testament. At one time there were two thousand lazarettos in France and two hundred in England. The patients were isolated in these institutions; and, after centuries of isolation, the disease has practically disappeared from Europe.

In this way the crusades were directly responsible for the building of hospitals and for a renewed interest in healing. These institutions had to be manned with nurses; therefore religious nursing orders, such as the Knights Hospitalers, were founded.

The Knights Hospitalers were orders of monks and laymen, primarily knights, who devoted themselves to the care of the sick in the hospitals. The Order of Hospitalers of Saint John of Jerusalem became the most widely known of these organizations, of which there were many. This order seems to have had its origin in the hospital at Jerusalem. With the co-operation of the crusaders, the hospital grew in size and importance. The members wore a black robe with a cross of eight points of white linen over the heart. Later members of the first class were permitted to wear a red mantle with a white cross.

Their chief hospital at Jerusalem was near the Holy Sepulcher, and was a large structure where hundreds of pilgrims received care. The order supported hospitals in other places also, Cyprus, Rhodes, and Malta being among the better known. Clothing, food, and wine were furnished by the hospitals, as well as other necessities for the sick. The most skilled physicians of the day were to be found in these institutions. As time passed, the knights became ever more engrossed in the warfare with the Moslems and had less time for nursing, and this situation caused the monks to out-number the knights in nursing orders.

The Knights Templars is another such order founded at Jerusalem about 1119. These were knights who organized themselves to protect pilgrims traveling from the coast to Jerusalem. Their garb was a white cloak that signified purity of heart; they gave every tenth loaf of their bread to the poor. This order received a sanction of the Church which was revoked in 1310; nevertheless it continued in existence and functions today chiefly among Protestants as an order of the Masonic Lodge. Today its primary beneficence is an educational fund that is used to help worthy students to com-plete their college education. It is also pledged to aid desti-tute widows and helpless orphans and is often called upon, individually and collectively, to render such service.

The Order of Teutonic Knights is another organization founded in Jerusalem that had the care of the sick as its pri-mary purpose. The members of the order were of German origin. It was organized in a field hospital during the siege of Acre in 1189. After the siege, members of the new order built a hospital and a church at Acre and called themselves the " Hospital of Saint Mary of the Germans in Jerusalem." It is interesting to note that this is one of the first orders that took Mary as its patron saint. It was sanctioned by the Church and grew in numbers and influence, especially in what is now Germany. As the years passed, it became mili-taristic, and castles of the order were built in many towns. The knights promoted commerce and offered protection for the people. Thus it lost its original purpose but served an-other.

In the foregoing discussion, a few of the Orders of Hospitalers are mentioned. However, these are not all of them. There were many more, such as: Alexians, Orders of Saint Anthony, Order of the Holy Ghost, Bethlehemites, Brothers of Charity, Orders of the Cross, Sack Brethren, and many more. The membership of these orders was composed of clergymen and laymen.

A full appreciation of the Orders of Hospitalers, however, should not give the impression that women withdrew from the care of the sick. When the Orders of Deaconesses, Widows, and Virgins were dissolved, other groups were formed to take their places. With the establishment of so many hospitals came great opportunities for women also to do Christian service. The Benedictines was one of the orders for women founded in medieval times which assumed nursing of the sick and ministering to the needs of the poor as its special duties.

This order was founded by Benedict of Nursia in 529 at Monte Cassino, a monastery in Italy that figured prominently in World War II. After the breakup of the Roman Empire it offered women a place where they could perform Christian service and cultivate intellectual tastes. Convent life was interesting when compared to the prosaic humdrum existence of women in those days when so many of the men were away from home in wars. Some of these Benedictine colonies or settlements were large; one in particular had 3,000 monks and nuns. They nursed the sick in hospitals and homes, and made a distinct contribution to the healing arts.

To the north, in the Netherlands, lived a priest, Lambert le Begue, who was a devout man. He saw the great need for service to the sick and the poor. With great earnestness he renounced his own property and used his wealth to build the hospital of Saint Christopher at Liége and also a church and a community for those who could care for the sick and the poor.

Many crusaders went forth from that territory, and many never returned. Their widows and other women, because of religious convictions, felt impelled to serve the Lord. Lambert invited them to join the society he formed at the cathedral. This order became known as the Beguines. Members of the society who owned property were permitted to retain it. At first they were required only to dress simply, but later they wore a sort of uniform. Permission was given members to withdraw from the order at any time or to marry if they so desired. They lived in a number of small houses grouped in the vicinity of the hospital and cathedral; the institution was enclosed by a wall.

While it was not required of them, many who had money and property renounced it and used it in the cause. They cared for the poor and the poor sick without cost to the patient, both in the hospital and in private homes. The order spread to France, Germany, and northern Italy, and acquired great wealth because many prominent and wealthy widows joined it; they built many hospitals and nunneries. The Beghards, a corresponding order for males, grew out of the spirit of the Beguines and was founded later.

There were other religious orders for women in the medieval period; and many more, such as the Sisters of Mercy, Sisters of Charity, and Little Sisters of the Poor, which are so well known today, were founded at a later time.

THE SACRAMENTS AND HEALING

Another important development in medieval times that had therapeutic value falls within the scope of this subject, namely, the sacrament of confession and penance. This sacrament is closely allied with the power of the clergy to forgive sins. During this period public confession of the members of the Church was replaced by private confession. As early as Origen, the Church Fathers were divided on whether confession of sins should be a private or a public practice. In the fourth century, Saint Basil advocated that a Christian should follow the same principles in spiritual illness that he does with physical ailments, that is, he should find a clergyman who is skilled in the cure of souls and make his confession. The order for the consecration of a bishop indicated his power to forgive sins, a power that went with his office because it was interpreted as promised by Jesus in Matt. 16:19, "And I will give unto thee the keys of the kingdom of heaven: and whatsoever thou shalt bind on earth shall be bound in heaven: and whatsoever thou shalt loose on earth shall be loosed in heaven." By the fifth century the pope clearly stated that it was sufficient for a person to make confession in private. A little later the Synod of Davin declared that any matters revealed in private confession must never be revealed by the confessor.

There arose out of this movement handbooks for priests to use in the confessional. The priest was regarded as the physician of the soul who should take into consideration the age, sex, condition, and status of the penitent in prescribing penance. The idea was to cure the sin by a corresponding virtue, much in the same manner as the physician prescribed a cold medicine to heal a fever or a dry medicine to cure a moist disease. Prayer, fasting, abstinence from meat and wine, assuming uncomfortable postures such as sleeping in water or on nut shells, giving of alms, and other remedies were prescribed by the confessor. With the penance the sinner could rehabilitate himself; the consequences of his sin were annulled and he was restored in the graces of God. All this had definite therapeutic value and helped the Christians to keep themselves well by preventing anxieties and neuroses. Its value was so evident that the Church finally decreed at the Council of Liége in 710 that everyone should make confession to the parish priest at least once every year. After that decree, in most of the hospitals and shrines a patient who came or was brought for cure made confession first, either to his parish priest or to the priests who were in attendance at the places of healing.

Medical science continued its development during this period. Contagion was recognized; and in anticipation of the discovery of bacteria, it was attributed to small, invisible demons. Uroscopy was developed at Salerno, and physicians tried to diagnose disease by inspecting the urine. Blood transfusion was considered as a possibility and attempted, but not generally accepted until a later period. Dr. Benjamin Lee Gordon, in *The Romance of Medicine,* tells of a transfusion given Pope Innocent VIII in the year 1491. Three donors were used, but the attempt resulted in the death of the donors, and the life of the pope was not saved. In the medical schools and the monastery hospitals clinical training for medical students developed in that they were taught at the bedside of the patient. Methods of diagnosis and treatment which anticipated the modern development in medical care were emerging in this period.

Part II

THE REFORMATION AND POST-REFORMATION PERIODS

IV. THE REFORMATION

TIMES OF CHANGE

The fifteenth and sixteenth centuries produced men, women, and events that are important because they touch in many ways the lives of those who are living today. This was a period of exploration in the physical, the mental, and the spiritual spheres. These centuries saw Columbus and other great explorers, Joan of Arc, Leonardo da Vinci, Martin Luther, John Calvin, Ulrich Zwingli, Paracelsus, and Vesalius. Some may not be well acquainted with all of these named, but they are worth knowing because they were great and interesting people.

The Church reached the height of its power, and it was believed that nothing worse could happen to a person than to be excommunicated from the Church. Nevertheless it was an age of much superstition and fear. No one knew about bacteria, there were no anesthetics, and how blood flows through the veins remained yet to be demonstrated and understood. Scientifically it was an age when the first omens of the Renaissance were making their appearance. The invention of printing with movable type would soon make the findings of the great scholars and scientists more generally available.

The fear and superstition of that day may have had something to do with the strange mental aberrations that swayed masses of people. There was, for instance, the dancing mania that followed the Black Death of the fourteenth century, a plague in which half the population of Europe perished. The physicians did not know how to control the plague. Terror spread with it; law and order almost disappeared. Some men left their families and fled; others tried to escape on ships; some hid in shrines, churches, and cathedrals. The disposal of the dead became a major problem. Some people gave all their possessions to the Church and moved to another place, where the disease found them and they were stricken down.

Along with all this went a common belief in demons and the practice of alchemistic experiments, in which men tried to convert base substances into gold and at the same time tried to conjure spirits. There were some notoriously cruel noblemen, such as the Baron of Rais with his blue-black beard, who, with his magicians, sacrificed many human lives in his bloody orgies. A person would simply disappear and no one saw him or her again. Mental aberrations can be expected from people living under such stress.

One such aberration was the dancing mania. It is supposed to have started in southern Germany and rapidly spread into France. People of both sexes danced madly in the streets, in and out of the cathedrals, until they were completely exhausted. People gathered to watch them and soon many joined the dancers. They saw visions; some imagined they were wading a stream of blood and jumped madly in the air trying to get out of it. Others saw Christ sitting upon the throne and leaped and danced with joy. Pious people often gave the dancers gifts, which may have caused some to join the dancing. Naturally, this extreme emotional expression often resulted in unsavory and immoral practices.

Nor would the dancers always stay in one city or town. A group might travel to the next town, go to the public square, form a circle, and begin to dance. A dance usually started rather slowly, then the rhythm increased in tempo while they jumped and screamed with saliva dripping from their mouths until they fell exhausted. By that time townspeople were ready to take the places of those who dropped out. Others followed the lead, and soon the whole town square was alive with dancers and the mania spread to the side streets.

This went on along country roads, and from town to city and city to town. The priests of the Church did not know how to cope with it. They believed the dancers were seized by devils and tried exorcism. They called upon Saint Vitus for the cure of the mania; " St. Vitus's dance " is a term familiar today.

Many of the people blamed the clergy for this malady. They said that they had been baptized by unworthy priests, and that for that reason the baptism was not divine enough to expel the demons. Others said they had been bitten by spiders, which caused them to squirm and dance. Village musicians tried to stop them with weird music.

There were other strange manifestations of mental aberration during that period, such as barking like a dog or mewing like a cat. Some of these even invaded the nunneries, where a nun would begin mewing and after a while others would be found doing the same thing. There were further manifestations of mass mania over a period of some three hundred years.

The belief in witchcraft was held by almost everyone in that period. The Church did not permit the shedding of blood, but it permitted many innocent persons to be burned to death or to be drowned. It was commonly believed that many diseases were caused by witchcraft. In epilepsy one could almost see the demon tearing the patient, and various prayers and exorcisms were used to break the spell. One common method was to burn the pillow of the patient, then the next person who died was considered to be the witch. There seems to be no record of what explanation was offered after that if the disease persisted.

Surgery was still relegated to the barbers. The educated surgeon wore a long robe, but hesitated to touch a wounded or a sick man. He gave directions; pointing to the place where the barber should make the incision. Only the privileged classes could command the services of a trained doctor such as this. For the common people, by and large, there were only the quacks, strolling physicians, and midwives. But there were still the shrines and the monasteries; there were faith and prayer and holy relics and charitable hospitals where the poor could go, but even in the hospitals there was little actual knowledge of the body structure.

This period saw the birth of Paracelsus, who was born in Switzerland of a German father and a Swiss mother. Theophrastus was his name given at birth but he chose Paracelsus as his writing and professional name. He studied medicine after the custom of the medical students of his day, learning from the same old authorities, Hippocrates, Galen, and Avicenna. As was customary in his profession, he traveled for a number of years, associating with common people, the barber surgeons, bathhouse keepers, and chemists. He worked in laboratories like the Arabians did, brewing substances that would aid mankind. " The wise man rules nature," he said, " not nature the wise man." Because he believed they were outmoded, he caused the books by Avicenna and Galen to be publicly burned. Departing from custom he actually studied the patient, and wrote about heredity and the predisposition to disease. He believed the primary causes of disease, however, to be in the firmament as cosmic causes; and he used the zodiac in diagnosis. After he succeeded in getting his works published, his great opportunity came when he was called to treat a really prominent patient, a wealthy printer of Basel whose name was Frobenius. The treatment proved to be beneficial.

Paracelsus was famous! He lectured in the German rather than the Latin and urged his students to learn by observation, trial, and reasoning. He was a great scholar and knew it. With bravado he bullied his students and made enemies of his colleagues. Contemporaries say he was egotistical, but he definitely helped to usher in the modern age in medicine. He is known as the first modern doctor, and the Church accepted the results of his research without protest.

THE BEGINNINGS OF REFORMATION

At the time when Paracelsus was leading the way in a break with the past, a Reformation and Counter Reformation were taking place in the Church. The man who is credited with the leadership in the Reformation was Martin Luther, a monk of the Augustinian order. Luther became the leader of a spiritual revolt against many of the practices and beliefs of the Church, and is known as the founder of the Protestant Church. Those were days of bitter theological controversies which have no place in this book except in so far as they have a bearing on the Church and its work of healing.

Martin Luther and his followers did not believe in the worship of the saints; neither did they accept the use of relics and shrines for healing purposes. But he was very much interested in the sick and used the medium of prayer and the Scripture for healing purposes. He accepted the scientific medical knowledge prevalent in his day and believed in demon possession. On one occasion, when he was translating the Bible into the vernacular, the devil appeared and Luther threw an inkwell at him. The spot made on the wall by the splattering ink could be seen in the castle at Wartburg for many years, and perhaps may be seen today.

At least one therapeutic miracle is attributed to the prayers of Martin Luther. The patient was Melanchthon, Luther's friend, who was the scholar of the Reformation. His illness may have been caused by a ruling made by Luther and Melanchthon regarding the bigamous marriage of the Landgrave Philip of Hesse. It is a story too long for inclusion here, except to say that the two Reformers gave an opinion permitting, as the lesser of two evils, the Landgrave to marry a second wife. This opinion weighed heavily on the sensitive conscience of Melanchthon, so much so that he became deathly sick.

When Luther arrived to visit his friend, he found him in a dying condition. He was semiconscious and could neither eat nor drink. Luther was much agitated at his appearance, and, after gazing at him awhile, went to a window in the room and prayed fervently to God. When he finished his prayers, he went over to the bed, grasped Melanchthon by the hand and said: " Be of good courage, Philip, you will not die; give no place to the spirit of sorrow, and be not your own murderer, but trust in the Lord, who can stay and make alive again, can wound and bind up, can smite and heal again." [5] After that Melanchthon began to improve, immediately became more cheerful, and regained his health and strength completely.

As was mentioned before, Luther believed in the efficacy of prayer and regarded it as a medium of confession. The formal confessional of the Church was abandoned, but some elements of it were retained. Confession of sin was to be made directly to God in prayer. Luther had become disgusted with the formality of the confessional of the Church, yet he realized its potential therapeutic values. He taught that confession must be voluntary on the part of the Christian. First the penitent should confess to Christ, and then talk with his pastor if he desired to do so. The pastor may assure him under what conditions he may feel that his confession is sincere enough to merit Christ's forgiveness, but the pastor cannot forgive sins.

" Do you want to confess? Come then! Jesus is here, who will forgive your sins, and will smother your iniquity. Because no human can absolve you, only Christ himself, through the mouth of the minister (His servant) and the minister's mouth is Christ's mouth, the minister's ear is Christ's ear, Christ sits in the confession, Christ hears: Christ's words are spoken and heard, not human words." [6]

We see the pastor emerging in the Reformation, one of the

great contributions this movement made to the healing arts. Luther himself was a great pastor, who felt that the visits of the spiritual adviser were just as important for the patient as the visits of the doctor. He was convinced that many physical ills have their origin in spiritual anxiety; sorrow, temptation, guilt, and fear were regarded as spiritual states that needed the cure of prayer and spiritual consultation with a pastor. As a result of his deep understanding of human problems, many people came to him for help. Many letters that he wrote to those seeking his help, whom he could not personally visit, indicate his deep concern. During a plague he visited in the homes of the afflicted, and some of them died in his arms.

He recognized the therapeutic value of love and forgiveness. " So you do not love your brother, then you belong to the devil, the way you go and what you stand for. He who will not receive counsel [in this matter] does it at his own risk and danger. You keep a loving and forgiving heart." [7]

It will be seen that Luther's attitude and thinking influenced Protestant thought and practices in relation to the Church and healing. He laid great emphasis on prayer, faith, love, the sacraments of Communion, Baptism, and private confession. The latter was no longer regarded as a sacrament but as a voluntary practice that the believer should exercise because he needs it for his spiritual health. Religion was for the home also; he directed his postils directly to the home, where they should be read for the spiritual nourishment of the members of the family.

The break with the Roman Church had been accomplished, and the Protestant movement soon could be seen spreading far and wide. To the south, in Switzerland, lived another spiritual leader of the Reformation, Ulrich (or Huldreich) Zwingli. He also was a priest of the Church and entered upon his parish work at Glarus. There he gave himself with unusual zeal and devotion to his pastoral labors. In 1516 he was removed to Einsiedeln, where there was a famous shrine to which many pilgrims went for help. He found religious conditions there so bad that he felt a great need for reformation. He started his campaign against religious abuses before he heard about Luther, who was doing practically the same thing in the north. There followed a permanent break with the established Church, and the Reformation movement was soon growing in that region.

Another great leader of the Reformation, John Calvin (1509–1564), was born in France. While his doctrines differed in various respects from the Lutheran teachings, they were in accord in their emphases upon the pastoral office and personal religious living.

Calvin was responsible for the establishment of a religious government at Geneva, in the French-speaking canton of Switzerland. In his theory of the Church, he held that it is an invisible company of those chosen by God who profess their Christian faith. The local church was to be governed by four classes of officers elected by the congregation: pastors, teachers, elders, and deacons.

Calvin found the care of the poor and the sick under the jurisdiction of the city government and accommodated himself to the situation as best he could. He made this phase of philanthropy a special responsibility of the deacons. Four of them were trustees of the city hospital that was in operation in Geneva at that time. Women were received into this order, and he wanted very much to revive the diaconate of the ancient Church. A surgeon and physician ministered to the sick at the hospital and much of the care of the patients was in the hands of deaconesses.

Names of candidates for the diaconate were submitted by members of the congregation to the elders and deacons. This took place during the week, after a sermon on the subject and the observance of Holy Communion. The actual choice of deacons and deaconesses was made by a meeting of all the elders and deacons; the elected ones were installed with an appropriate ceremony.

Some contemporary critics accused Calvin of a lack of interest in the poor and the sick. Uhlhorn relates that Kampschulte accused the clergy of neglecting the sick in the pest hospital when an epidemic was rampant in Genf in 1543. Calvin's critic said that the author of the *Institutes of the Christian Religion* applied himself diligently in bringing to light the great truths of the faith, but did not evidence the same diligence in exercising love for the afflicted. He based this criticism on the fact that Calvin did not visit the hospital himself. But the truth of the matter is that he wanted to go there, but the council forbade him because they felt it was too much of a risk for the one whom they felt was indispensable to the Church and the State. The patients did not go without spiritual nurture because Calvin always managed to find clergymen who were willing to serve in that capacity.

His interest in the poor and the sick was a matter of conviction, because he was very conscious of the social welfare of the people. Modern scholars who have studied Calvin's life carefully write of his intense interest in the well-being of the people. He would not tolerate beggary; any person in need could apply to the deacons whose business it was to care for them.

As far as deaconesses were concerned, their primary purpose was to minister to the sick. When Calvinism spread to other parts of Europe, local congregations revived the deaconess order for that purpose.

The doctrine of predestination, believed and preached by Calvin, had its effect upon the attitude of the sick. Since that which happens in the individual's life is ordained by God, this belief helped the sick to resign themselves to the will of God rather than rebel against their condition. On the contrary, it also caused some to accept a condition as the will of God when a conscious effort to overcome it might have had definite therapeutic value.

As far as confession was concerned, Calvin held with Luther and Zwingli that it was a personal matter between the individual and God. However, confession, although not compulsory, could be made to the pastor. A general confessional was used in the observance of Holy Communion.

While the genius of John Calvin expressed itself primarily in his great organizing ability and his power as a preacher and teacher, he also recognized the therapeutic values of Christian virtues and the transforming power of the gospel. In his *Institutes,* Book III, Chapter I, when referring to the Holy Spirit on the basis of the invitation of Isaiah 55:1, " Ho, every one that thirsteth . . . ," he says that it corresponds to the invitation of Christ: " If any man thirst, let him come unto me " (John 7:37; 4:14). The Holy Spirit is referred to as water because it has a " purifying and cleansing energy." This purifying energy has beneficial effects upon the total personality.

All the Reformers rejected the belief in the efficacy of relics and shrines and laid the emphasis upon the prayer of faith. Confession to God and consultation with the pastor were emphasized as important for the health of the believer. It was taken for granted that the physician and the clergyman should co-operate for the benefit of the total personality.

This was a period of transition from the old, of theological controversy; and yet, it was an age in which spiritual foundations were formed upon which the modern Church has built its structure. Man was regarded as a total personality, and religion became an expression of his whole life. The modern Protestant pastor owes much of his philosophy of life to these pioneers.

ADVANCES IN MEDICAL PRACTICE

Some valuable contributions were made to the advancement of medicine and surgery in this period, and they also should be considered here. Much of the progress was due to a man whose life was saved by a special decree of the king of France. Ambroise Paré was a Protestant physician at the time when the massacre of the Huguenots was planned for Saint Bartholomew's Day in 1572, and King Charles IX ordered that this great physician should not be molested. Paré was one of the most colorful and self-sacrificing physicians of the sixteenth century. At the age of nine years he apprenticed himself to a barber, where he first learned how to shave, cut hair, and comb wigs. Six years later he went to Paris and apprenticed himself to a barber surgeon. Each morning at four o'clock he attended lectures on anatomy given by physicians on the staff of the Hôtel-Dieu.

The Hôtel-Dieu was a great stone building, lighted by small dirty windows; and it contained long rooms with canopied beds in rows. There was no thought of isolation. Patients with all kinds of diseases were placed in the same hall, often in the same bed. Sometimes two or three or more were put in one bed. There were piles of straw in the halls where others lay. The nursing care was done by the Sisters of Charity who were mentioned in the preceding chapter.

The operating room was a corner of the hall, or perhaps a vestibule. Sanitation did not figure in the scene. In such an operating room Paré learned how to bandage a wound, remove an arm, or apply a splint. The anesthetic was strong men who held the patient while the operation was performed. In some cases a drink of rum was added.

When he was twenty-six years old, Paré was called into the army as a physician and became a regimental surgeon. He followed the army and became acquainted with indescribable scenes of suffering. One thing that particularly characterized Paré was his compassion for suffering people. One day he was horrified when he went into a barn to stable his horse, and found four dead soldiers and two more alive, sitting against a wall, their faces mutilated, clothes burned by gunshot powder, their eyes gone. As he stood there a moment, looking upon those suffering men, an old soldier came by, who asked him if he could cure them. Paré said that he did not think he could. Without further ado the old soldier cut their throats so that they could die. Paré was shocked at such cold-blooded treatment, but the only answer he got from the old soldier was that he hoped if he were in such a condition someone would as mercifully relieve him.

Gunshot wounds were a new feature of warfare at that time. The sword or lance made a clean wound, but gunshot made a narrow, deep wound and usually carried bits of clothing or dirt along with it. Infection soon followed. The customary way of treating a wound was to pour boiling oil into it to cauterize it, or to use a red-hot iron for that purpose. Paré tried the same method until one day he ran out of oil. He substituted the yolk of egg, oil of roses, and turpentine. That night he did not sleep well because he worried about the patients upon whom he had applied his remedy. Early in the morning when he made the rounds he found that those who had been treated with boiling oil were in pain, the wounds swollen and inflamed, while those upon whom he had used his treatment were feeling better. Then and there he made up his mind that he would not again torment wounded men with the boiling oil treatment.

In this he was an exceptional physician for his time, in that he learned by experience regardless of the medical authorities. His keen observation and his compassion led him to find other valuable methods of surgery. The use of the ligature was revived, to tie the ends of bleeding vessels rather than seal them with a red-hot iron. He improved artificial eyes, arms, and legs, and became the first dental surgeon by implanting teeth.

Dentistry was practiced by bathhouse keepers, barber surgeons, and old women. It consisted almost entirely of pulling aching teeth. There were some who were skillful enough to wire in teeth made of bone or ivory to fill the vacancy. But that was done only for the rich. Paré found that he could implant a tooth in the jaw when one was pulled, the jaw would heal, and the tooth remain useful for quite some time. Of course, in order to do this, it was necessary to find someone who was willing to part with a tooth for a certain sum of money.

He used his medical knowledge and skill to prove that certain medical practices were nothing more than superstition. One of these was the use of the bezoar stone as an antidote against poison. Legend said that the bezoar stone was the hardened tear of a deer bitten by a snake. It was, however, nothing more than a gallstone taken from a goat or some other animal. It was believed if a person were poisoned all he needed to do was to swallow such a stone and the poison would not affect him. King Charles IX had one of these stones that was dipped in his food to make sure it was safe for him to eat it. Paré decided to prove it was mere superstition. There was a cook in prison who was sentenced to be strangled or hanged for stealing two silver plates. He was given the choice of taking poison and using the bezoar stone, or hanging. The prisoner decided to take a chance; they gave him the poison and then the bezoar stone. The poor fellow died a few hours later. When the stone was removed and returned to the king, he threw it in the fire. That was, among others, one of the reasons why the king gave orders not to molest Paré during the persecution of the Huguenots.

Another medical superstition was the use of "mummy," a powder that was supposed to have been made from mummies in Egypt. This was applied to heal wounds and sores. Paré said that most of the mummy in use was made in France from bodies stolen from gallows. But he thought such mummy had just as much healing power as that which came from Egypt. He was denounced by the physicians of the Hôtel-Dieu for not using it, but he persisted in his belief and no one could shake him from it.

Ambroise Paré was a great man and would have been a great man in any age. He is mentioned in this story of the Church and healing because he was a religious man, and in this chapter because he was a Protestant in a land that was predominantly Roman Catholic. He was recognized because of his ability. Another distinct contribution he made to the field of medical science was the spirit of compassion exemplified by his Lord and Saviour. His writings abound with that spirit, which was destined to do so much for the medical arts in the future. Although his exterior was roughhewn according to the pattern of the day, he devoted his life and intelligence to alleviating suffering and pain.

V. THE COUNTER REFORMATION

CATHOLIC HEALING MINISTRIES

The Protestant Reformation supplied the incentive for a Counter Reformation in the Roman Catholic Church. The Catholic Reformers worked with zeal to abolish abuses that caused the Reformation, and at the same time evidenced an equal zeal against any heresies. One of the first leaders of this movement was Saint Philip Neri, born in Florence, Italy, in 1515. He founded the Roman Catholic Order of Oratorians. This order was designed for the care of strangers and the convalescent poor people. The house of the order breathed a spirit of friendliness and service. Saint Philip believed that a Christian should be friendly and happy. Several times a week he and his friends went to the hospitals to tend the sick and performed the most menial tasks to relieve suffering. They cared for sick people in their own establishment also. The order emphasized purity of life on the part of its members; there were no vows and they could withdraw at any time.

Saint Philip Neri is credited with many instances of spiritual healing. On one occasion he was called to the home of Pietro Vittrici, of Parma. This man was in the employ of a cardinal, who later became Pope Gregory XIII. The physicians had despaired of saving the man's life and, as a last resort his relatives sent for Philip. Father Philip, when treating a sick person, always first engaged in prayers for the patient. This he did in the sickroom, and then put his hand on the patient's forehead. Pietro revived immediately, and in two days' time was well enough to leave the house and tell his friends how he had been cured by Father Philip.[8]

He is even credited with healing Pope Clement VIII. It must have required a lot of courage on Saint Philip's part to accomplish this cure. The pope was afflicted with what was called " gout of the hand." It made his whole body ache, and when Father Philip came to see him, the pope asked him not to come near the bed because he was afraid the bed might be jarred. But Father Philip came ever nearer, over the protests of the patient, until he could reach out and touch him. Trembling with fear as he approached the bed, he re-assured his patient that he would not hurt him and then quickly took him by the sore hand and pressed it. To the amazement of the pope, the pain ceased and he was healed from that moment. After his miraculous cure the pope spoke about it often and referred to the life of Father Philip as be-ing saintly.

Father Philip used the laying on of hands and prayer in healing, and reassured the patient by inspiring confidence in his ability to heal. There was the case of a woman who had a cancer of the breast. The physician decided to apply the hot iron, a method used to cauterize a cancer. Before she would permit the operation to be performed, she went to see Father Philip. He inquired about her affliction and asked to see it. After seeing it, he assured her she would be healed. Then he prayed to the Lord in her behalf, reached forth his hand, and touched the cancer. After the ceremony was completed, he told her to go home and rest assured that she was healed. It happened on the way. When the physician came to cauterize the cancer, he was amazed to find her perfectly healed.

Saint Philip Neri had many followers in his Order of Ora-torians. While these followers did not possess the ability to heal by faith as did their leader, they devoted themselves to nursing and other care of the sick. The brothers of the order would at times leave the monastery for days and travel in the community doing nursing duty and practicing medicine.

In this post-Reformation period much progress was made in the medical field. At the same time that religious leaders were successful in faith healing and shrines and relics were being used by many, great men of science loyal to the Church were devoting their talents and ability to the development of medicine and surgery.

Vesalius, a Roman Catholic layman, was born in 1514, two years before Martin Luther nailed his Ninety-five Theses to the church door at Wittenberg. Even as a boy he dissected mice and frogs. It is interesting to notice that the Church did not forbid dissecting animals. He wanted to see what was on the inside much in the same manner as a boy today takes an alarm clock apart to find what makes it tick. He wanted to be a surgeon, and when he grew up, that is the profession he followed. Furthermore, he decided to specialize in anatomy, and thereupon became the first surgeon to follow that course.

His decision presented one great difficulty and that was to get human bodies for dissection. The medical school where he studied managed to get one or two a year. These were unclaimed bodies of criminals. The student rarely touched the body; he watched, the surgeon pointed, and a barber did the actual dissection. On one occasion, when he was a student, Vesalius asked permission, and received it, to take the barber surgeon's knife and do the dissecting himself.

His zeal knew no bounds. On another occasion he stole the skeleton of a criminal that was hanging on a gallows — which was taking a chance, for if he had been caught he might have been hanged on the same gallows. He studied anatomy carefully and found things different from Galen's ideas. He found also that a man has just as many ribs as a woman, despite the fact that God used one of Adam's ribs to create Eve. No man could contradict the great Galen, and yet Vesalius did that very thing. He set himself to work preparing a new book on anatomy. It was published in 1543 and contained many woodcuts. He was only twenty-nine years old at the time of this great accomplishment.

Once his book was well known, Vesalius became a haunted man because he contradicted Galen. It was not from the Church that he suffered persecution; neither did the Church defend him. His fiercest opposition came from his colleagues, and he had to abandon his position as an anatomy instructor. In disgust he burned his books and gave up the study of anatomy altogether. Later he was made a court physician. It is fortunate that he was not able to burn all his books and many remained in other hands. In due time these books proved that Vesalius was far ahead of his day.

NEW RELIGIOUS ORDERS

A religious order of this period that indirectly made a contribution to the healing arts was the Society of Jesuits, which was founded by Saint Ignatius of Loyola. Ignatius was born in a noble family, probably on Christmas night in the year 1491. A chivalrous knight, he was seriously wounded in battle in 1521 and suffered severe pain during the illness that followed. Someone gave him a book on the life of Christ to read and some legends of the saints. At that time he vowed to devote the rest of his life to self-denying labor and to try to emulate the saints about whom he read. As the years passed, he found other noblemen who were like-minded, and they banded themselves together in an order and took vows of poverty, obedience, and celibacy. One of the requirements of a recruit was that he spend a month in a hospital doing menial work and another month traveling as a mendicant.

The order was named after Jesus — " the Jesuits "; it grew in numbers, and the members became known for their reforming zeal. They are mentioned in this connection, not because they made any contribution to the healing arts or were in any way especially devoted to healing, but because a brother of the order, Saint Francis Xavier, who was a personal friend of Loyola, did make a contribution in healing.

Saint Francis Xavier is the founder and pioneer of the

modern Roman Catholic missionary enterprise. He traveled as far as India, Japan, China, and the East Indies in missionary endeavors, and set the pattern in missions that was followed by the Roman Church for many centuries. He was undoubtedly a gifted and courageous man, even though many would not agree with the methods he used in converting the heathen. Like others of his day, he helped to fight the plague with the usual medical practices and all his life he was interested in the sick. Besides using his medical knowledge, he also cured by faith, and he is credited with a number of miraculous cures.

Among those cures is one that occurred while he was in China. A four-year-old child had been ill with a fever for several months. One day Father Francis called at the home when the fever was high. The parents despaired of the child's life because they had tried everything they knew to help the child to get well. Father Francis came over to the bed where the patient lay, and placed his hand upon the forehead as he assured the parents that the child would be healed. Then he read a portion of the Scripture and offered a prayer, and when he made the sign of the cross, the child opened his eyes and smiled. The little one immediately showed a marked improvement because he was free of the fever and was soon completely well again.[9]

Saint Francis Xavier may be regarded as a pioneer in medical missions, a field of Christian service that grew in the practice of the Church in subsequent years. There were many others, less well known than Saint Philip Neri and Saint Francis Xavier, who engaged in faith healing in this period. Almost all of them used medicines with their healing practices. There seems to have been no prejudice against the use of medicine or surgery. In fact, these methods of healing were usually tried first.

Other religious orders continued to minister in the hospitals and to found new hospitals. Sometimes they worked in hospitals that were built by municipalities because the

Church was not the only source for the construction of hospitals any longer. Town or city officials or a feudal lord, seeing the need, might build such an institution. It was not only a matter of constructing the building; it was also important to have people to nurse the sick and operate the hospitals when they were constructed. In the latter capacity, religious orders made contributions to the healing arts also.

One of the new religious orders of this period was the Sisters of Mercy founded by Saint Vincent de Paul, who received his early training from the Franciscans in his home town, Dax, in Gascony. In his youth he was " shanghaied," as often happened in those days, and found himself in Tunis, North Africa, where he became the property of a renegade from Nice. His religious influence over this renegade was so great that the man came back to the Church and also brought Vincent back to France.

Vincent had been ordained a priest. It was during the post-Reformation period, and he himself went through a time of skepticism that worried him tremendously until he vowed to devote his entire life to helping the poor, a decision that enabled him to find peace. He became the parish priest in the town of Châtillon-lès-Dombes, where poverty was rampant and many people lived in hovels. Here he organized his first sisterhood of charity, composed of women who were willing to give personal aid to the poor. This organization was so successful that he organized others, one for the specific purpose of giving attention to galley slaves. Because he was very much interested in their plight he established a hospital for their care, and in 1619, King Louis XIII made him royal almoner of the galleys of France.

Then he interested other priests in the care of the poor and organized the Order of the Lazarists in Paris. He must have been an excellent money raiser because he secured a number of very large gifts to carry on this work. The house of Saint Lazarus in Paris became the headquarters of the order. Some priests were detailed to visit the soldiers, others to care for the blind and the sick, and others to visit the poor and the laborers. The influence of this order was felt in far places, and Vincent did not overlook Tunis, where he once won his own freedom. Workers were sent to Ireland, Genoa, Poland, and even to the island of Madagascar; but with all this activity he did not forget the sisterhoods.

In 1634 he devoted attention to the great, ancient hospital of Paris, the Hôtel-Dieu; and there he established a sisterhood of matrons to care for the patients. A few years later he established a large hospital for the poor in Paris, which later became known by the name Salpétrière. The great physicians and surgeons of the day practiced the art of healing in these institutions. The care of the patients was under the Church orders which also managed the institutions.

Saint Vincent did not practice faith healing. He felt constrained by a great compassion to do everything in his power to relieve the sick and the poor through care and charity. He was canonized or sainted by the Church in 1737 and in 1885 he was made the patron saint of all Roman Catholic charitable and healing institutions that were influenced in any way by his spirit. For that reason there are many Roman Catholic hospitals with his name.

There were some distinguishing characteristics of the sisterhoods organized by Saint Vincent. They pledged themselves to care for the sick regardless of how loathsome the disease might be. They were never to fear death or leave the impression that death is to be feared, and they were to minister to the needs of each patient as if they were doing it to Christ personally. Each patient must be treated like the others; there must never be partiality or any favoritism. No matter how disagreeable the patient was, they were always to be kind and agreeable. Neither were they to become intimately friendly with one another. It was a large assignment, perhaps too large, and perhaps in some ways inadvisable, but one thing is certain, they devoted themselves unstintingly to the care of the sick.

HEALING RITES

The use of relics and shrines for healing purposes continued during this period in the Roman Church, but the custom of anointing with oil in healing declined and was replaced by extreme unction. After the Council of Trent (1551), the sacrament of extreme unction became even more regarded as a means of preparing the patient for death. That, however, had not always been the significance of this sacrament. In the early days of the Church it was intended to restore bodily health to Christians. Oil, especially blessed by the bishop, was used by the priest to anoint the five external senses — the eyes, the ears, the nostrils, the lips, the hands, and the feet. When the male patient could be moved, the loins were also anointed. This latter practice was omitted in English-speaking countries and always forbidden in the case of women. As the oil was applied, the priest said, " Through this holy unction and His own most tender mercy, may the Lord pardon thee whatever offences thou hast committed by sight [hearing, smell, taste, touch, walking, carnal delectation]."

In the Eastern or Orthodox Church the sacrament was administered by a number of priests — three, five, or seven. The oil was applied to the forehead, chin, cheeks, hands, nostrils, and breast. The form used was, " Holy Father, physician of souls and bodies, who didst send Thy only-begotten Son our Lord Jesus Christ as the healer of every disease and our deliverer from death, heal also Thy servant [name], from the spiritual and bodily infirmity that holds him, and restore him to life, through the grace of Christ by the intercession of [certain saints who are named] and of all the saints." Each participating priest repeated the formula as he anointed one of the parts.

Origen (?-254), in mentioning the ways in which to acquire forgiveness of sins, lists this sacrament as one of them.

He writes that it was administered after confession to the priest and was regarded as a salutary medicine. From the fourth to the seventh centuries, the cure or alleviation of bodily sickness was a result added to the forgiveness of sins. Saint Bede (?–735) says that the then current custom of the Church was that the sick should be anointed by the priests with consecrated oil and through the accompanying prayer be restored to health. By 789, Theodaelf, the Bishop of Orleans, warned the priests that no one should die without it because it signified the forgiveness of sins and prepared the person for death.

During the twelfth and thirteenth centuries a change of practice took place and the sacrament came to be regarded by many as intended only for the dying. There were various reasons for this change of meaning and one of them was the demands made by the clergy for the administration of it. The poor people could not afford it except as a last resort, and waited as long as they could before they asked for it. Then too, certain superstitions became associated with it; many believed that if a person recovered after receiving the sacrament he could not use the rights of marriage or eat meat or make a will. In the third place, because it meant the forgiveness of sins, many thought it should not be administered until the patient was so near death that he probably would not sin again.

The edict of the Council of Trent is interpreted to mean that this sacrament should be administered only to a person whose sickness is such as to excite apprehensions of approaching death. According to the Catechism of the Council of Trent for Parish Priests, page 312, it can be administered to no one who is not dangerously sick; not even to those whose activities might lead them into death, such as a soldier or one on the way to execution.

This interpretation sets it apart as a preparation for death, but its healing efficacy is not denied under certain conditions.

The Acts of the Council of Trent on Extreme Unction, Session XIV, Cap. 2, state that at times there results the health of the body where it is expedient for the health of the soul: *" Et sanitas corporis interdum, ubi saluti animae expedierit, consequitur."*

VI. RELIGION AND HEALING IN ENGLAND

The Protestant Reformation spread to England and became official there during the sixteenth century. In England the kings had for many years controlled the ecclesiastical appointments because there was a strong national feeling against the encroachment of foreign power of any source.

It is not necessary to go into the reasons for the royal change to Protestantism because that is a long story, but the effect it had upon the Church and healing is of interest. The same practices and methods were employed by the Roman Catholic Church in England that were prevalent on the Continent, so the Reformation did affect this field of service.

King Henry VIII was determined to make the break with *Heresy* the Roman Catholic Church complete. On the Continent, the Reformers, in their anxiety to get away from image and relic worship, went to extremes in depriving their churches of beauty. In England, since the Protestants simply took over churches that were already constructed, the beauty was there in the original construction. The altar, the stained glass, and the Gothic architecture became a heritage of the Protestant Church in England. The Episcopal Church has retained this heritage to the present time. Their churches often are built beautifully, in the form of a cross, with a high altar and the cross as the center of attention. In " high " Episcopal churches the service of worship is called " the Mass," and the clergy are elaborately robed according to the season of the Church year. For these reasons many Protestants regarα the Episcopal Church or the Church of England as a middle way between the Protestant and Roman Catholic Churches.

While these outward appearances retain much of the Roman influence, the doctrine or teaching is Protestant. When the Reformation reached England, the Roman monasteries were dissolved, and their lands were taken over either by the government or by the Church of England. Protestant Episcopal orders of monks and nuns were formed to replace the Roman orders. But belief in the efficacy of relics and shrines, as well as faith healing, was discarded because they were regarded as Roman Catholic customs. The ancient practice of bringing the sick to holy shrines also was discouraged. Even though many believed that such healing was still being wrought, when the Reformation came to England the practice was frowned upon by the Protestant Church.

Luther emphasized the importance of faith and the power of prayer. Even though he exercised faith healing, yet the importance of faith and prayer became ever more regarded as being efficacious only for the soul. Jesus' miracles of healing were attributed to his divine power, and the part the Protestant clergyman could exercise was to help the patient to find a greater faith and a sense of having his sins forgiven. Jesus emphasized the importance of these elements before he healed, and the Protestant clergyman felt that was as far as he should go. He could not presume to possess the same divine powers as his Lord. In England we see the priest emerging as a pastor, as was the case on the Continent.

THE KING AS A HEALER

While faith healing was discarded officially by the Protestant Church there still were many people who believed in it. The belief in demons was prevalent and the common person reasoned that a holy influence should be powerful enough to overcome the evil spirits of demons. It is not astonishing that after a number of years faith healing was attributed to another institution or authority — the king of England himself.

Scrofula was a disease prevalent in England in those days. It is a tuberculous condition of the lymphatic glands and is marked by swelling of the glands, particularly those of the neck, and inflammation of bones and joints, and often results in discharging abscesses. This disease became commonly known as "the King's Evil." It was during the period when the divine right of kings was a commonly believed doctrine. From this it was rather easy to draw the conclusion that the king should also be able miraculously to cure disease. Just why this miraculous power should be confined to one disease remains unexplained, except on the basis that the excitement of visiting the king and the faith in his power to heal might have beneficially influenced a patient with this affliction.

The custom originated with King Edward the Confessor, but it was his successor, Henry VII, who in 1485 had a form prepared for use in the ceremony. The sick were brought to the king in great numbers. Each kneeled as he was touched while the king's chaplain intoned, " He put his hands upon them, and he healed them." After they had all been touched, they were brought back in the same order and each one was presented with a gold coin on a ribbon that was placed by another chaplain around the patient's neck. Then followed the reading of a portion of the holy Gospel, usually Mark, ch. 16, beginning with the fourteenth verse.

Later the ceremony was changed and the monarch touched the patient and placed the coin around the neck at the one kneeling. While the monarch performed the act, the chaplain prayed aloud that God would bless this work and grant healing to those upon whom the monarch laid his hands. When all had been blessed, there was a responsive prayer, led by the chaplain, and the benediction was spoken. Then the lord chamberlain brought a basin and towel, the king washed his hands, and the ceremony was over for that day.

The custom spread to the Continent also and was practiced by the rulers of France until the time of Louis XIV. Louis XIV touched twenty-four hundred sick people on the day of his coronation. An investigation of sorts was made, which reported that only five of them showed improvement. Some of the monarchs themselves did not want to participate in these services, but felt impelled by expediency to continue the custom. It is said that William of Orange considered the practice to be superstition and touched only one person. He is said to have muttered when he did it, " May God give you better health and more sense."

Right after Charles I was beheaded, Cromwell ruled England. This ruler refused to practice the royal touch for the King's Evil, so the people turned to another man, a soldier named Greatrakes, who said that he had a vision that told him he could heal. He treated almost every disease that came to him; thousands of sick people came or were brought for his touch and many said they were cured. Prominent people believed in this healing. Even Robert Boyle, the great chemist, voiced his praise of the man Greatrakes and his healing.

With the restoration of the monarchy in England the custom became the prerogative of the crown again. Royal physicians and surgeons believed in the ceremony, and helped the patients and examined them when they were brought for the healing service. A ritual for this service was included in the *Book of Common Prayer* of the Church of England for many years. Dr. John Browne, the royal surgeon, records that ninety-two thousand were touched for scrofula between the years 1660 and 1682, and it is said that the disease became much more prevalent during the years of the Commonwealth when Cromwell refused to conduct these services.

Queen Anne was the last of the English rulers to practice the touch. One of the most famous of the people whom she touched was the infant Samuel Johnson in 1712. The child was brought by stagecoach for the ceremony. She touched about two hundred that day. Samuel was a little over two years old at the time and James Boswell, Johnson's biographer, says that his mother brought him on the advice of the family physician, Sir John Floyes. Later in life Johnson talked about it and said that he had a faint recollection of the queen in diamonds and a long black hood, but he was not healed and suffered with the disease more or less all his life.

Since the monarch of England was the secular head of the Church of England, the royal touch had a distinct religious sanction and was observed for more than two hundred years.

THE HEALING WORK OF GEORGE FOX

Another man who wielded great influence in the Church during the Cromwell period in England was George Fox, who became the founder of the Society of Friends or Quakers.

It is rather surprising to read biographies of the life of this remarkable man and to find the biographers saying nothing about his healing activities. A recent book entitled *George Fox's Book of Miracles,* edited by Henry J. Cadbury and published by the Cambridge University Press, corrects this oversight. In his introduction, Cadbury points out that many people of seventeenth century England believed in miracle healing and that George Fox considered himself a healer. The publication of his *Book of Miracles* was indefinitely postponed because its appearance would have caused further attacks upon the Friends, who already had suffered enough because of their convictions.

George Fox was born in Leicestershire, England, in 1624, at a time of dissension in the Church in England. Baptists and Puritans and other nonconformists felt that the Church had lost its spiritual vitality. The Puritan ministers preached long sermons about the fall of man, sin, guilt, and wickedness. They told their hearers over and over again that God had elected some to be saved and some to be damned. The damned, even if they were children, would suffer forever in a hell designed for the devil and his angels.

George Fox never liked these sermons. He felt that the Christians of his day talked a lot about being saved, but they did not act as if they were. He saw " professors," as he chose to call people who said they were Christian and contradicted their words with their actions, sit through long sermons and then go to the tavern and guzzle liquor. George Fox set out to find the truth. In his search he went to London, where he visited churches and clergymen, but he could not find what he was seeking. For two years he wandered about until in 1646 he realized that God was speaking to him from within. " I heard a voice," he wrote in his *Journal*, " which said, ' There is one, even Christ Jesus, that can speak to thy condition; and, when I heard it, my heart did leap for joy.' " Christ became as real to him as a friend.

At first he called his followers " Children of the Light." He went about the land preaching; and his sermons were short and simple, different from the long Puritan addresses. He refused to remove his hat for any person, high or low; and he used " thee " and " thou " in addressing anyone, rich or poor, for in the sight of God all persons are precious. The religious authorities soon began to censor him. He would attend a service of worship in a church and ask permission to speak, but he scarcely had time to get started before the congregation was ready to throw him out. And he was thrown out and beaten unmercifully on many occasions. The authorities imprisoned him time and again so that he spent many years of his life in prison.

But this strange, sincere man made followers who were as sincere and determined as he was. At first he attracted only a few here and there, but as time went on the following grew in numbers. Probably the one incident that did most to further his cause in that early period was the enlistment of the interest of Mrs. Margaret Fell, a very religious woman who was dissatisfied with her Church and longed for a more real experience of God. It happened at a time when her husband, Judge Fell, was away from home. When he returned in a few weeks, he found his house turned into a meeting place, with Fox and two other leaders staying there. He must have been a very gracious man to accept such an upheaval in his home life. He knew and trusted his wife, and she said he behaved like a sensible man. At the evening meal on the day the judge returned, Margaret Fell began to quake and tremble as they did occasionally in the meetings. The children too were changed; now they were quiet and thoughtful.

The clergy and others in the neighborhood tried to induce Judge Fell to get rid of them but he would not. He never became a Quaker himself, but he never forbade them the privilege of meeting in his home. Years after the judge died, George Fox married Margaret Fell, but they never had much home life together because Fox was almost constantly on preaching tours. His great zeal impelled him to travel all over England, into Scotland, Wales, Ireland, Holland, Germany, and the English colonies along the coast line of America.

Percy Dearmer, in his book *Body and Soul,* gives a number of instances of faith healing that were accomplished by Fox. They are taken from the *Journal* of George Fox published by the Friends' Tract Association. On one occasion a man with the name Richard Myers was healed in a meeting at Arnside. The incident reminds one of the healing of the man with a withered hand by our Lord. Richard Myers' arm had been lame for a long time and Fox knew it. At the meeting Fox was " moved of the Lord " to tell the man to stand up. Myers stood and reached forth the arm that had been lame so long. After the meeting they took off his doublet and examined the arm. They found it sound and healed, and after that Richard Myers freely declared that the Lord had healed him.

On another occasion at a meeting of Friends, James Claypole and his wife were present. Claypole was wont to have attacks of a stone, evidently kidney or gallstone attacks. In those seizures it was often necessary for him to be inactive for two weeks, sometimes a month. Here at the meeting he had a severe recurrence. He cried out in his misery, and could neither stand nor lie down. Fox went to him and talked with him, trying to reassure him, and then laid his hand on the suffering man and prayed the Lord to give him relief. Fox tells us that the spirit of the Lord went through Mr. Claypole and he was immediately relieved and fell asleep. The next day he rode twenty-five miles in a stage-coach with Fox. He had been completely healed the day before.

Once when he was passing through Leicestershire Fox came to a town where some Friends asked him to visit a man who had been sick for a long time, of whose recovery they had despaired. Fox called on the man and talked with him about the Lord and then he was moved to pray with him. He prayed to the Lord for the man's welfare, and the man was restored to health again.

These are a few instances of the faith healing exercised by George Fox. He believed that the Lord could heal the sick through prayer, and he practiced the laying on of hands but did not use oil. Although he did not devote his ministry to healing practices, and that was not the main emphasis of his preaching, yet on occasions when he did practice it, he was usually successful. As a matter of fact he never used healing as a lure to win followers, and the Society in the succeeding years did not publicize his healing activities. It is only in these later years that his success in this field is becoming more widely known.

WITCHCRAFT

Since it was commonly believed that some people were possessed of a spirit that enabled them to heal others, it was also believed that other people could be possessed with the devil to do evil. The belief in witches is about as old as history. The incident about the witch of Endor in the Old Testament is well known. There were witches in Israel, and sometimes it is hard to distinguish whether the person had an evil or a good spirit. Ancient Israel set the pattern in dealing with the pagans whose land they conquered in that they treated the priests and priestesses of the conquered people as witches. When King Saul was abandoned by his prophets, he turned for help to the suppressed pagan witch of Endor.

Among the non-Jewish peoples, too, Africans as well as the Greeks and the Romans, there were witches. However, in these pagan religions they were regarded as sorcerers or magicians. The Christians attributed their spirit to the devil; Paul speaks of a person as being possessed of an evil spirit. Thereafter Christians regarded witches as dangerous people, but there were few who were executed for witchcraft until the Middle Ages because it was hard to decide whether the person in question was a witch or not. In some instances, such as Joan of Arc, the same person was regarded by some as a benefactor and by others as a witch.

During the Reformation and the post-Reformation period, witchcraft became an absorbing topic of conversation. The first pronouncement of the Church that really started the witch hunt was the decree of Pope Innocent VIII in 1484. In this bull he mentions specifically, " That in some parts of Northern Germany . . . many persons of both sexes, unmindful of their own salvation and straying from the Catholic Faith, have abandoned themselves to devils," etc. In order to discourage this practice he commissioned Heinrich Krämer and Jacob Sprenger as inquisitors. These priests were professors of theology, and as such should be capable of discerning a witch when they saw one. Of course it became an easy way to get rid of heretics also.

Krämer and Sprenger made a thorough study of the subject and wrote a book on how to discern a witch, which is

usually referred to as *The Witches Hammer*. It contained
the edict of Pope Innocent VIII against witches and quoted
or interpreted numerous Church Fathers. Ralph H. Major, M.D., in his book *Faiths That Healed,* writes that he
examined the book himself. It was first published in 1489,
and was "packed with information concerning demons and
their servants, the witches." In it, we learn that "witches
slay and devour children, cause hail, lightening, thunder-
storms, and tempests, make horses kick, foretell the future
and raise up the dead." [10] In 540 pages the authors left no
doubt that there were witches, and they gave directions how
to find them and how the witches cast spells.

The book started a terrible witch hunt that resulted in
the execution of many people. Catholics found Protestant
witches and Protestants found Catholic witches. The witch-
hunting grew until no person felt safe. After a while it became expedient to accuse someone of witchcraft in order not
to be accused.

The witch hunt spread from the Continent to England.
The king, who was instrumental in causing the English ver-
sion of the Bible that is dedicated to him, was the first English sovereign to write against witchcraft. King James liked
to write, and finished a few other books before he produced
his *Daemonologie*. He was quite positive that he had been
bewitched himself because on a number of occasions a storm
arose each time he wanted to undertake something important, such as a voyage by sea. He started a search for the
witch; his witch-hunters soon found him in the person of a
Dr. Fian, a sorcerer, who had quite a group of Catholic ad-
mirers. The king was a Protestant. Dr. Fian was arrested
and put to torture. In his pain he confessed, but as soon as
the pain was eased, he denied his confession. Then he was
put through it again; even his fingernails were torn out. He
confessed a second time and was sentenced to death. He and
several women were burned at the stake.

The tortures used to extract confessions from witches

were indeed the crudest forms of sadism. The rack was used, the body stretched until the bones came out of their sockets. Bones were broken, and the body on a rack was burned with a candle. Another method used was to seat the victim, tie his wrists together behind him, and then suspend him by his wrists in this position. If he did not confess, weights were tied to the feet and the inquisitor jerked the rope. If the victim still refused to confess, he was left to recover as best he could.

King James devised two methods for testing a witch. One method was to find witch marks on the victim's body. A " pricker " stuck the victim with a needle to find an insensitive spot. If one was found, it was definite proof that the victim was a witch. It is well known today that there are portions of the body less sensitive to pain than others and that it is possible through hysteria for a person to become insensitive to pain in certain areas. But King James did not know this.

His second method of determining the guilt of a witch was the water test. The victim's hands and feet were tied together and he or she was thrown into a pond. If the suspected witch went down in the water and drowned, that was a definite proof of innocence. If the victim floated, the sentence was passed and the stake came next. Either way, the person lost out.

Parliament passed laws against witchcraft and the hunt was on in earnest. There were some brave men who spoke and wrote against the belief in witches, but they had to be very careful lest they be accused and found guilty. Some scientists of the day, such as Dr. William Harvey, voiced their unbelief. On one occasion Dr. Harvey was commissioned to examine four women who were accused of changing boys into greyhounds and white horses. He found no witch marks on them. When the boy who brought the charge admitted that he had lied, the women were released from custody.

However, many of Dr. Harvey's colleagues did believe in

witches. Not only did the medical scientists hold such beliefs but the clergy did also; some went so far as to say that the Christian faith was dependent upon the belief in witchcraft. A few clergymen tried to refute the arguments. One of them was John Webster, who was a clergyman before he became a physician. In his parish he heard about a boy who had found some witches, which caused much excitement in Webster's congregation. He went to see the boy, but when two people who seemed to have charge of the child would not let him answer Webster's questions, the clergyman became suspicious and refused to believe the whole affair. Later he wrote a book in which he tried to expose witchcraft.

The witch hunt spread to the new colonies in America, where it centered in Salem, Massachusetts. Here the men of the Mather family, which figured so prominently in American history, used their influence to encourage witch-hunting. Rev. Cotton Mather wrote a book in which he told instances of witchcraft he had personally seen or heard about. A witch could, beyond a doubt, " afflict a person with diseases of astonishment, fits, epilepsy, torments, distempers, and pain."

The witch hunt was inadvertently augmented by a Rev. Mr. Parris, a businessman turned preacher. He had spent several years in business in the Barbados, and when he came to Salem with his family, he brought a native female servant along. She was half Negro and half Indian and knew the voodoo practices of her people. With her weird stories she amused the Parris daughter and a niece, Abigail Williams. Other children in the neighborhood came over and were intrigued by her tales. The same children heard all kinds of witchcraft stories in their homes also and it is to be expected that some of them would start acting peculiarly. That happened when a few of them crept under chairs and talked in an unfamiliar language. Parents called doctors, who could not diagnose the affliction. A few clergymen were called, and they were baffled also but did offer a cure: fasting and prayer. The remedy did not cure the affliction. A visiting clergyman saw some of the children in action and was convinced that they were bewitched. The witch hunt was on again, and the Negro servant and others were arrested. Some were burned; the Negro was sold into slavery.

The agitation grew in intensity. Twenty people were executed, many more were tried. The peak was reached in America about the same time as in England. Then people began to doubt the rightness of all this cruelty and began to listen to the voices of those who were trying to speak above the spiritual din. One such voice was that of Rev. George Burroughs, who was, before his retirement, the respected pastor of the Salem Village Church. From his retirement at Wells, Maine, he continued to speak and write against witch-hunting. Along with other victims he was suspected of having an alliance with the devil. In due time he was arrested and brought to Salem, where he was examined by lawyers and clergymen. The children who claimed to be bewitched started to cry and have fits when they saw him. One boy said he saw Rev. Mr. Burroughs carrying a molasses barrel with his thumb in the bung of the barrel. Other accusations were brought. Burroughs declared his innocence, but he was sentenced to be hanged.

At the execution he continued to declare his innocence and offered a prayer, closing with the Lord's Prayer. A witch was not supposed to be able to say the Lord's Prayer, and when they saw that he could do it, the people started to mumble. They did not like this execution. This man was surely innocent. At that moment Rev. Cotton Mather made his appearance and saw that the hanging might be avoided. He took a hand in the matter and quieted the crowd. Then he told them that the victim was not an ordained minister and to beware because the devil often disguises himself as a saint. As a result of his oratory, Rev. Mr. Burroughs was hanged.

This execution seems to have marked the change. Many

people did not like it. Some children who had accused others had now grown to maturity and realized what they had done. They confessed that the accusations they had made in childhood were not true. The witch hunt waned and left an episode in history that has been studied by many scholars who attempt to find an explanation for it.

The belief in witchcraft has never disappeared from the American scene. While the Church did support that belief, once it was convinced of its error, it used every Christian means at its disposal to discourage the superstition. But many living today remember stories about witches that they heard in their childhood. Voodoo ceremonies are still held among the Haitians and some other nationalities in our cities. Charms that are supposed to cast or break spells can be purchased in our metropolitan areas.

Many people wear medals that they believe will protect the wearer in various situations. While religious authorities may not officially teach that medals can cast or break charms magically, many who wear them feel that they were blessed for that purpose.

VII. HEALING AND COMPASSION

PROTESTANT PASTORAL MINISTRIES

In the post-Reformation period very little was done by the Protestant Church to establish female nursing orders. Luther himself did not re-establish the diaconate, chiefly because he did not have the time to do so although he considered it. What he really would have liked to see accomplished was a systematic division of a city into four or five parishes, each with a pastor and a number of deacons and deaconesses. They could divide the ministry among themselves, with some to have responsibility for the church property, the pastor to preach and visit the sick, and others to care for the needy. But Luther never put the plan into effect, chiefly, he said, because they would have to wait " until the Lord God makes enough Christians to do it."

He did regard the cloisters with much interest and probably should have reformed some of them that he caused to be abolished. In other instances he championed the cause of the cloister when he felt that the nuns were doing a Christian work. One of these was the cloister at Herford in Westphalia. The town council wanted to disband it and forbid the nuns to wear their garb. They appealed to Luther for help, and he wrote to the town council and begged them to permit the cloister to exist and the nuns to wear their dress. He based his plea on the fact that they did not hinder the work of the pastors and were a useful and elevating influence in the community. On other occasions, when he felt that the situation merited it, he used strong language against cloisters. He did not favor any retreat from the realities of life and felt that nuns and monks should be useful in their communities. For that reason any associations resembling Roman orders in the Protestant Church would never have received his approval.

He did recognize woman's special ability to care for the sick and said that the inclination to pity others is greater in the female than in the male. Christian women have special grace to comfort others and to soothe their pain. He even went so far as to recommend the use of female teachers in girls' schools, quite a revolutionary idea in his day, when males only were used in teaching.

Many years were to pass before the Lutheran Church revived the diaconate. There were some attempts to use Christian women in the Church to minister to the sick through the period of the Thirty Years' War and the years that followed. But these attempts were local and on the part of volunteers and did not have the sanction or the authority of the Lutheran Church.

The Reformed Church in Switzerland, however, regarded the diaconate as one of the offices indispensable to the Church. The religious nature of the care of the sick and the poor was recognized, and many sincere women devoted themselves to this work. But the Reformed Church did not maintain institutions to train these deaconesses. Synods farther north often seriously considered the establishment of an order of deaconesses, and there were resolutions for it and resolutions against it. A number of individual congregations here and there had deaconesses, and they were regarded much in the same manner as the widows of the Early Church. The office was by appointment for an indefinite period, and the deaconess could quit her office if she so desired. She lived in her own home and went out to visit and care for the sick and the poor. It required another one hundred and fifty years before any definite steps were taken by the Protestant Church to establish a diaconate.

This was the period in which the Protestant pastorate developed. Luther regarded health as a term that includes the various phases of man's being. Inner regeneration or conversion was emphasized. " Faith is a living, daring confidence in the grace of God so sure that it would die for it a thousand times. And such confidence and apprehension of divine grace make us cheerful, bold, and joyous toward God and every creature, which is the work of the Holy Ghost in faith. Hence, without compulsion, a man is willing and glad to do good to every one, to serve every one, to suffer all things, for the love of God and to His praise, who has shown such grace to him; so that it is impossible to separate works from faith, yea, just as impossible as it would be to separate burning and shining from fire." [11]

Luther developed the observation that out of faith flow love to God and joy in him, and out of love a spontaneous, happy life, in the free service of one's neighbor. He set the pattern for much of the Protestant preaching. His emphasis upon private confession led to the custom of regarding the pastor as the *Seelsorger*. The *Seelsorger* is the one who is concerned about the health of the soul. Even though much of the preaching of this period was polemic in nature, there was also an abundance of preaching of a personal, spiritual nature. This naturally invited the confidence of the people in the pastor, and they consulted him about personal spiritual matters. Pastoral counseling, especially pastoral counseling with the sick, really has its origin in this period of the Church's history. It grew spontaneously out of the preaching that inclined or directed the individual to examine himself in the light of the gospel.

THE NEED FOR NURSES

While the office of the pastor grew out of the Reformation, the lack of interest in nursing care caused many hospitals to close. It is estimated that in England alone at least one hundred hospitals were closed that were previously staffed with nuns. This situation presented a tremendous problem in the care of the sick. It caused municipalities to build and operate hospitals. This period is regarded as the " dark period " in nursing history. The matrons chosen for these municipal hospitals rarely knew anything about nursing care. The lay nurses who were employed were usually lacking in both skill and morals. They were overworked and ill-treated women who took to nursing when they could not find employment elsewhere. The picture is not a very pretty one. From old records there is information about the duties of the nurse:

" She must stupe as often and in such a manner as the doctors shall direct, and shall attend to the workings of all vomits.

" She is to make all the beds on one side of the ward, and to scour and make clean the beds and floors of the whole ward, the passages, stairs, etc.

" She must keep clean scoured the cans for beer, and the dishes fouled at dinner.

" She must attend the butler at the ringing of the beer bell and of the bread bell, . . . and at the ringing of the cook's bell must receive from her the exact amount of provisions appointed for each patient.

" She may take to help her such patients as the sister (head nurse) shall see fit." [12]

Other rules forbade nurses to throw rags, dirt, or bones out of the windows and forbade drunkenness and quarreling. Many of these nurses were ill-bred and immoral, and it was not until a few centuries later that lay nursing became an honored and consecrated profession.

In the midst of this there were some local efforts in the Protestant Church to revive the nursing orders. The spirit of compassion still motivated Christian people. As early as 1530 the Protestant Church in Minden formed an order of district nurses. They were not called " deaconesses," but were religiously motivated. In 1567, Pastor Keppel established a charitable institution for the care of the sick, with an order of Protestant nurses in charge. At Walsdorf there was a similar organization, and their members were called sisters. It is interesting to notice that a girl had to be at least eighteen years of age before she was admitted and she served a one-year probation period. If her character and ability were of a sufficiently high standard, she was consecrated with a religious ceremony. The sisters were free to leave or marry at their discretion. They were also especially trained in various fields, nursing, teaching, visiting, and the care of the poor. In the Reformed Church at Wessel the deaconesses were chosen by the congregation and employed by the congregation to nurse the sick. But the General Synod did not confirm the action of this congregation, and the movement was discouraged.

The Protestants in the city of Amsterdam attempted a plan similar to Luther's suggestion. The city was divided into four districts for nursing service and they chose sisters or deaconesses for this visiting nursing service. They were chiefly elderly Christian women and the work was strenuous. Each year new ones were consecrated and others were released from service with thanks. Still others served in that capacity for many years.

The Moravians, a Protestant group founded by Count Zinzendorf, also had sisters who were chosen to do this work. Mennonites in Holland, founded in the sixteenth century, also had deaconesses.

So it can be said that there were local attempts in the Protestant Church to make the care of the sick a religious work, but the effort grew rather slowly for a few centuries after the beginning of the Reformation. There are those who maintain that the Reformers and those of the post-Reformation period in Protestantism made no contribution in the field of healing, but that observation is not based on facts. It is true that much of the old was discarded, especially the veneration of relics and other sacred things that were used in the Roman Church. The practice in faith healing almost disappeared in the Protestant Church and was taken over by secular religious people. But the Protestant leaders did recognize that health is a matter of the total personality. This conception laid the basis for the future development of the pastoral office which has such an important place in the Protestant Church today.

JOHN WESLEY — THE PASTOR

John Wesley (1703–1791) attributed his conversion on the evening of May 24, 1738, to the influence of Martin Luther. Rev. Mr. Wesley was an ordained rector of the Anglican Church, but until that time he felt that he was not saved. On this particular evening he went unwillingly to a society in Aldersgate Street where the leader was reading Luther's *Preface to the Epistle to the Romans.* Wesley mentions the exact time of his conversion, and says it was at a quarter of nine that evening, as the leader of the meeting was reading about the change that God works in the heart through faith in Christ. Then John Wesley felt his own heart strangely warmed. " I felt I did trust in Christ, Christ alone for salvation; and an assurance was given me that He had taken away my sins, even mine, and saved me from the law of sin and death." [13]

John Wesley became one of the greatest preachers of any age. He is regarded as the founder of the Methodist Church, one of the largest denominations in the world. While he was primarily a preacher, he was a great pastor also. He made it his business to visit many people who evidenced undue emotional and spiritual stress at his preaching services. He was a man of prayer and believed that prayer has therapeutic value. In his *Journal* of Friday, May 8, 1741, he wrote: " I found myself much out of order. However, I made shift to preach in the evening: but on Saturday my bodily strength quite failed, so that for several hours I could scarce lift up my head. Sunday, 10, I was obliged to be down most part of the day, being easy only in that posture. Yet in the evening my weakness was suspended, while I was calling sinners to repentance. But at our love-feast which followed, beside the pain in my back and head, and the fever which still continued upon me, just as I began to pray, I was seized with such a cough, that I could hardly speak. At the same time came strongly into my mind, 'These signs shall follow them that believe.' I called on Jesus aloud, to 'increase my faith,' and to 'confirm the word of his grace.' While I was speaking my pain vanished away; the fever left me; my bodily strength returned; and for many weeks I felt neither weakness nor pain. 'Unto thee, O Lord, do I give thanks.'" [14]

This great preacher and pastor also used prayer when he called upon the sick. In his pastoral call he usually used prayer as a medium of reassurance. While he never laid the main emphasis upon its curative powers, there are many instances when he used it effectively for that purpose. On Monday, March 14, 1745, he wrote: " I took horse, and rode away for Bristol. Between Bath and Bristol I was earnestly desired to turn aside, and call at the house of a poor man, William Shalwood. I found him and his wife sick in one bed, and with small hopes of the recovery of either. Yet (after prayer) I believed they would 'not die, but live and declare the loving kindness of the Lord.' The next time I called he was sitting below stairs, and his wife able to go abroad." [15]

On one occasion his brother Charles set out for the north but had to return because he was taken ill. When John came home in the evening two days later, he found his brother much worse. He had not slept for several nights, except with the use of opiates. After visiting with him, John went down to some friends who were in the house and they prayed for his recovery. When he went up to see him later, he was asleep and slept through the night until morning.

He believed that the prayer of faith has healing virtues and

seemed to think that it might be used for animals also. At
least he did use it in that manner on one occasion as he related in his *Journal* on Monday, March 17, 1746: " I took my
leave of Newcastle, and set out with Mr. Downes and Mr.
Shepherd, but when we came to Smeton, Mr. Downes was
so ill, that he could go no further. When Mr. Shepherd and
I left Smeton, my horse was so exceeding lame that I was
afraid I must have lain by too. We could not discern what it
was that was amiss; and yet he would scarce set his foot on
the ground. By riding thus seven miles, I was thoroughly
tired, and my head ached more than it had done for some
months. (What I here aver is the naked fact: let every man
account for it as he sees good.) I then thought, ' Cannot God
heal either man or beast, by any means, or without any? '
Immediately my weariness and headache ceased, and my
horse's lameness in the same instant. Nor did he halt any
more either that day or the next. A very odd accident this
also! " [16]

There are other instances of faith healing in his ministry.
Even though he usually used prayer in connection with his
calls upon the sick, it is doubtful that he expected instant
healing. He seemed rather startled himself in these three
cases that are quoted from his *Journal*. But many people
were grateful for the prayers he offered in their behalf when
they were sick. His contribution was rather in the sick calls
he made, in the spirit of compassion that he awakened in his
followers, and in the hymns he wrote. Many of these hymns
are a means of expressing and releasing strong emotions;
they relieve tensions and express hopes and aspirations. As
such, they have definite therapeutic value. John Wesley encouraged people to sing.

Anyone of Wesley's nature who comes into contact with
so many people cannot help becoming interested in their
physical well-being. He was no exception, and his compassion for the sick was such that he felt impelled to do something about their condition in addition to his prayers and

preaching. With characteristic diligence he applied himself to the study of diseases and remedies. With keen observation and wide reading in the medical field, he gained a considerable knowledge of medicine and published the results of his research in a book entitled *Primitive Physic*. The prescriptions in this book must have been approved by physicians of that day, because the man who wrote what is considered to be the first good biography of John Wesley was a physician named Dr. John Whitehead. Undoubtedly Wesley also got much of his medical information from physician friends.

In this it is seen that he was sincerely concerned about the health of people. Even though he recommended medical care, he also realized that a sick person needs more than that, and he never neglected to minister to the spiritual needs also when he called upon the sick.

This deep interest in healing was transmitted to his followers, who founded dispensaries, orphanages, strangers' societies, refuges for widows, hospitals, and other philanthropic institutions. Today there are many institutions of mercy and love in our country that were founded and are supported by the Methodist Church. Among them are some of the finest hospitals in the land.

THE CONTRIBUTIONS OF NURSING ORDERS

In the Roman Catholic Church during this period the established nursing orders continued their work and many new ones were formed. One of these was the Brothers of Saint John of God founded by the Portuguese Juan Ciudad. In his youth he lived a life of dissipation and adventure in the army of King Ferdinand I of Hungary. While fighting the Turks, Juan was converted and took his conversion very seriously. He imposed such penances upon himself that he was regarded as insane. Having been wounded in battle, he was taken to a hospital, where he was treated like an insane person. Here he experienced what treatment these unfortunate people received and vowed to devote his life to the care of the sick, especially the insane.

He went to Granada, where he turned his rented house into an asylum for the sick from the poorest classes. People observed his self-sacrificing work of love and soon there were other religious men who joined him. Among them were Martino and Velasco, two laymen. After ten years Juan died and Martino took over the direction of the work. The institution at that time did not have monastic rules. But others joined the organization and soon there were other houses in operation, especially a large hospital in Madrid. A bull by Pope Pius V in 1572 made the brethren an order of the Augustinian rule. They were given the privilege of presenting some of their number for the priesthood. The rules of the order made it necessary for the members of the hospital staff to have a thorough knowledge of medicine. The number of their institutions grew to about one hundred. The brothers still nurse in some of their Roman and Austrian hospitals.

Another order of men started about this time is known as the Agonizants or Agony Fathers or Fathers of the Good Death. This order was founded at Rome by a pious priest, Camillus de Lellis, who was born in 1550. His life experience was similar to that of Juan Ciudad. He was converted in the hospital of Saint James at Rome, and decided to become a priest and devote his life to service to the sick in hospitals. The Order of the Agonizants grew rapidly in numbers and wealth, and spread beyond Italy to Spain, Portugal, and France. He also instituted a similar order for women known as the Camellines or Daughters of Saint Camillus. It was their special work to nurse victims of the plague. They gave themselves so unstintingly to their service that the entire order died while nursing the plague victims in Barcelona. Camillus and Juan Ciudad have both been canonized by the Roman Church and are patron saints of Roman Catholic hospitals.

Another person who is a prominent figure in this period is Virginia Bracelli, who was born in Genoa in 1587. She became the founder of the Daughters of Our Lady of Mount Calvary, better known as Brignoline, because Emanuele Brignole later redirected the order. She started by taking orphans and girls into her house. Later she rented the deserted convent of the Friars of Bregard, which was known as Mount Calvary. It was from this convent that they took their name. She cared for the girls here out of her own funds until the government gave her a certain number of " protectors." " Protectors " were wealthy people who sponsored an institution. Among them was Cardinal Brignole, who thought the girls should serve some useful purpose and trained them in the care of the sick. An epidemic soon came, and the Daughters of Our Lady of Mount Calvary demonstrated so much devotion and skill that they were recognized as a nursing order. One peculiarity of this order was that the daughters cared only for female patients.

There were other orders founded by Roman Catholics in this period, mostly of the same pattern except that some specialized in the care of male or female patients or in the care of certain diseases.

Part III

THE MODERN PERIOD

VIII. NURSING ORDERS AND CHURCH
HOSPITALS

The Reformation and Counter Reformation were events of the past. Napoleon (1769–1821) was responsible for a series of wars and revolutions that spread over most of Europe. The beginning of the nineteenth century was a period of horror and uncertainty, and in such circumstances moral laxity and spiritual stupor usually follow. Europe was no exception to this rule. Nevertheless, uncertainty provides an incentive for many to examine their moral and spiritual standards, and a period of laxity is often followed by a wave of revival. That is what happened in the nineteenth century. Conditions became so corrupt that some people awakened to the seriousness of the situation. Great preachers and pastors felt called by God to counteract the influences of moral and spiritual degeneracy, and men of great ability were moved to use their talents to stimulate higher moral and spiritual standards. Many people turned to religion for assurance and security as they became aware of their spiritual needs. So it was that in many places the nineteenth century was marked by a wave of religious earnestness and service.

THE DIACONATE AND PROTESTANT HOSPITALS

There were feeble local efforts in the eighteenth century to revive the diaconate, but in the nineteenth century, from 1820 to 1845, at least four different religious leaders in Germany succeeded in re-establishing this order of Christian service in the Protestant Church. In 1820, Pastor Kloenne published a pamphlet entitled *The Revival of the Deaconesses of the Ancient Church in our Ladies' Societies*. In it he suggested that the choice of deaconesses be made by the synod or presbytery rather than by the individual congregation. They should be single or widows and be trained to work among the sick and the poor. This pamphlet received a wide circulation, and a few years later Count von der Recke-Volmerstein started a periodical, *Deaconesses, or Life and Labors of the Handmaids of the Church in Teaching and Training and in Nursing the Sick*. These writers, representing both the nobility and the clergy, influenced the Protestant rulers.

Some Christian women of their own accord, and without connection with a healing order, dedicated their lives to healing. One of these was Amalie Sieveking, a young Lutheran girl. When a cholera epidemic broke out in Hamburg, she offered herself for service in the cholera hospital. She and the doctors attempted in vain to interest other women. After a short time the doctors turned the whole management of the hospital into her hands. There she labored until the epidemic subsided, and after that she succeeded in forming a Society for the Care of the Poor and the Sick. Her organization was imitated in other cities, and years later Theodor Fliedner tried to get her to come to Kaiserswerth, but she preferred to continue her work in Hamburg. She felt that she was called by God to minister to the sick there. While her efforts were not fostered by the Church, her reputation and influence did much to promote general interest in nursing care in Protestant circles.

Baron von Stein was instrumental in the restoration of Prussia after the Napoleonic wars. He was a religious man who heard about Amalie Sieveking and also admired greatly the work of the Sisters of Mercy of the Roman Catholic Church. Through his influence Pastor von Bodelschwingh, who was well known and respected, became convinced that the Protestant Church should have a similar female diaconate and furthered the cause through his preaching. But the man who actually put all these hopes and wishes into practice was Pastor Theodor Fliedner.

When he visited Holland, Pastor Fliedner saw Mennonite deaconesses at work in their local congregations. He was so impressed with their usefulness and consecration that he decided to begin a similar order in his own Church. While visiting in England, he inspected the hospitals and was impressed with the buildings, but terribly disappointed in the lay nurses. Upon his return to his church at Kaiserswerth, he was determined to begin a female diaconate. A guide or constitution was prepared that contained principles for the training of Christian women in nursing. This document was entitled *The Order of Deaconesses for the Rhenish Provinces.*

Beginning without money, but with great faith and a sincere interest in the welfare of the sick, he managed to buy the largest and handsomest house in Kaiserswerth. There he opened his first training school for deaconesses; and Gertrude Reichard, the daughter of a local physician, was the first student to enter for training. Mrs. Fliedner became the mother superior. The house served both as a mother house for the deaconesses who entered training and as a hospital. The first patient was a Roman Catholic servant girl. A few other girls followed Gertrude's example, and two years later one deaconess was sent from the mother house for service in the city hospital at Elberfeldt.

Fliedner's Kaiserswerth institution grew in size. Other buildings were acquired. More girls entered training and it became known all over Europe, and finally its reputation spread to America. But that is getting ahead of the story. Fliedner branched out. He educated three kinds of deaconesses: the first group to care for the sick, the poor, and unmarried pregnant girls; the second group to teach; and the third group to do parish work.

Christian character, as well as a healthy constitution, was regarded as essential on the part of those who were admitted for training, and after a period of probation the deaconess was consecrated in a special ceremony. Although there were no vows regarding celibacy, the deaconesses did promise to serve at least five years. They were permitted to wear a simple distinctive garb, but even that was optional.

Fliedner acted in the capacity of rector or chaplain and was assisted by a mother superior who had charge of the domestic life of the institution. Most of the deaconess hospitals today, in Europe and in the United States, still have clergymen in the capacity of superintendent and chaplain. The clergyman's work was primarily administrative, and he did not minister to the spiritual needs of the patients except as an avocation.

Soon after the Kaiserswerth institutions became known, others were established on a similar plan. Many deaconesses were trained who were sent into hospitals, orphanages, and other institutions; but they always regarded the mother house where they received their training as their home. Theodor Fliedner himself was active in establishing many such institutions. He traveled extensively, and during his lifetime founded deaconess homes and hospitals in Jerusalem, Constantinople, Smyrna, Alexandria, Hungary, Holland, France, England, Scandinavia, and the United States. In twenty-five years twenty-seven institutions were founded. At the time of his death there were thirty mother houses and sixteen hundred deaconesses in active service.

The idea of the female diaconate was regarded with favor everywhere. These consecrated women served without remuneration, except for a stipend, and devoted their lives to a healing ministry. When Florence Nightingale decided to become a Christian lay nurse, she traveled from England to Kaiserswerth for some of her training. It was here that she found an expression of her ideals.

The second oldest deaconess mother house was in connection with the Elizabeth Hospital in Berlin. It was founded in 1837 by Rev. John Gossner, who was formerly a Roman Catholic priest. After he became a Protestant pastor, he established a deaconess mother house in Berlin. He did not believe in fixed forms or vows, which was a reaction from his Roman Catholic training. Everything about the deaconess order in his mother house was on a voluntary basis. As long as he lived everything went well, but after his death it was hard to find a successor who could dominate the institution with his personality as Gossner had done. So the order was reorganized on the Kaiserswerth plan.

There were other leaders in this movement to re-establish the diaconate of the ancient Church. They were such men as Franz H. Haerter in Strassburg, Loche in Neuendettelsau, Froelich in Dresden, Schultz in Bethany, and Von Bodelschwingh in Bielefeld. There is extant a translation of a handbook for the instruction of probationers in the Neuendettelsau institution.[17] In this book, Rev. Frederick Meyer, who was the rector of the institution at the time of the writing, states the aims of the deaconess school. Emphasis was placed upon personal religious living: " Her whole behavior, including her outward appearance and manner, should conform to these requirements, and be simple and truthful, sincere and honorable." As far as the " requirements " were concerned, she had to be thoroughly familiar with Luther's Small Catechism and know the books of the Bible and Biblical history. In order to meet the spiritual needs of her patients, she must memorize a number of Scripture verses and hymns that are appropriate for the sick, the dying, and the bereaved. She should also be able to sing some hymns that are comforting. The liturgy of the worship services was also important, and instruction was offered to help the deaconess to understand its construction and the attitude of the hearer, which is so important in the effectiveness of the sermon.

As far as general culture is concerned, it was required of

the probationer that she read fluently and write legibly and know enough arithmetic to be able to do bookkeeping if that be required of her. She should know the geography of her own country and of the Holy Land.

As a competent nurse, she must master the medical instruction and know how to deal with the sick, the dying, the melancholy, the troubled, the young, the feeble-minded, and the fallen. In all this she must exercise the compassion exemplified in the early Christian diaconate and remain unmarried.

There were some young Christian women who wanted to be nurses, but looked askance at the strictness of the Church diaconate and the supervision of the clergy, so they caused independent orders to be established, such as the Sisters of the Red Cross and the Sisters of the Lazarus Cross. These became rather large numerically and were religiously motivated, but their religious training was not so thorough nor their supervision so strict as that of the Church-related organizations with their rectors and chaplains.

On the Continent, most of the mother houses and hospitals were under the direction of the Lutheran, the Reformed, and the Evangelical Churches. But the Methodists in Frankfort also had a deaconess home.

The diaconate spread to England, where some of the more progressive physicians became interested in better nursing care in the hospitals and turned to the Church for help. One physician, Dr. Robert Gooch, attempted to interest the Methodists and the Quakers in this movement. He wanted the student deaconesses to receive their nursing training in the hospitals of London and Edinburgh and their religious training in a mother house supported by the Church. In 1840, Dr. Gooch, with the poet Robert Southey, succeeded in starting the Protestant Sisters of Charity. The mother house was in connection with Guy's Hospital in London, and this is regarded as the beginning of the nurses' training school in connection with a municipal or secular hospital. After they had received their training, the sisters were permitted to nurse in private homes. This order was rather more secular than ecclesiastical, although religious motivation was not overlooked.

The first thoroughly religious nursing order in England was founded by the Church of England in 1848 at Saint John's House in London. The Kaiserswerth principles were followed, in that it was required of the nurses that they be members of the Church and of good Christian character. There was a clergyman in charge who acted as rector and chaplain and a mother superior. The students received their medical training at the hospital nearby and lived in the mother house. Six of these sisters went with Florence Nightingale to the Crimea to nurse the wounded soldiers there.

The diaconate was established in the United States through the interest of an English Lutheran pastor, Rev. W. A. Passavant, in Pittsburgh, Pennsylvania. Dr. Passavant's name will always be associated with a ministry of mercy in healing. He was interested in the relief of the sick and insane and the care of the poor and destitute. A hospital was desperately needed in the section of the city in which he worked because there was no place where the sick poor could be taken for adequate treatment. Having heard about the Kaiserswerth institutions, Passavant journeyed there and received encouragement from Fliedner. Both felt that a similar institution could be established in Pittsburgh, if some of the deaconesses from Kaiserswerth would be willing to go there and help to get it started.

With the encouragement he received, Passavant returned to Pittsburgh, and in his enthusiasm rented a house in the spring of 1848 that should serve as a hospital. The first two patients were soldiers, and since he could not find nurses he took care of them himself, with the aid of a divinity student. Then came a cholera epidemic and the house was too small to meet the needs. Still hoping that deaconesses would soon arrive from Kaiserswerth, he purchased property that was large enough to provide forty beds. Then word came from Fliedner that he was coming himself and would bring four deaconesses with him. Mrs. Passavant was acting as matron of the hospital, and Louisa Marthens was assisting her. In June of 1849, just when the gold-rush enthusiasm was at its height, Fliedner and the deaconesses arrived at the Pittsburgh infirmary. This institution is regarded as the first Protestant Church hospital in the United States.

Other people became interested in the project and contributed funds so that a mother house could be established to train deaconesses who would devote their lives to the care of the sick poor. This latter project was not successful enough to meet Passavant's expectations because in the first thirty-five years only sixteen candidates entered the institution with this purpose in view. But even this small number of consecrated women had a far-reaching influence in that they were instrumental in starting hospitals in Milwaukee, Wisconsin; Chicago, Illinois; and Jacksonville, Illinois.

Christian people of different denominations watched this experiment closely, and soon there were other synods and presbyteries that were interested in doing the same thing. Miss Dorothea Dix, a lay nurse, became well and favorably known because she investigated conditions in poorhouses, prisons, and insane asylums and gave much publicity to her findings. Then at the outbreak of the Civil War the Secretary of War appointed her to act as superintendent of female nurses for the Union Army. She came into contact with the work of the deaconesses and praised them highly for their efficient and Christian service. All this helped the cause of the female diaconate.

An Association for Works of Beneficence was formed in the Iowa Synod of the Lutheran Church. Its purpose was to instruct in God's Word, to found institutions of healing, and to train deaconesses. Anna Lutz, of Toledo, Ohio, was sent to Neuendettelsau in 1872 to be educated in the principles of the diaconate, but shortly after her consecration she had to give up the work because of ill health. American pastors called upon the mother houses in Germany to send deaconesses over here for the purpose of establishing the diaconate. In response to these pleas, a few deaconesses came over, but the net results were not very encouraging.

One such venture that did prove successful occurred in Philadelphia. John D. Lankenau, a wealthy philanthropist of German extraction, was interested in the German hospital there and served as president of its board. He was dissatisfied with the management and the nursing in the institution, and in 1884, with the help of a few prominent Lutheran pastors, he appealed in vain to several mother houses in Germany to send deaconesses. Their attention was called to an independent group of sisters in Iserlohn. It was this small deaconess community, consisting of six sisters and their mother superior, who answered the call and took over the management and nursing in their German hospital at Philadelphia. Mr. Lankenau supported them financially, and two years later built the beautiful Mary J. Drexel Home for older people and the Philadelphia mother house for deaconesses. This institution grew in size, members, and influence, and has been a leader in deaconess work for many years. With the help of the board of trustees and Mr. Lankenau, the sisters of their institution founded a children's hospital, Easton Hospital, Saint John's Hospital at Allegheny, Pennsylvania, and the Kensington Hospital for tubercular patients.

The next Lutheran denomination to establish hospitals in the United States was the Norwegian Lutheran. Sister Elizabeth Fedde, of Oslo, Norway, a deaconess nurse and pharmacist, came to New York at the invitation of Mrs. Anna Boers, the wife of the Norwegian consul general, and Rev. Mr. Mortensen, the pastor of the Norwegian Seamen's Church in Brooklyn. They felt the impelling urgency to establish an institution of healing, and appealed to people of their faith to help to build a hospital where Christian care could be given to the sick. After Sister Elizabeth served as a visiting nurse for a year and a half, they began to realize a dream; a deaconess home and hospital was built with thirty beds.

The Norwegian Lutheran Church was strong in the Northwest, and their second hospital was founded in 1888 in Minneapolis, through the instrumentality of interested pastors and Sister Elizabeth Fedde, who went there for that purpose. Three years later the hospital was functioning well and Sister Ingeborg Sponland was left in charge of the institution located at Fifteenth and East 23d Streets. In 1897, the Norwegian Lutheran Deaconess Home and Hospital was founded in Chicago with the purpose of offering adequate medical and nursing care to people who needed it and to train deaconesses who would be willing to dedicate their lives to that cause.

These institutions also trained deaconesses for Christian work in orphanages, in old people's homes, in parishes, and for the mission fields in China and Madagascar. In each institution a Norwegian Lutheran pastor acted as superintendent and chaplain.

The Swedish Lutheran Church also started hospitals, primarily through the efforts of Pastor E. A. Fogelstrom, of Omaha, Nebraska. Omaha was a growing frontier community, where adequate care of the sick was direly needed. In order to get the work started, Pastor Fogelstrom sent Sister Bothilda Swensen to be trained in Philadelphia; and after she visited hospitals and deaconess homes in Europe, she became the mother superior of the Swedish Lutheran Hospital of Omaha. This institution grew in size and was taken under the care of the Augustana Synod of the Lutheran Church. Later, in 1898, Sister Bothilda went to St. Paul, Minnesota, where she assumed charge of the Bethesda Hospital. This hospital in St. Paul was started by the Minnesota Conference of the Swedish Lutheran Augustana Synod and in 1901 opened a training school for lay nurses.

Augustana Hospital of Chicago was incorporated in 1882 for the purpose of the " training of well qualified nurses, the establishment and support of hospitals, the care of the aged, the education of the young and in general the exercise of mercy among the suffering." [18] It started in a house at first rented and later purchased from Rev. Dr. Erland Carlson, and the nursing care was in charge of deaconesses. From that modest beginning it grew, through the efforts of pastors and members of the churches who were willing to pray and sacrifice for what they considered to be a practical expression of Christ's love for man, until today it can care for four hundred and fifty patients at a time.

Other hospitals started by Lutheran groups are Bethesda Hospital, Crookston, Minnesota; Deaconess Hospital, Northwood, South Dakota; St. Luke's Hospital, Fergus Falls, Minnesota; St. Luke's, Fargo, North Dakota; Ebenezer Hospital, Madison, Minnesota; St. Olaf, Austin, Minnesota; Passavant, Milwaukee, Wisconsin; Eben-Ezer, Brush, Colorado; and the Lutheran Hospital, Sioux City, Iowa. The same altruistic motives prompted Christian people in every instance to engage in this ministry of healing in their Lord's name.

Among the Episcopal clergy there were many who were interested in the ministry of healing, one of whom was Rev. Horace Stringfellow, the rector of St. Andrew's in Baltimore. He took it upon himself to journey to Germany to visit the Kaiserswerth institutions. When he returned in 1855, he was so enthusiastic about the idea of offering care for the sick that he was instrumental in getting two young women of his parish to decide to become nursing deaconesses. At first they were residents in the rectory of St. Andrews. The bishop of the Maryland Diocese assured them a livelihood if they devoted their lives to nursing the sick members of the parish, and he recognized them as deaconesses. This was the beginning of the St. Andrew's Infirmary, which was consolidated with another institution in 1858 and became the Church Home and Infirmary of Baltimore. The deaconesses became an order known as the Sisters of the Good Shepherd.

Other young Episcopal women were inspired by the unselfish service of these sisters and started the Deaconesses of Long Island, which later became the Community of St. John the Evangelist. St. Mary's Free Hospital for Children was opened in New York City in 1870 by another order, the Sisters of St. Mary, who had as their ideal a ministry to the needs of poor children who could not otherwise afford medical care. St. Luke's, New York, was started by the rector of the Church of the Holy Communion, with Sisters of the Holy Communion in charge of nursing care. St. Luke's, St. Louis, Missouri, and St. John's, Brooklyn, New York, were also started in a similar way by the clergy, consecrated laymen, and sisterhoods.

Other hospitals of the Episcopal Church were founded without the aid of deaconesses, by clergymen and laymen and laywomen who were sincerely interested in the care of the sick. Some of the well-known institutions are the Episcopal Eye and Ear Hospital of Washington, D. C.; St. Barnabas Hospital for Women and Children, Newark, New Jersey; St. Luke's, Chicago, Illinois; St. Luke's, Boise, Idaho, and others. The compassion of the Saviour was expressing itself in these institutions. The sisters and other nurses did not hesitate to perform the most menial tasks if they could thereby alleviate suffering or hasten the recovery of a patient.

The Methodist Church also founded institutions of healing. In 1888 a group of Methodist men met in Chicago and, after careful planning, founded Wesley Hospital. A missionary training school, previously organized by Mrs. J. S. Meyer, herself a physician and the wife of a Methodist minister, became the first home of Methodist deaconesses in this country. She intended to be a missionary, but the death of a friend somehow caused her to change her plans. She and her deaconess young women worked among the poor in the tenement districts of Chicago. She saw that many of these people who died might have lived if only they had had adequate hospital care. Other prominent Methodist people were interested enough by her work to found a hospital. When they started Wesley Hospital, it was their purpose to take care of the needy poor without charge.

Deaconesses became influential in founding a number of Methodist hospitals, such as Christ Hospital, Cincinnati, Ohio; Bethesda, Cincinnati, Ohio; Montana Deaconess Hospital, Great Falls, Montana; Sibley Memorial Hospital, Washington, D. C.; Asbury Hospital, Minneapolis, Minnesota; Methodist Deaconess Hospital, Louisville, Kentucky, and many more.

In other instances Methodist Church conferences started hospitals, and supported them financially through the efforts of the district superintendent or the bishop of the area. With all the gratuitous care that was given the poor, these institutions had to be supported by the people of the churches. Today there are seventy-one hospitals affiliated with the Methodist Church [19] under the direction of the Board of Hospitals and Homes, which has headquarters in Chicago.

The Evangelical Synod of North America, now included in the Evangelical and Reformed Church, also founded hospitals and deaconess homes, the first one in St. Louis in 1889 with the name, The Evangelical Deaconess Hospital. The Evangelical Deaconess Hospital at Lincoln, Illinois, was started in 1900; and similar institutions were started in Faribault, Minnesota, in 1908; Chicago, Illinois, in 1910; Milwaukee, Wisconsin, in 1910; Marshalltown, Iowa, in 1913; Detroit, Michigan, in 1918; and Cleveland, Ohio, in 1923. The former Reformed Church started the Fairview Park Hospital in Cleveland, Ohio, in 1892. [20]

The Protestant Deaconess Hospital of Evansville, Indiana, was founded in 1892 by pastors and laymen of the Evangelical and Reformed Church, the first German Methodist Episcopal Church, and Salem Evangelical Church. A Deaconess Aid Society, composed of women from the churches, worked to support the hospital. They gave bazaars, canned vegetables and fruits to be used as food for the sick in the institution, and sewed the pillow slips and sheets. Sister Mathilda Sterling was called from the Bethesda Hospital in Chicago and took charge in 1893. Other deaconesses were trained in the institution, including Sister Carolina Braun, who administered the hospital for many years and Sister Lina Appel, who followed her in that capacity and is today associated with the chaplain. Sister Sophia Bartelt, who was supervisor of nursing for many years and now has charge of certain phases of housekeeping, also received her training there.

In recent years the hospital underwent an expansion program under the guidance of Dr. Albert G. Hahn, the administrator, with the support of Mr. Gilbert H. Bosse, the president, and the hospital board, all of whom are eager that the hospital shall offer the best service possible.

Characteristic of the founding of these institutions are the purposes of the Evangelical Deaconess Society of St. Louis, which was originally organized to offer care of the sick poor by nurses who were motivated by Christian love and charity.

Interdenominational Protestant deaconess groups were also organized, and founded hospitals such as the Deaconess Home and Hospital of Cincinnati, Ohio. In Dayton, Ohio, a hospital was started by a similar group, and when deaconess training was discontinued, the hospital became known as the Miami Valley Hospital Society and Training School for Nurses.

The Mennonites also had deaconesses and started the Bethel Deaconess Hospital in Newton, Kansas, in 1907. Other hospitals were founded by them in Mountain Lake, Minnesota, and Beatrice, Nebraska. The deaconesses nursed for a pittance or the institutions could not have continued to function.

As far as deaconesses are concerned today, the complaint

common to all their institutions is that there are not enough young women entering deaconess training, and as the older deaconesses pass away, there are not enough younger ones in training to replace them. Lay nursing schools are taking over the field, and the Church-related hospitals also have lay nursing schools in connection with the deaconess training. In their training schools some of them offer courses in religion that are designed to motivate religiously the young women who are preparing themselves for the nursing profession. But the time may not be too far away when the deaconess order will vanish from the scene of healing again unless the Church does something that will inspire more young women to enter this religious service with the purpose of dedicating their lives to it.

The Presbyterian Church in the United States of America has about eleven hospitals. One of the first to be founded was the Presbyterian Hospital of New York City. In 1868 a number of Presbyterian churchmen met in the lecture room of the First Presbyterian Church and made provision to apply to the state legislature for a charter. On March 26 of that year James Lenox, Esq., was elected president of the board of managers. In this instance the founding was easier, because the entire plot of ground upon which the hospital was built was given by Mr. Lenox, and to this he added the sum of two hundred and fifty thousand dollars. Other liberal citizens gave one hundred and eighty thousand dollars, but the rest of the cost had to be raised by private subscriptions. The complete cost of the institution was in excess of a million dollars.[21]

The Presbyterian Hospital in the City of Philadelphia grew out of a reunion of New and Old Schools of Presbyterianism in 1870. The organization of the churches was known as the Philadelphia Presbyterian Alliance, and they combined their interests to do thorough and systematic evangelism and to provide hospitals and homes for the care of the needy. Among the standing committees was one on hospitals, with a number of the clergy and some prominent laymen as the personnel.

Ephraim D. Saunders, D.D., generously offered the property located on Powelton Avenue, Filbert, Thirty-ninth, and Boudinot Streets for the erection of a Presbyterian hospital. This offer was accepted by the committee, and the Executive Committee of the Alliance was asked to secure a charter for the hospital, which was granted by the State of Pennsylvania in 1871. Then Dr. Saunders was appointed as agent of the hospital and funds were raised for its erection.[22]

The Presbyterian Hospital in Pittsburgh, Pennsylvania, dates its origin on May 4, 1895, when a charter was granted by the State of Pennsylvania for the Presbyterian Hospital of Pittsburgh. In the charter it states that the purpose of the hospital is to afford medical and surgical aid to sick and disabled persons of every creed and nationality, together with ministrations of the gospel.[23] The Christian ideal of the universal brotherhood of man is clearly indicated in the purpose. (It is interesting to note that the charter members consisted of sixteen women.)

The Presbyterian Hospital of Newark, New Jersey, started as a dispensary initiated by Rev. A. N. Stubblebine, who was the pastor of Bethany Presbyterian Church. It was known as Bethany Presbyterian Hospital. He saw the great need to care for the sick of the neighborhood, without regard to the individual's ability to pay. In October, 1909, a number of the charter members met and changed the name to the Presbyterian Hospital of Newark, New Jersey, elected officers, and applied for an amended charter, which was granted in 1910. The Christian purpose of the institution appealed to sincere people who were willing to have a share in that work, and support it generously with their gifts.

Other Presbyterian hospitals are: The Presbyterian Hospital of the City of Chicago; The Presbyterian Eye, Ear and Throat Charity Hospital, Baltimore, Maryland; Abbott Hospital, Minneapolis, Minnesota; Presbyterian Hospital, Denver, Colorado; Presbyterian Hospital–Olmstead Memorial, Hollywood, California; Harper Hospital, Detroit, Michigan; and the Southwestern Presbyterian Sanatorium and Hospital at Albuquerque, New Mexico.

The Baptist Church has many hospitals also. Chaplain Richard K. Young, of the North Carolina Baptist Hospitals, Inc., Winston-Salem, North Carolina, is making a study of the hospitals of the Southern Baptist Church. In his research he found that the motives that prompted the founding of many of these institutions were: (1) the benevolent idea; (2) the attempt to carry out the healing example of Jesus as found in the New Testament; (3) the effort to provide a distinctly Christian atmosphere for the sick; (4) the purpose of training godly young women in the field of nursing and to furnish an avenue of service to nurses and doctors who feel a specific Christian call; (5) the Catholic impetus behind the Baptist movement in the field of hospital ministry, especially in Louisiana.[24]

Nearly all the major Protestant denominations, including the Salvation Army and the Seventh-Day Adventists, have Church-related hospitals, and the motives for founding them were quite similarly altruistic. Religious principles, the desire to carry on the healing ministry of Jesus, concern for the poor sick and any who needed medical and spiritual attention were the motives that prompted people to pioneer in the healing ministry in this age. The compassion of Jesus found an expression in the unselfish service, the consecration, and sacrifice that started these institutions of mercy.

Today there are 516 Protestant Church-related hospitals in the United States,[25] which admitted 2,035,535 patients last year. These institutions have 74,047 beds and 11,093 bassinets, with an average daily occupancy of 60,629 patients. Four hundred of these institutions, through their representatives, are affiliated with the American Protestant Hospital Association. These numbers indicate the tremendous growth of the hospitals from the humble beginnings of most of them and the sacrificial effort and foresight of those who had the vision to start them.

In modern times the Roman Catholic Church also has made great contributions to the fields of healing and nursing. Many of the clergy in this country in the nineteenth century were of European origin and were acquainted with the work of the nursing orders in Europe. Until this time nursing in American hospitals was done by lay women and men hired by the management. There were no training schools, and the standards of nursing were not high. Credit for the high standards of nursing today must go to the Protestant and Roman Catholic sisters, who carried on until Florence Nightingale came on the scene in lay nursing in 1860. Some of the American Catholic clergy of this period were dissatisfied with the nursing conditions and set about organizing Roman Catholic orders. The first of these communities in the United States was founded in 1809 at Emmittsburg, Maryland, near Baltimore, by Mother Elizabeth Ann Seton. She was married and had three children when her husband died. Two years later she entered the Roman Catholic Church and became an indefatigable worker. Archbishop du Bourg, then president of St. Mary's Seminary, recognized her devotion and ability and called her to found the Sisters of Charity of St. Vincent de Paul. The community was established at Emmittsburg, and became very influential in establishing hospitals and nursing orders through the ensuing years.

A few years later the Sisters of Nazareth was founded in Kentucky by Father David, an exile from France, and at about the same time Father Nerinkx, an exile from the same country, founded the Sisters of Loretto, also in Kentucky. These beginners started in a very humble and modest way. In Kentucky their mother house was a log cabin, and the sisters traveled on horseback and nursed the poor sick of the surrounding country. In 1829 the Sisters of Our Lady was started in Charleston, South Carolina, by Bishop England.

By this time the European orders noticed what was happening in America and started organizing branches of their orders. Soon there were many functioning here. By 1823, the Sisters of Charity, founded by Mother Seton, were strong enough in numbers and well enough trained in nursing to assume charge of the Baltimore Infirmary, which is now the University of Maryland Hospital. This institution was leased from private owners for ninety-nine years. There were four wards, and the sisters were trained in nursing care by professors. Their work was in the kitchen, in the laundry, and with the patients in the wards. They did not overlook the spiritual welfare of the patient, for a portion of the Bible was read each day audibly in each ward. The sisters also were trained in administering simple medication.

In 1828, four sisters from the Emmittsburg Community arrived in St. Louis to take over the work in the Mullanphy Hospital there. This institution soon outgrew its small building, and in 1832 a brick structure was completed. This is known as the first Catholic hospital in the United States.

Then the order in Charleston took over hospital work. A Catholic brotherhood rented a house, furnished it as a hospital, and the sisters assumed the management and nursing care. Others followed in quick succession: the Charity Hospital in New Orleans, Lousiana; St. Vincent's Infirmary at Louisville, Kentucky; the Infirmary at Richmond, Virginia; and thus the movement spread. From 1840 to 1871, seventy hospitals were either built or staffed by the sisters of the various orders. The number of orders grew also from four in 1840 to seventeen in 1871, and still there were not enough sisters to meet all the demands. In some instances, such as St. Johns in Nashville, Tennessee, Catholic girls from an orphanage nearby were trained by the sisters to help in the nursing care at the hospital.

The Catholic Church continued to build, supervise, manage, and staff hospitals. The Catholic Hospital Association of the United States and Canada [26] lists the total number of Catholic hospitals in these two countries in 1947 at the impressive figure of 1,038, with 160,058 beds and 25,384 bassinets.

IX. HEALING BY FAITH AND BY MEDICINE

CATHOLIC HEALING SHRINES

In the area of healing, the nineteenth century was marked by popular confidence in miraculous cures and faith healing on the one hand and by the rise of scientific medicine on the other.

While the diaconate was developing in the Protestant Church, Lourdes became a name synonymous with healing in the Roman Catholic Church. Lourdes is a city in France that became famous throughout the world as a healing shrine. It all started in 1858 when Bernadette Soubirous, a fourteen-year-old girl of a poor peasant family who could neither read nor write at the time, had a vision of the Virgin Mary.

On February 11, 1858, she, with her sister Marie and a playmate named Jeanne, went to gather sticks outside the city. They came to a millrace near a grotto. The other two girls went ahead while Bernadette stayed behind to remove her shoes and stockings. She was rather frightened by a sudden wind and her attention rested on a brier bush that grew before the grotto. Then she saw a golden cloud above the bush, and above that appeared a beautiful, youthful woman in a white robe and a blue sash. On each of her bare feet was a golden rosette and she held a white rosary in her hand. She motioned to Bernadette to approach, and as the girl came nearer, reciting the rosary, the vision said the Gloria Patri with her at the end of each decad.

The two companions returned in the meantime and were amazed when they saw Bernadette on her knees praying.

They could see nothing and laughed at her; later, when she told her parents about the experience, they thought it was an illusion and forbade her to return. But the child begged, and on the following Sunday (February 14) they permitted her to visit the place again, but with other children. The vision appeared again, and Bernadette was overcome with ecstasy. The girls became frightened and called a woman who lived nearby, who aroused her, and her companions took her home.

The children talked about her strange actions and her vision although they saw nothing unusual. While her parents did not want her to go back, some women of the town were curious to see what would happen, so they took Bernadette back to the place four days later. The vision appeared again and asked Bernadette to return daily for a certain period of time. In the meantime the news of these incidents spread, and when the girl made her daily visits ever more people gathered at the scene. These people did not see anything unusual, but three times Bernadette reported that she had seen the vision, and the crowd marveled at the child's ecstatic expressions. It was on February 24 that she heard the command from the vision to dig a hole in the ground at the entrance of the grotto. When she was digging with her hands, a stream of water started to flow from the hole, which became a permanent spring of water.

The vision appeared to Bernadette on February 26 and 27, when it told her to instruct the priests to build a chapel there. On February 28 there was a crowd of more than two thousand present when the phenomenon occurred. The crowds increased in numbers. The vision appeared again to her on March 4. In the intervening days there was no appearance until March 25, the Feast of the Assumption, when the vision told the girl that she was the Immaculate Conception. There were two more appearances, on the seventh of April, and the last one, on July 16, 1858.

All this caused considerable controversy. The local priests

were reluctant about accepting the story of the appearances. Ecclesiastical and civil authorities questioned the child thoroughly, but she told her story without contradiction under intense cross-examination. Those who questioned her were at last convinced that she was sincerely telling what she had experienced, and it was their opinion also that a child so young and unlearned would scarcely think up a scheme such as that to deceive people. Bernadette never tried in any way to capitalize on this experience.

As a matter of fact, shortly after this she went to live in the convent of the hospital sisters, where she learned to read and write. Later she took the vows of the order, and died in the convent of Nevers at the age of thirty-five.

Crowds continued to frequent the place of her visions and there were reports of miraculous healing. There was so much talk about it that the Church had to make a thorough investigation. Monsignor Lawrence, the bishop of Tarbes, appointed a commission to study the occurrences and their character, and in 1862, after four years of investigation and observation, the bishop announced that the apparitions appeared to be authentic and the faithful could believe them. But there seems to have been some reservation in his opinion because he left the final decision to the judgment of the pope. Official investigations of Lourdes continued and are still in process. Various popes have expressed their personal belief in the apparitions and the miracles although, it may be said, there has never been an official declaration to that effect by a pope.

The pilgrimages to Lourdes for healing continued. In 1872 the first big pilgrimage from all over France was made, about August 15. A beautiful chapel was dedicated above the grotto in 1876, and the Church of the Holy Rosary was completed in 1901. Sick people of every kind are brought to Lourdes and are lined up in the space before these churches. When the consecrated Host is carried past them in procession, the healing is effected.

It is interesting to note that the cures have been tested by medical men over a period of many years. The first medical committee was formed in 1882 to investigate the cures. Each patient was given a certificate that he was examined by a physician, and the members of the medical committee made a thorough examination. Any doctor, a skeptic or a believer, can secure permission to examine a patient, and it is said that an average of about two hundred different doctors examine patients there each year.

James J. Walsh, M.D., Ph.D., has told of his experiences at Lourdes in an article in *The Ecclesiastical Review*.[27] Dr. Walsh spent a semester at the University of Paris and used much of his time observing and investigating cures at Lourdes. Dr. Boissarie, the president of the Bureau of Medical Investigations, became his personal friend. He writes that each patient was examined by a physician before the cure and was given a certificate to that effect by the examining physician in the clinic at Lourdes. In three years, from 1923 to 1925, almost two thousand physicians took some part in the work of the bureau.

Here is a typical example of a cure presented by Dr. Walsh in his article. As a child, Gabrielle Durand was not well. She had tuberculous keratitis of the left eye, which healed and left an opacity. Also she had had tuberculosis of the cranium and several joints that had left scars. She also had scrofula, or a tubercular disease of the glands of the neck. She contracted diphtheria, which left her with a cervical abscess. At eighteen she went to a hospital at Ville Pinte, but there was no improvement. Then she had a pulmonary hemorrhage and developed abscesses of the back, arm, and both hips. She remained in the hospital at Ville Pinte for two years, when tuberculosis of the lungs made it necessary to take her to St. Joseph's Hospital in Paris. The diagnosis was pulmonary tuberculosis of the second degree. After a period of time in that institution, the surgeon found Pott's disease, a tuberculous spinal disease. She was put in a cast and ordered absolute rest. She constantly grew worse and was transferred to the hospital at Pan, because it was hoped the fresh air there might help her. In June of 1907 she developed symptoms of tuberculous meningitis, and her fever went up to 104. She was in a stupor. But later she became a little better, and in August of that year was taken on a stretcher to Lourdes.

Her certificate from the attending physician at Pan, Dr. Monod, stated the case. She was at Lourdes for four days without any change, until on Sunday, when the procession of the Holy Sacrament passed, she tried to raise herself in her splint but the pain in her back was so severe that she collapsed. She was unconscious from that evening until Monday, when she regained consciousness and requested to be carried to the bathing room where patients are placed under the water from the spring.

When this was done at her insistence, she felt terrible pain as if her body was being straightened out. She saw her leg turn itself in the hip and take its normal position, she felt herself cured, and began to walk there in the room.

When she was given a thorough examination, the physicians present believed she was cured. She walked, did bending movements involving the spine, in fact, did every movement to prove that she was healed. Then she reported to her physician at Pan, who reported her to be completely healed.

Dr. Le Bec succeeded Dr. Boissarie as president of the Bureau of Medical Investigation. Five years after this cure (1915) he examined Gabrielle Durand and found her in good health. He found indications of hypertrophy of some of the bronchial glands, but this did not inconvenience the patient. A year after this examination Dr. Le Bec operated on her for appendicitis, and the internal organs that he examined were normal.

However, the impression should not be gained that no one in authority questions the genuineness of the cures effected at Lourdes. In fact, many books have been written by both believers and skeptics. One of the most widely known instances of fraud was perpetrated by a hospital orderly named Pierre Delannoy. Working as an orderly in a Paris hospital from 1877 to 1881, he became discontented with the long hours and hard work and decided to become a patient so that others would attend him for a while. He feigned locomotor ataxia, and did it so well that he duped doctors and others for six years. When at long last the physicians made life very uncomfortable for him with their treatments, he left the hospital.

The climax of his hoax came when he visited Lourdes. Here he threw away his crutches and claimed to be cured. Since he possessed the necessary medical history from his former confinements in hopitals, the cure seemed absolutely authentic. Some of the clergy were so impressed that they took him to various places and presented him as a proof of the cures effected there. When he was placed in charge of a home for invalids, he absconded with the funds of the institution. Then he feigned insanity, and his case was diagnosed as incurable by a physician. He was committed to a hospital for the insane, and a little later disappeared with the funds again. Finally, the law caught up with him and he was sentenced to prison.

Such deceptions cause the authorities at Lourdes to take every precaution against repetition, but no precautions are foolproof. Some skeptical physicians say that about ninety per cent of the cures are nervous disorders. But nervous diseases are just as serious as physical disorders, if not more so. A bad dream is only a dream, but it is very unpleasant while it is happening.

Many neurologists believe that the religious anticipation and the excitement of a cure at Lourdes help the body to fight organic disturbances also, and such diseases as tuberculosis may be healed, sometimes instantaneously under those conditions. No one will deny that cures are effected there. A difference of opinion may exist as to how they are wrought. Many Catholics and people of other denominations believe that the cures are miraculous; at the same time, many Catholics and people of other denominations believe that the cures are psychosomatic. At any rate, sick people continue to visit this healing shrine, and it is well known all over the world.

The healing shrine in America that attracts the most attention is the one at Beaupré, a town in Montmorency County, Quebec, Canada. The town itself has a population of about two thousand, predominantly French-speaking residents. Its reputation as a healing shrine began about 1658, when some storm-tossed sailors from Brittany vowed that if they were afforded a safe landing, they would build a shrine. They were blown safely ashore and proceeded to fulfill their promise.

The first healing occurred in the laying of the foundation. An inhabitant of Beaupré, who had suffered from chronic rheumatism until it almost crippled him, helped with the work. While he was bending, laying the third stone of the foundation, the pain became very severe. He prayed to Sainte Anne to relieve his suffering, and the pain disappeared. He stood erect and felt healed. In his joy he jumped, shouting that a miracle had been performed. That was the beginning of the healing reputation of Beaupré.

The basilica burned on two occasions, the last time in 1926; but after each such misfortune a more beautiful structure was built. The church contains the miraculous statue of Sainte Anne, the mother of Mary, and the patron saint of sailors. In Transept Chapel, back of the statue, is a relic, a bone presented to the shrine by Bishop Laval in 1870 as from the wrist of Sainte Anne. In one of the fires this sacred relic was almost lost. A rescuer risked his life to snatch it from the flames when heat had already blackened it. But the statue of Sainte Anne weathered the fires unharmed.

This miraculous statue is surrounded by hundreds of crutches and offerings which are evidences of the healing that is wrought there. The stations of the cross go up the hillside to Calvary high above the church. There is a candle-light procession once a year on the feast day of Sainte Anne, July 26. Thousands of pilgrims come for the occasion. However, healing may occur at any time, not only on the feast day.

The healing principles are much the same as at Lourdes. There is not, however, the strict medical supervision that is practiced at Lourdes. While the shrine is Roman Catholic and there are priests in attendance who conduct the Masses and the processions, it may be said that it is difficult to find any official pronouncement from Rome concerning its efficacy as a healing place. It is widely known, however, as a healing center, and visited by many sick people each year who hope to find there the answers to their prayers; and there are evidences that many do. Again, as in the cures at Lourdes, there are those who accept them as miraculous, others who regard them as psychosomatic, and many who deny that the cures occur at all.

PROTESTANT FAITH HEALERS

While the revival of the diaconate and the institution of hospitals were the most important Protestant contributions to healing and the care of the sick during the nineteenth century, this period also brought into prominence some significant Protestant leaders who believed in healing by faith. Probably the best known of these healers was Pastor John Christopher Blumhardt (1805–1880), a Lutheran pastor who was born at Stuttgart, Germany. He possessed a remarkable intellect, and, although he came from a poor family, managed to graduate from Tübingen and became a professor at the missionary institution at Basel in 1830. He married in 1838 and became the Lutheran pastor of a village church. It was in this capacity that he had his first experience in faith healing.

There were two sisters, Gottliebin and Katharina Dittus,

who were strangely affected by apparitions and noises of all kinds. The house where they lived was closely examined and nothing could be found that should cause the sisters to become so possessed. Pastor Blumhardt prayed for them over a period of about two years. During this time Katharina recovered but Gottliebin became worse. She was seized with convulsions, sometimes through a whole night while strong men tried to hold her in a chair and Blumhardt prayed. An unnatural voice came from her during such convulsions and argued with the pastor while her body trembled. During one of those nights the voice said it was from Satan and only Christ could cast him out with a miracle. The pastor prayed on until the voice cried through the woman, "*Jesus ist Sieger*" (Christ is Victor). Toward morning the convulsions subsided. She was healed and thereafter lived a normal life, married, and became a co-worker with Pastor Blumhardt at an institution he later purchased at Boll.

This cure was followed by a religious revival over a large area. On Good Friday, 1845, people came from 176 different places to worship at his church. He practiced the laying on of hands as a token of absolution, and many people claimed they were healed at these services. His house was besieged by people wanting help. As many as the place would hold were lodged there, and he counseled with them regarding their spiritual life.

A little distance from his church was a watering place at Boll, noted for its sulphur springs. In 1852 the pastor purchased this institution and dedicated it to Christian healing. One hundred to one hundred and fifty patients could be treated there at a time. The pastor devoted most of his time to personal interviews with people in stress and to a large correspondence with those who wrote him for guidance. He never professed that he could be instrumental in healing all kinds of diseases and never opposed the ministration of physicians; in fact, he appreciated the services of doctors. " Healing in prayer " was a term he disliked; he felt that God could not be influenced against his will miraculously to effect a cure. The continuance or the healing of a disease was according to the will of God. He felt that he had a special gift for discerning whether God would heal a patient or not. On the patient's part there must be a sincere conversion, expressed in repentance and faith.

His institution became a haven for many sick, who came there for a cure and left the place converted. There were daily prayers and teaching and the patients are said to have learned to love God and their fellow men. The cures went on year after year until his death in 1880.

Pastor Blumhardt possessed a keen knowledge of human nature and was far more interested in the salvation of the soul than in the healing of the body of the patient. He was convinced that the former must come first. Most of his cures would be recognized as religiously and medically authentic.

During the eighteenth and nineteenth centuries a number of sects started in the United States; many of them were communities, such as The Brotherhood of Perfection, The Brethren of Solitary, the Mennonites, the Old Order Amish, the Dunkards, the Shakers, and others. According to the census of 1916,[28] there were two hundred and two denominations; seven tenths of them had less than ten thousand members; two fifths, less than five thousand; and one fifth were below one thousand in membership.

Many of these sects emphasized healing, and the most notable was the United Society of Believers, known as the Shakers, who really started in a Quaker revival in England in 1747. The original leaders, Jane and James Wardley, were succeeded by Ann Lee. To escape persecution a number of them came to America under the leadership of Mother Ann and arrived in New York in 1774, where they remained for two years before settling in the woods at Watervliet near Albany, New York. In 1780 there was a revival in New Lebanon and some of the converts joined the colony.

Mother Ann became a crusader, traveled the country, and

became well known as a faith healer. The community believed they had power over physical disease. They held all property in common, practiced celibacy, confession of sin, separation from the world, and wore a plain garb as a protest against vanity. During the nineteenth century they had colonies in New York, Massachusetts, Connecticut, Ohio, Kentucky, Indiana, and Florida. In 1874 there were 58 communities, with 2,415 members, which owned 100,000 acres of land. By 1905 the members were reduced to 1,000, and today the sect is almost extinct.[29]

The Shakers are typical in some ways of many of the various communities that were founded by religious leaders. Their primary aim was security for this life and eternity. Some of them are in existence today, such as the Amish communities. For the most part, however, they served the needs of their time and have vanished from the American scene except where their community buildings are preserved for their historical value, such as the old Rappite buildings at New Harmony, Indiana.

SCIENTIFIC ADVANCES IN MEDICINE

Scientifically speaking, the nineteenth century may be regarded as the golden age in the development of medicine, surgery, and the medical care of the sick. In this period the medical profession broke the chains of traditions and customs that held it in bondage with the past. Keen minds and adventurous spirits dared to forge ahead, retaining the truths of the past but discarding foppery and magic and substituting scientific research.

This new spirit, which actually started with the French Revolution, resulted in developments in medicine and the allied sciences, such as the use of ether and chloroform in anesthesia, the use of antiseptics, vaccination, and hypodermics. New methods of diagnosis were evolved, as well as better sanitation and construction of buildings for the use of the sick. Investigations were made of the care of the insane and the conditions existing in prisons, and, with all this, lay nursing was also raised to a professional status.

Many leaders in medicine and science of the last century live as familiar names in the conversation of doctors today: Corvisart, Laënnec, Roentgen, Beaumont, Long, Wells, Warren, Lister, Jenner, Pasteur, Pinel, Koch, and others. In the laboratory Pasteur found bacteria and isolated them; Lister discovered how they infect wounds; Koch classified them and found that they cause specific diseases. The fight against bacteria was on, yellow fever was conquered, as well as hookworm, smallpox, typhoid fever, and other dread killers.

In surgery new techniques were evolved. The surgeon became equally respected with the medical physician. The American Medical Association was founded, and in 1881 the French Academy of Science announced that the virus of rabies was discovered in the saliva of animals that had the disease. The journals of these worthy organizations report, year by year, the tremendous progress that was made in the medical and surgical fields.

The nursing care of the sick kept pace with this advancement, and Dorothea Lynde Dix and Florence Nightingale made great contributions in the lay nursing field. The former investigated conditions in the asylums and aroused the concern of the people for better care of these unfortunate people. Florence Nightingale established standards and motives that transformed lay nursing into a worthy profession. She is regarded as the founder of the modern nursing profession; and her birthday, May 12, is widely observed by nurses as a memorial to the contribution she made. The standards of lay nursing were brought to a par with those of the religious orders. And when lay nursing excelled in professional and clinical requirements, the religious orders accepted the new standards. There was a mutual exchange of benefits.

X. CHRISTIAN SCIENCE

Christian Science owes its origin to Mary Baker Eddy, one of the most enigmatic persons of our modern times. In order to understand Christian Science and its growth, it is necessary to know something about the person through whom it was promoted. The facts of her life have been studied very thoroughly, and there are probably few persons of our modern age who have engendered so much personal loyalty and devotion and so much adverse criticism.

Mary Baker was born July 16, 1821, in Bow, a small town near Concord, New Hampshire. Her parents were of sturdy pioneer American stock. If she had lived the normal number of years for a person of those times, her name would probably be unknown today, because it was not until 1875, when she was fifty-four years old, that the first edition of her *Science and Health with Key to the Scriptures* was published.

Mary Baker was an impressionable child, of delicate health, and strongly religious. When she read stories in the Bible, she identified herself with the characters, and felt that God spoke to her as he did to the people of the Scripture. In her childhood she heard voices calling her and became very religious, so that at the age of twelve she confessed her faith at a service in the village church. It was not until five years later that she united with the Congregational Church at Tilton, Massachusetts. Her pastor, Rev. Enoch Corser, often visited in the Baker home and admired the girl and the poetry she wrote.

She met George Washington Glover, a friend of her brother Samuel, and they were married two weeks before Christmas (1843) in the farmhouse at Tilton, where her parents had previously moved. The two made their home in Charleston, South Carolina, where the question of slavery was a burning issue and Mary Glover voiced her opposition to that institution. Her health was delicate during this period. When George Glover died the summer following their marriage, he left her almost destitute; and she went back north to her father's home. In September she gave birth to her only child, a son, whom she named after his father.

Mary Glover was too weak physically to care for her son; in fact, her health never permitted her to care for the child personally. As her health grew steadily worse, she went to live with her sister, Abby Tilton, where she continued to have seizures that made her very nervous. During this time she wrote poetry that was published in local papers. Her mother died and her father married again. In looking for help to relieve her physical condition, she heard about mesmerism, which was destined to influence her life so much.

In 1853 she married again — Dr. Daniel Patterson, a roving dentist — hoping to make a home for her son, but the stepfather refused to have the child. After the marriage, they moved to Franklin, where Dr. Patterson had made a payment on a house. For three years she lived there, and during most of this time she was ill. A " Dr." Phineas P. Quimby, of Portland, Maine, was at that time receiving much publicity because of the miraculous cures he achieved by mesmerism. Mrs. Patterson was interested, and Dr. Patterson wrote Dr. Quimby, telling him about his wife's long illness, and said he would like to see him when he came to Concord. But Quimby did not come, and Mrs. Patterson made up her mind to go to Portland to see him. In October of 1862 she made the journey and, when she had registered at the hotel, went to Dr. Quimby's office, where she gave him her unreserved confidence. Quimby, who was a doctor by courtesy only, used hypnotism or mesmerism in healing. He had been taught by the French hypnotist Charles Poyen, when he visited this country, and it was Poyen who induced Quimby to use hypnotism in healing. Quimby taught that the mind gives form to the animal spirit, and that the animal spirit gives form to the body as soon as the less plastic elements of the body are able to assume that form.[30] In treating a patient, first he sat beside him to absorb the illness and then put him into a mesmeric sleep. Quimby said that he often suffered from the diseases of his patients.

He did not pretend to be a religious man, but Mrs. Patterson read religion into his practice. She came to him with that preconceived idea and she was temporarily healed. She remained with him for quite some time thereafter and tried to analyze his methods. Just how much Quimbyism she incorporated in her writings, and how much he influenced her thinking, is a matter of controversy to this day. Be that as it may, she was convinced of the reality of faith healing.

At home again she spent much of her time writing, but an incident occurred at Lynn, Massachusetts, on February 3, 1866, that she considered the crucial experience of her life. She fell on the icy sidewalk and was carried unconscious into the home of Mr. S. M. Bubier, and Dr. Alvin Cushing was called to attend her. He found her injuries to be internal and felt that there might have been a concussion; at any rate, she was badly hurt. The following morning, after visiting her twice during the night, he found her semiconscious and asking to go home. So they wrapped her warmly and put her on a long sleigh and took her to her home in Swampscott, Massachusetts. There she says, she asked to be alone, took her Bible, and, when she opened it, read the account of Jesus' healing of the man with palsy. If miracles were performed then, she felt that God could perform them now. At last she found the " lost chord of Truth." Love invaded her, lifted her; God said to her, " Daughter, arise! " and she was healed at that moment.

Mrs. Patterson attributed her healing entirely to divine intervention. She says that in this experience she discovered the Christ science or divine laws of life, truth, and love, and she named her discovery " Christian Science." [31] After this she retired from the public for three years, during which she devoted herself to study, prayer, and the task of writing the principles of health and life. It was at this time that Dr. Patterson left her and eloped with the wife of a wealthy patient. In 1873 she secured a decree of divorce from him and thereafter took again the name Mary Baker Glover.

During the next months she had a number of healing experiences. Her first demonstration of " Mind Science " was upon a lad with a bone felon. His name was Dorr Phillips, and when she visited in the home, she found the boy in agony. He had heard his mother and father discuss divine healing, and when Mrs. Glover asked him to promise not to use any more medication if she would heal it, the boy consented. The finger was healed that night. The boy could not tell what she had done, but he knew the finger did not hurt any more. When the parents declared it to be a miracle, Mrs. Glover insisted that it was not — just natural, divine healing.

There are extant other instances of healing during this period of her life. She felt that she had grasped a great truth and the next step was to teach it to others. With Richard Kennedy, a young man who had received instructions from her, she went to Lynn and found an apartment. Later she rented the second floor of a three-story building for sleeping rooms and offices, where she formed her first class in Mind Science. The first pupils were from the shoeshops. Patients soon came, and she instructed young Kennedy in giving treatments. A number of other students received instructions also, and went out to practice on their own. These were troubled years, and she saw that she had to try to divorce herself entirely from all the practices that Quimby had taught her.

The manuscript of *Science and Health* was finally completed in 1875. She had difficulty in finding a publisher, but after much effort found a printer in Boston who was willing to undertake the task for a payment of one thousand dollars. One thousand copies were printed that fall, and then the controversy over her healing began in earnest. Many of the clergy and the physicians opposed her ideas, but she was determined to keep on with her mission. Some of her students went from door to door trying to sell her book, and they succeeded in disposing of the thousand copies. In June, 1879, about seven students chose a treasurer, rented a hall in which to meet, and pledged to pay a certain amount each week to engage Mrs. Glover as their teacher. This may be regarded as the beginning of the Church of Christ, Scientist. The hall was small, they sang to the accompaniment of a melodeon, and the audiences usually numbered about twenty-five people.

With her teaching, preaching, and writing Mrs. Glover also healed. It is said that she cured a case of tuberculosis, caused a painless delivery, healed the finger of a patient after the physician had advised its amputation. Then some friends sent to her a Mr. Asa Gilbert Eddy, a bachelor who was in ill health. After he was healed, he entered a new class that she was forming. She found him to be a man of character and business ability. When the first edition of *Science and Health* was disposed of, she was ready with a second for a printer. Mr. Eddy undertook the management of this work. This caused jealousy in the ranks of the followers, and in the midst of the controversy Mrs. Glover and Mr. Eddy were quietly married on January 1, 1877. The ceremony was performed by the Unitarian clergyman, Rev. Samuel B. Stewart.

Litigation and disruption followed in the ranks. Suit was brought against her by George Barry for twenty-seven hundred dollars, which he claimed she owed him for services rendered. Others were dissatisfied for one reason or another, while students continued to bring patients to be healed. All this drove the harassed Mrs. Eddy to leave her home for a time so that she could finish the editing of the second edition of *Science and Health*.

Once the lawsuits were over, it seemed that the atmosphere cleared for a time. She realized that if the healing of Christian Science were to continue, a college of instruction must be founded. Since she had experienced enough controversy in Lynn, and Mr. Eddy had much larger audiences in Boston, it was decided to organize the college in the latter city. So in 1879 the Christian Scientist Association was formed and incorporated as the Church of Christ, Scientist, to be located in Boston. There were twenty-six members, and for a year and a half they met in the homes of the members. Then a hall was rented on Park Street in Boston and Mrs. Eddy became the pastor of the church. But the sailing was not on smooth waters by any means. Again students protested and withdrew from the Association, and some tried to get the leadership of the organization away from her. In the meantime she wrote the third edition of *Science and Health,* this one with a preface by Mr. Eddy.

Through all this her husband became quite ill. She believed he was suffering from a suggestion of poisoning. It is said that when Dr. Noyes, a resident of the city hospital, was called, he diagnosed the illness as heart disease. Mrs. Eddy could relieve her husband with silent treatment for a time, and he would fall asleep. But the attacks occurred again and he died at dawn, June 3, 1882.

In January, 1881, she founded the Massachusetts Metaphysical College and students were soon enrolled. She taught from thirty to fifty students a month and preached every Sunday. Then the *Journal* was founded in 1883, and it became the official publication of the Church. The *Journal* was inaugurated to bring health and healing into the homes. This was a wise move on her part, and this *Journal* has been more instrumental than any other medium of spreading the teachings of Christian Science. One of its results was that students came to the Metaphysical College from far and near.

The Christian Science movement spread to California; then the Illinois Christian Science Institute was founded in Chicago, and in 1886 a National Christian Scientist Association was founded. By the time the California Metaphysical Institute was functioning on the West Coast, Christian Science had spread across the country. Mrs. Eddy's activities were zealous, and with them she rewrote *Science and Health* again. This time the manuscript was read by Rev. James Henry Wiggin, a man who professionally read and edited the works of a number of authors of that day.

In 1888, the National Christian Scientist Association met for the first time in Chicago. Mrs. Eddy attended the meeting, accompanied by her secretary, some friends, and a young doctor, Dr. E. J. Foster, whom she later adopted as a son. About four thousand of her followers came to this meeting from all parts of the country. Mrs. Eddy was escorted to the platform for her address. It was an expectant audience which anticipated a wave of healing. In the emotional upsurge after her speech, they rushed forward to greet her, to touch her hand, and to tell of the healings. Others who could not get near cried aloud for help, and many said they were healed at that moment. She stayed at the Palmer House, where a reception room was arranged for her to receive the many people who came to interview her personally.

While this was going on in Chicago, the shades of Quimby were at work again in Boston. Some of the students there withdrew and took a following with them which became known as the New Thought movement. Its teachings go back to students of Quimby, Mr. Julius Dresser and Rev. Warren F. Evans. This group took the Association's books with them, in the absence of Mrs. Eddy and her secretary, and upon their return informed her that the books would not be returned to her until she gave them an honorable dismissal from the Association. When this desire was acceded to, this same group tried unsuccessfully to expel her from the Church.

Mrs. Eddy was convinced now that a total reorganization of the Church was necessary. She felt that it was built too much around her personality, and that if Christ was to be the head of the Church in reality, she must withdraw. To accomplish this end, she closed the Metaphysical College and discontinued teaching classes. In October of 1889, the organization of the Boston Church was discontinued. An article appeared in the *Journal* in which she stated that she was no longer to be consulted by her students concerning family, church, or personal problems, or even on healing disease. The students and churches were henceforth on their own.

The Boston Church started anew, supposedly on its own power this time. Mrs. Eddy gave a piece of ground, and on September 1, 1892, trustees were elected and plans were made for a new building. The mother church was built with the contributions of students and completed in 1894. The board of trustees elected Mrs. Eddy to the position of pastor emeritus, and it was her intention to withdraw from active direction of the organization. Since she had previously made her home in Concord, she had a haven there where she could write articles and revise *Science and Health* from time to time. On occasion she would visit the mother church and preach there, and although she tried to withdraw as much as possible, her followers still held her in great esteem.

In 1906 the large new granite and stone church next to the original mother church was completed at a cost of two million dollars. At the dedication it was estimated that forty thousand Christian Scientists were in Boston for the occasion. They came from all parts of the United States and England. These figures are mentioned to give the reader an idea of the vast spread of Mrs. Eddy's teachings. At the dedication ceremonies the large church was crowded, the balconies filled, people were standing, and many could not get in. Each one present was given an opportunity to testify about the healing that had occurred in his life, a custom still practiced in the churches at the midweek meetings.

But despite all this acclaim, criticism and trouble followed Mrs. Eddy all her life, and there was some of it even after she retired in extreme old age. Her relations with her son, George W. Glover, were always questioned by those who wanted to discredit her. At this time he was living in Lead City, South Dakota. Newspaper reporters interviewed him about his life with his famous mother. He is reported to have had some grievances because he could not always see her just when he wanted to and because he resented her secretary, Mr. Calvin Frye. Somehow George was influenced to take steps to have a share in the management of his mother's affairs. A lawsuit grew out of this effort which was long and involved, causing much publicity. As a result, Mrs. Eddy set aside a trust fund of about $125,000 for him and his heirs, but that did not seem satisfactory to him and there was more litigation before it was finally settled.

After about a year in retirement at Concord, she decided to move to Boston again. When she left Concord, the city council passed resolutions of regret and expressed appreciation for the kind relations that had existed between her and the people during her residency there. She was eighty-seven years old when she went back to live in Boston. The year before, ground had been broken to build a publishing house. Now it was completed, and her first move in Boston was to ask the publishing board to make plans for a daily paper. The first issue of *The Christian Science Monitor* appeared November 25, 1908, with an editorial by Mrs. Eddy. Other publications of the organization were: *The Christian Science Sentinel, The Christian Science Journal,* and *Der Herold der Christian Science,* the latter in the German language.

These publications reached a wide audience. The mother church is reported to have had forty-eight thousand communicants at that time.

In 1909, The First Church of Christ, Scientist, was dedicated in London. It cost approximately four hundred thousand dollars and was debt-free at its dedication. In the same year a large edifice was dedicated in Edinburgh. As the organization grew, it seems that dissension diminished. Her son George was reconciled, and she transferred to him and his family the sum of $245,000, and to Dr. Foster Eddy, her adopted son, the sum of $45,000. The sum to George included the trust of $125,000 transferred to him in the previous arrangement. It is estimated that she accumulated about $2,000,000 during her lifetime.

Active to the last, she passed away quietly, December 3, 1910, after she had retired for the night. The funeral service was held in her home on Chestnut Hill on December 8. About fifty persons — members of the immediate family, her household, and distinguished guests — were present. Judge Clifford P. Smith, First Reader in the mother church, read the Ninety-first Psalm and portions of the Gospel of John. Mrs. Carol Hoyt Powers, Second Reader, read Mrs. Eddy's poem, " Mother's Evening Prayer," and all united in the Lord's Prayer. It was a simple, dignified service, and then her remains were laid to rest in a steel and cement vault at Mount Auburn.

By that time the Christian Science movement was so thoroughly and well organized that it could continue without its founder and leader. Through the ensuing years there has been a steady growth in membership until today there are about 275,000 Christian Scientists in our country.

The doctrine of this Church emphasizes the power of mind over matter. There is no matter, and the idolatrous claims of sin are that matter exists, that it has substance, that it has intelligence, and that it produces life and death. The physical senses, being material, can only testify for their own evidence, consequently their testimony is false. There is only one reality, and that is mind and mind is God. The divine science enables the individual to understand life, truth, and love, and these cast out error and heal the sick. As the believer accepts this principle, he achieves a oneness with God that denies the existence of sickness or pain.

A Christian Science member of a family may not object to medical treatment for another member of the family who has not embraced the divine science. In other instances, the contrary may be true. A husband and father became a " Scientist " and insisted that his family join him in this faith and refused to call a doctor when a member of his household became ill. Generally speaking, however, they are quite ethical in this regard with nonbelievers.

This healing movement was opportunely timed. For the most part the physicians and surgeons of that day regarded religion with toleration or opposition. Their attitude can be justified by the fact that much of the preaching was otherworldly, and revival movements used the psychology of fear to bring sinners to repentance. The clergy were primarily interested in saving souls for eternity and played this one string on the harp of the gospel until the sound became monotonous, to say the least.

The physicians and surgeons were interested in saving lives for this world and this apparent divergence of interests caused them to regard the aims of the clergy with more or less disdain. They knew very little about the influence of the mental or spiritual states on the physical organism, and the clergy regarded the soul as something entirely apart from the body. It seems the prevalent attitude was that the physician should take care of the body, the clergyman should save the soul, and the two aims should have little or nothing in common.

In practice, however, it was not working that way. Many people died under the care of the most competent physicians when faith might have saved their lives, or when the Word of God might have brought them the comfort or courage that was needed. Some more progressive physicians and clergymen were observing that mental or spiritual states influence the digestion and assimilation of foods and accelerate or slow down the functioning of the endocrine glands. While people could not explain what happened to them, they knew that religion and mental attitudes helped them. Mrs. Eddy came upon the scene with Christian Science, and many people found in it what neither the physician nor the clergyman had offered them.

Both professions owe a debt of gratitude to this movement in that it caused them to re-evaluate their approach to the patient. It caused religious leaders to study and investigate the interaction of the spiritual and physical phases of the human organism. The Emmanuel Movement, which will be studied in a later chapter, was the result of the new understanding of human nature that grew out of study and research prompted by the spread of Christian Science, primarily on the part of clergymen who succeeded in getting the interest and co-operation of some leading physicians. Christian Science was not accepted as a recognized Church by either the Protestant or the Roman Catholic Church, and is not recognized as such by most of these groups today.

It can be easily seen that the movement encroaches upon the field of the Church and the physician and almost any individual does not regard with favor anything or anyone who professes to do his job better than he does. If he is wise he will observe techniques and accept that which brings results and disregard what is irrelevant or harmful.

The membership of Christian Science churches is composed to a large extent of people who have received their religious education in the older, established Churches, and they carry many of these religious concepts with them into their new Church. The doctrines of Christian Science that cannot be accepted by other Churches are often disregarded by these people. The atonement, which is an important belief of the Church, is variously interpreted by the clergy and not so readily understood by the average church member who may go into Christian Science. There he is taught that salvation is the result of oneness with God that he can achieve through his own efforts, and the atonement no longer seems to bother him.

It has succeeded also because it appeals to the educated and cultured people who have made it socially acceptable. It is doubtful if Christian Science will ever be a mass movement because it does not use methods that stimulate the emotions but demands that its followers read and think, and these activities have had little religious appeal for the masses. It offers an emotional outlet in its testimonial midweek meetings that seems to meet this need of the members.

Christian Science admits no defeat so far as healing is concerned. There is no disease so fatal as to make it necessary to call in a physician.

Another observation that may have some truth in it is that this religious faith finds its growth among the class of people who are economically better situated than the average. These people have fewer children and have more time for selfish or altruistic interests and those who choose the former have a tendency to neural disorders. The physician who concentrates only on physical healing does not have the time or the ability to deal with psychological states that cause people to turn to Christian Science, where they feel they find what they need.

XI. NEW THOUGHT AND UNITY

Phineas P. Quimby's name is not only connected histori-
cally with Christian Science but with other healing
faiths, among them the New Thought movement. It was
mentioned in the previous chapter that "Dr." Quimby
gained quite a reputation as a healer. By profession he was
a watchmaker until he became interested in hypnotism
through the influence of the Frenchman, Charles Poyen,
who came to this country to demonstrate his art. Quimby
found that he could hypnotize people also, so he influenced
Mr. Lucius Burkmar, who was interested, and these two
traveled the country giving exhibitions of the art of hypnotism. When the tour was finished, Quimby went back to
watchmaking, but Burkmar went with another hypnotist
on a protracted tour. Quimby noticed that they used hypnotism for healing purposes, and when the tour was completed, he decided to use Burkmar again and go into the
healing business. Burkmar would prescribe the medicine for
the patient, and if the medicine was too expensive, he could
change the prescription. Quimby observed that with many
of his patients one medicine seemed to do just as much good
as another remedy. So he came to the conclusion that the
disease was largely in the mind of the patient and could be
treated just as well without medicine. He tried hypnotism
and suggestion and decided to use these in faith healing.
However, he continued to rub the patient's head with his
hands and left the sick one under the impression that he
absorbed the sickness himself.

Quimby wrote many notes about his healing, and at his death in 1866 these manuscripts became the possession of his family.

One of the patients who claimed to have been cured by him was Mr. Julius A. Dresser. Before Mrs. Eddy disclaimed any doctrinal relationship with Quimby, she urged Mr. Dresser to carry on the work of healing as he had learned it from Quimby, but Mr. Dresser at first demurred.

Another former patient, who was to figure prominently in the New Thought movement, was Warren Felt Evans, a Swedenborgian clergyman who also attributed his healing to Mr. Quimby. After Quimby's death Rev. Mr. Evans wrote about the Quimby methods of faith healing. Since he was trained in the Swedenborgian doctrine, he was conditioned to carry on such work.

It might be of interest here to mention some pertinent facts about Emmanuel Swedenborg, a contemporary of John Wesley. He was born in Stockholm, Sweden, in 1688, and lived until 1772. The son of a Lutheran bishop, he became one of the great minds of his age and made a reputation for himself in the scientific world. In his fifties, when he felt that he sufficiently understood the physical world, he turned his inquiring mind to the field of theology.

In the field of religion he gradually developed a " second sight." In three ecstatic years he prepared his soul, and claimed to have been elevated into heaven where he found the answer to what happens to the soul after death. Thereafter his chief interest was the soul of man, and he taught that the physical realm is but a symbol of the real which is the spiritual. Like Christian Scientists, he denied the reality of the physical being except as a symbol. The state of man's inner, spiritual life is what makes heaven within. It is possible for a believer to have heaven here and now. No one will go to heaven who does not have heaven in his heart. Death is not what it is commonly regarded to be, but is a continuation of the life begun here.

He thought of heaven as a place where life continues at its highest and best. There will be sexual love also, and if one has not found the ideal mate on earth (Swedenborg never married), he will find that person among the unmarried in heaven. He spoke of the spiritual life with familiarity, and contended that he could do that because he had been in heaven a number of times in his ecstasy. With the emphasis upon the reality of the spirit world over against the unreality of materialism the influence of the mind over matter is obvious.

Although Emmanuel Swedenborg never founded a Church or even preached a sermon, after his death societies were formed to study his voluminous writings. The writings were translated into English and the societies were organized into a Church. This Church spread to America in 1792 and became known as the General Convention of the New Jerusalem in the U. S. A. They established a theological seminary at Cambridge, Massachusetts, adjacent to Harvard University, for the training of their clergy.

Warren Felt Evans was a clergyman of this denomination and became a prolific writer about Quimby's teachings. He traced the cause of disease to wrong beliefs and felt that people could be cured through right beliefs. Faith, he advocated, was employed by Jesus in healing; it should be used now.

Rev. Mr. Evans and Julius Dresser knew each other and, with the encouragement Dresser had received from Mrs. Eddy, became the founders of the New Thought movement. They believed that it was applied Christianity, the original Jesus way of healing.

Their teachings spread, and with the growth of the movement came diversity of opinion; hence a number of organizations grew out of it, such as Divine Science, Church of Advanced Thought, Institute of Religious Science, and others. Aside from the encouragement of Mrs. Eddy in the very beginning there is no organic relationship to Christian Science, although some concepts are similar. These various groups that have some teachings in common keep in touch with each other through conventions. In 1899 they came together in Boston and adopted the name " New Thought " as inclusive of all of them. In 1917 a national convention was held in St. Louis, where they adopted a Declaration of Principles that generally expresses the views of those who adhere to New Thought. They regard the human body as shaped, ruled, repaired, and controlled solely by mental influences. God is regarded as Universal Love, Life, Truth, and Joy, and through oneness with God these virtues have healing power. Their theology is largely unitarian, and Jesus is regarded as the one who demonstrates God's way of life.

New Thought is composed of so many groups, each with its distinctive and unique teaching, that to tell the complete story would require more detailed discussion than can be presented in this book. Their literature, under one name or another, is widely circulated and read by many people, some of whom find help in it and praise it highly.

The New Thought groups believe in the divinity of man, and that since God dwells within the individual, and the Kingdom of God is within, heaven is experienced here and now. This heaven within expresses itself in health, harmony, happiness, well-being, and prosperity.

It is not necessary for a follower of New Thought to leave the Church where he holds membership. This may account to some extent for its growth and the widespread use of its literature. Church members who follow it, however, are usually those who are not much interested in the doctrines of the Trinity and the atonement.

Its approach is primarily intellectual and does not appeal to the masses. Its followers are among the educated, but at the same time there are many people without much formal education who read New Thought literature and claim to be helped by it. It seems that helpful thoughts of various religions, not only the Christian faith, are accepted by this movement.

Since New Thought is directed to the individual, its message can hardly be called a "social gospel." These groups support few if any orphans' homes, hospitals, or other institutions, so it does not urge its followers to give to causes.

Probably its greatest appeal lies in the fact that its followers are taught to affirm what they want in their prayers, whether it be health or success. What is anticipated is accepted as coming in the natural course of events if the mind is made up to that effect. The mind controls the whole individual and will create for him as he directs.

UNITY

Closely akin to New Thought is the Unity movement, with headquarters at Kansas City, Missouri; however, it differs theologically from New Thought in that it recognizes the three Persons in the Holy Trinity and has a more compact and centrally controlled organization.

Unity's origin can be traced to Christian Science also. A Mr. J. S. Thatcher started a school of Christian Science in Kansas City in 1887. Eugene B. Weeks, of Chicago, came there to teach a class, and Charles and Myrtle Fillmore were pupils in that group.

This young couple were in financial and physical difficulties. Those were depression years and Mr. Fillmore was sick; there were debts to be paid; his real estate business had failed also. Mrs. Fillmore was expecting another child and at the same time she was seriously ill; her ailment was diagnosed as an extreme case of tuberculosis. Almost as a last resort they went to the class to study Christian Science in the hope of finding help. Here Mrs. Fillmore found the power of God and applied it to her life through faith. She claimed to have found healing, and in due time gave birth to a normal, healthy son. Enthusiasm for Christian Science caused her to win over her husband when, a few years later, he was healed of what doctors had diagnosed as tuberculosis of the bone. However, he claims to have used a different technique in healing himself. He went regularly to a quiet place where he could be silent and wait for God. In this frame of mind he found he could send spiritual impulses to any part of his body he desired and said the impulses resembled a " crawling feeling." Through the daily practice of the presence of the Universal Mind he said that new tissue was formed in his body and he was healed. In this he was convinced that he had found a new healing force, the Jesus power.

Mr. and Mrs. Fillmore then advertised themselves as healers and teachers, and soon there were followers. Every evening at nine o'clock a group met in their home for silent thinking. They sat quietly for fifteen minutes, dwelling on a positive thought that was spoken audibly at intervals to aid concentration.

Soon there were reports of cures: a Negro laundress got rid of her asthma; a crippled man was healed; a boy about to go blind had his sight restored.[32] Enthusiasm grew. They called themselves " The Society of Silent Help," and in 1889 acquired a meeting place large enough to accommodate the two hundred followers. They started a monthly magazine, *Modern Thought,* edited by Charles Fillmore. It was another voice amid the unorthodox writings of Christian Science, Spiritualism, New Thought, Rosicrucianism, Transcendentalism, and others. In fact, it seems that this new movement contained elements of all these beliefs and at first there were literary contributions to the magazine from writers of all of them. The name of the magazine was changed from *Modern Thought* to *Thought, Christian Science,* and then after Mrs. Eddy forbade the use of any of her material, it was changed to the one word, *Thought,* and finally to *Unity.*

The name of The Society of Silent Help was changed to Silent Unity, and Unity is now the name by which this healing movement is popularly known. In 1914 it was changed officially to Unity School of Christianity.

The Unity Church in Kansas City was dedicated in 1906, and the plant combines a church, a publishing house, a school, and a health building. Other Unity centers are to be found in many cities. An almost unbelievable amount of literature is published and widely read. Among the regularly published magazines are *Unity, Weekly Unity, Wee Wisdom* (for children), *Good Business, Progress,* and *Daily Word.* The Fillmores have written a number of books that spread their teachings also, and thousands of tracts come off the presses every day.

It is estimated that the institution answers over a half million telephone calls, letters, and telegrams every year; these requests for help cover about every imaginable subject, from health or sickness to a prayer for the success of a business transaction. There are workers on duty all hours of the day to take the calls and offer help.

Once in 1919 the Fillmores identified themselves with the New Thought movement and went along with that group for three years. The New Thought convention, meeting in Cincinnati, invited them to enter the alliance. After negotiations in which the Fillmores' emphasis on the " Christ message " was accepted, they decided to become a part of the alliance. But in 1922 the directors of Unity voted to withdraw. Since that time it has had no relation to New Thought.

The chief source book of Unity teaching is the *Metaphysical Bible Dictionary,*[38] in which Jesus Christ is recognized as a person of the holy Trinity; their beliefs about his position in relation to the other two Persons are sufficiently orthodox to satisfy almost any old-line denomination. But other teachings are not — such as the belief in reincarnation and in the regeneration of the body. As the believer becomes ever more like Jesus, a spiritual body replaces his physical one, and in the final analysis it should not be necessary for anyone to die if there is a firm belief in the Christ life.

To make the teachings easier to understand, the twelve powers of man are classified and identified with the twelve disciples. The center of the brain is the seat of faith exemplified by Peter; the loins, strength, Andrew; the pit of the stomach, wisdom, James; and thus the faculties are described, continuing with the back of the heart, the root of the tongue, the front brain, and so on.

Like God, man's nature is threefold — spirit, mind, and body. The mental processes are generative, and thoughts produce either health or sickness. Every thought produces living organisms after its kind which are let loose in the world to do their work in human lives. These results of thought are referred to as microbes. If one uses the mind to see God, these thoughts kill disease microbes.

The teachings are far too involved for inclusion here. A great wealth of literature has been produced and is read by many church members as well as others. Unity has many ardent followers, so many — and so much demand is made on the Kansas City facilities — that there are plans now for a much larger new plant on grounds about fifteen miles from that city.

Unity is not officially recognized by any of the orthodox or old, established denominations. Although it has much in its teachings that is not out of line with these denominations, there is so much that is unorthodox that it probably will never be accepted by them. But some church members will continue to read and study Unity and feel that they are helped by it.

Unity employs prayer, the Scriptures, and silence as healing means. Its literature is filled with prayers and Scripture quotations, and for that reason it appeals to Christian people who are not too much concerned about its teaching on cardinal Christian doctrines. They find help in prayer and healing in the Word, just as they do in their churches and their church literature. The average Christian who reads *Unity* does not discern anything out of line with his denomination's teaching. Only those who seriously study it find that on many points, some previously mentioned, there is divergence.

Unity also emphasizes affirmations of a truth. *Good Busi-*

ness, the monthly magazine, may carry a calendar of the month with a daily affirmation such as, " I newly acquaint myself with God," " I refrain from negative conversations," " I waste no time in dispute or controversy," " I keep my head clear and my body strong," " I express the praise of God that is in my heart," or " I consider the outcome of an undertaking before launching upon it." [34] The approach is positive, rather than negative, and that appeals to many people.

Autosuggestion plays an important part in its effects upon the individual. He affirms until he believes, and a person's beliefs influence his actions either consciously or unconsciously. This may explain how many people are convinced that Unity helps them.

XII. THE EMMANUEL MOVEMENT

RELATING FAITH AND HEALING

While Christian Science was spreading rapidly in the early nineteen hundreds, another healing movement was inaugurated in Boston under the guidance of Elwood Worcester, D.D., Ph.D., the rector of Emmanuel Episcopal Church, and his associate, Samuel McComb, M.A., D.D. Isador Coriat, M.D., of Tufts Medical School, whose interest was aroused when the two clergymen came to him for advice, assisted in a new work which came to be known as the Emmanuel Movement.

Dr. Worcester was born in Massilon, Ohio, in 1862. When he decided to prepare himself for the ministry in the Episcopal Church, he was advised by the bishop to graduate from the General Theological Seminary of the Protestant Episcopal Church. Prior to that he had graduated from Columbia College. With a desire to pursue his studies further, he spent three years at the University of Leipzig, where he was privileged to study philosophy in the classes of Dr. Gustav Theodor Fechner, psychology with the world-famous Wundt, and Hebrew under the two authorities, the Delitzch brothers. Here he received his Ph.D. degree, *magna cum laude*. His extraordinary ability was recognized with honorary degrees from Hobart College and the University of Pennsylvania. The officials of Lehigh University chose him for the position of professor of philosophy, and he taught there successfully until the call came to become the rector of St. Stephen's Church of Philadelphia.

There was one member of his parish in Philadelphia in whom he found an especially kindred spirit, S. Weir Mitchell, M.D., the well-known neurologist. Dr. Mitchell had become famous because he pioneered in neurology and was interested in the deplorable conditions he found in state mental institutions. He was deeply concerned about the unscientific approach to mental patients. These two humanitarians had much in common, and undoubtedly their association influenced Dr. Worcester to such an extent that when he accepted the call to Emmanuel Church at Boston in 1904 he was prepared to enter the field of healing.

Fortunately his associate in Boston was a man also well prepared to undertake such a mission. Rev. Samuel McComb was born in Ireland and a graduate of Oxford University. Being intensely interested in psychology, he did postgraduate work at Berlin University, and after that accepted a professorship in ecclesiastical history at Queen's University in Canada. He studied abnormal psychology under Dr. William Graham, and was made a Doctor of Divinity by Glasgow University.

One might expect something unusual from a combination of two such capable individuals. Both were interested in the entire field of mental therapeutics and were convinced that it has a place in the healing ministry of the Church. They studied Christian Science also, and tried to analyze the reasons for its spread. Although they say modestly that their movement had no relation to Christian Science, by way of either protest or imitation,[35] yet they profited by what was commonly regarded by the old, established Churches as its errors. The power of the mind over the body was clear to them, but they felt that more was involved than that. The therapeutic value of medication, surgery, good habits, and healthful Christian living and thinking were also to be considered. They did not attempt to prescribe medication, and before they started their healing classes, they consulted leading physicians, such as Dr. Joseph H. Pratt, Dr. James J.

Putnam, Dr. Richard C. Cabot, Dr. Isador Coriat, and other leading physicians, neurologists, and psychiatrists. It was through one of these consultations with Dr. Isador H. Coriat that this physician decided to associate himself with them as a counselor in their healing movement.

Dr. Coriat was a Jew, a man who was learned in his profession and respected by other physicians as an unusually expert diagnostician. He was interested in psychotherapy, as were other well-known authorities of that day, among them William James, Morton Prince, Lewellys F. Barker, James J. Putnam, Boris Sidis, and Frederick Peterson. During the first years of his association with Worcester and McComb, he collaborated in the preparation of the official Emmanuel book, *Religion and Medicine,* and was a liaison between these clergymen and the medical men of Boston.

Worcester and McComb believed that people turned to cults because they offered something that the Churches were not giving. Although clergy, physicians, editors, teachers, and even humorists criticized these cults and presented them as false and erroneous, yet the undeniable fact remained that many people turned to them for help and evidently found something they did not find in the established Churches. Thus they came to the conclusion that people found that tangible something in the healing the cults professed to offer. The established Churches ignored healing as if it were a charism that ended with the postapostolic period. It was the contention of Worcester and his associates that Christ heals today, just as he did in New Testament times, using the prevailing medical skill and knowledge.

They worked on the basis that God has the power to cure disease, but does not cure all disease by the same methods or with the same materials. If the disease needs medicine or surgery, God uses these to serve his purpose. If the disease is functional, God heals through the mind or the spirit. The therapeutic value of the gospel of Jesus should be used in the individual's life. Physical blessings follow spiritual exercises, and it was their purpose to return to the Christ of the gospels and accept his teachings in a more literal sense. The Christian religion was regarded as the greatest of all therapeutic agents, if applied wisely and sincerely.

They made a thorough study of Christ's miracles of healing. It was these miracles that caused many to follow him, but since the second century they seem to be the portions of the gospels that are hardest to accept. The reason for this incredulity, they contended, is a lack of understanding of the underlying principles of healing. They found that modern medical research admits that many cures are effected by other than physical means. In these cures personality is a dominant factor: the personality of the one to be healed and that of the healer. Undoubtedly the Great Physician was one who inspired an overwhelming confidence in his ability to do what he intended to do. He could say to a man with a withered hand, " Stretch it forth." The man knew that he could do it because Jesus so instructed him, and he reached forth his hand and was healed.

There is no record that Jesus healed all diseases, but the Gospels do tell us that he healed fever, leprosy, paralysis, a withered hand, demoniacal possession, uterine hemorrhage; brought to life or reanimated at the point of death, and cured epilepsy and blindness. In other statements the Gospels tell us that he healed " many," but do not describe these diseases. In these cures Jesus recognized the moral causes that were sometimes basic, used faith as a spiritual condition necessary to healing, and depended upon God for his own ability to heal. These factors are fundamental to healing in his name, and with these principles in mind Worcester and McComb started a healing program.

As far as they could, they explored the influence of the subconscious on behavior; the power of suggestion, autosuggestion; functional neuroses; the causes of hypnotism; psychic and motor re-education; fear and worry; faith as a therapeutic power; prayer and its therapeutic value; suicide and its prevention; the healing wonders of Christ and the way these can be used by the Church in healing. The approach was both scientific and religious; they did not make that distinction, because they felt that religion can be applied scientifically to human needs.

Dr. Worcester and Dr. McComb first ventured into the field of healing at the invitation of a brilliant young physician, Dr. Joseph H. Pratt, a graduate of Johns Hopkins who was concerned about the welfare of the poor consumptives who lived in the tenement districts. The plan consisted of organizing the patients into a class, which met once a week when Dr. Pratt and his assistants could examine them and give directions and medication. The patients were to be healed in their homes, and a patient without a home could not be accepted. The open-air treatment, relaxation, and rest were prescribed. For that purpose the doctors often had to erect little white tents on the roofs of tenements or build lean-tos in back yards. Each patient was provided with a diary, so as to record every three hours: nourishment, sleep, temperature, and coughing, and the time spent relaxing in the air. At the weekly class meeting each person was weighed. Even in cold weather, the patient was ordered to rest in his open-air room. Since these people were almost all poor, they were provided with milk and pure olive oil. One or two nurses were employed to visit them, which helped to keep up their morale.

Those who were able were brought to the weekly class meeting, where Dr. Pratt inspired their confidence and the two clergymen offered religious service and strengthened their faith. The results were astonishing, as good as those in the most favored sanatoria.

The personalities of these three men were significant in the healing. This is evidenced by the fact that when the health authorities of the state took over the work, it steadily declined, and in a few years was discontinued. The state offered to take over the responsibility for the work since the

Church had borne the expense of it for so many years. Dr. Worcester did not regard this move with favor, but the state authorities and the vestry of the Church argued that with the better facilities the Government was in a position to provide, better results would follow. But it did not take long to find that morale, faith, and hope are not provided by the state, and that these are of great importance in the cure of tubercular patients.

While the tuberculosis class was in progress, Worcester and McComb decided to form a class for the moral and psychological treatment of nervous and psychic disorders. It was not their intention to intrude into the field of the physicians, but to co-operate with them, and they brought their plans to the attention of leading physicians for their advice. They felt that their healing plan was based on sound religion and sound science, and it was accepted as such by many of the physicians. It was launched with four Sunday evening services in the parish house of Emmanuel Church. Dr. James J. Putnam, of the Harvard Medical School, spoke at the first meeting; Dr. Richard C. Cabot spoke at the second; Dr. McComb at the third; and Dr. Worcester at the fourth. The latter two gave discourses on the Lord's ministry of healing, and, at the close, the clergymen said they would be in the parish house on Monday morning to consult with any who might have moral or psychical problems.

They did not know whether anyone would come or not; they were amazed when they came to the church the next morning and found one hundred and ninety-eight men and women. The physicians who were there had more than they could do and, to add to the confusion, someone sent down several hack loads of patients from a nearby insane asylum. While the examinations were in progress, the people were taken into the guild hall, where the ministers talked to them and prayed with them, and hymns were sung. Out of this grew the health conference for prayer and instruction that met weekly for many years.

Indifference and abuse were lavished on the Emmanuel group by many physicians and others. Newspapers found in the movement a tasty morsel of news and often exaggerated what was done and made it appear ridiculous. The papers called it the " Emmanuel Movement," a name that remains today. Many men of the cloth attacked the healing practices also, probably because they thought this was something similar to Christian Science. Faith healing had been taken over by the cults, and many of the clergy felt that it had no place in the Church. The clergy and the physicians who were responsible refused to answer the abuse, hoping thus to silence it. In the meantime Worcester, McComb, and Dr. Isador Coriat were writing *Religion and Medicine;* once it was published, there was more controversy. This book was reviewed, criticized, praised, and censured by all the leading newspapers.

Notwithstanding the criticism, a constant stream of people came for help. Each received personal attention as far as it could be given. In addition to that, and the regular parish work, the ministers were called to preach and lecture on weekdays in other cities, at colleges, medical meetings, and church gatherings, and to engage in debates. Dr. McComb was especially adroit at debating because he possessed a wit that was rare and used it as the occasion arose.

Certain information about their work reached England, and the ministers were invited by the archbishop of Canterbury to attend the Lambeth Conference and make a statement about their work to a committee appointed to study it. Dr. McComb made the trip and when he was called on at the meeting, the bishop in charge gave him twenty minutes. In his inimitably witty way he excused himself from speaking until the meeting granted him all the time he wanted. Then he presented his subject cautiously; after he finished, the Church of England endorsed their position, and legitimized spiritual healing in the Church.

The Emmanuel Movement specialized in psychotherapy

after the state took over the work with the tubercular patients. Every person who came for help was first examined by a competent psychiatrist or physician, who referred to the ministers those whom he thought could be helped by them. Then the psychiatrist examined the patient from time to time to determine what progress was being made.

As pastors of the congregation of Emmanuel Church, Worcester and McComb did not confine their pastoral calls to the psychoneurotic, but visited all their parishioners who were suffering with any illness, whether organic or functional. They believed that a clergyman can give spiritual help, which is beneficial to a person who is organically ill. The will to live is an important factor in recovery. Then also there is therapeutic value in a mind made peaceful by faith in God's care and love. Hope and confidence are healing forces and help tremendously in restoring health. These ministers were interested in applying Christian virtues to specific conditions that produce illness and in helping the patient to dispel any anxiety, fear, or despair, for these emotions have a negative influence.

Dr. Worcester also used hypnotism when he felt that the patient could be helped with it. One such patient was an architect, whom Dr. Mumford, who was in charge of a sanatorium in New York, referred to Dr. Worcester. The architect was on a job in Colorado when he collapsed; the next morning he found his right arm paralyzed and his right leg drawn up so that the knee almost touched his chin. Prior to that, he had had difficulty with his wife and she had left him, taking their only child with her. Since the man had been in this taut position so long, Dr. Mumford had to amputate two of his toes.

When Dr. Worcester saw him the first time, the patient was in a nasty mood and cursed both him and God because he blamed God for bringing all this sorrow upon him. The clergyman spoke with him and tried to reason with him that God is good and can offer a way out of difficulties. Once he becomes reconciled through faith, God will give him a new way of life.

The next day, when Dr. Worcester called again, the man was in a different frame of mind. After thinking over the suggestions of the previous call he was ready to express the confidence that Dr. Worcester could help him. During the ensuing conversation he told about things that troubled his conscience, and after listening to a complete confession and assuring him of God's willingness to forgive, Dr. Worcester used suggestion, or hypnotism, to cause him to fall into a deep sleep. While he was under the spell, the minister commanded him to obey, suggesting that he was not paralyzed at all, and then told him to move his arm. Without much effort he moved his arm above his head, out to the side, and then shook the minister's hand. Then Dr. Worcester told him that since he could move his arm he could also move his leg, whereupon he moved and straightened it. Dr. Mumford and the nurse were called into the room and the patient performed the same flexing movements for them. Then they left him sound asleep.

The cure was permanent. The next time Dr. Worcester saw this man was when the latter came to Boston and made it his business to visit the clergyman. He came up the steps two at a time, shook hands vigorously with the arm that was once paralyzed, and said that he had gone into another kind of architecture. Now he was a physical therapist, and, with the help of some wealthy friends, had established a " Consolation House " where physically or functionally handicapped people could learn crafts and arts. During World War I he was invited by the British and French Governments to do occupational therapy with wounded soldiers, but he was so engrossed in his work that he could not leave it. He had found, as Dr. Worcester told him in the first interview, that God could help him to make a better future for himself.

Scripture and prayer were nearly always used to relieve

pain, as was the case with a woman of fifty-two who was sent to Dr. Worcester by her physician.[36] She had just been informed that she was suffering from an internal cancer and her only hope was an operation that should be performed immediately. The shock of the news, combined with her misery, completely unnerved her, and she paced the room, wringing her hands in anguish. The physician sent her to Dr. Worcester because he did not want to operate while she was in this agitated condition.

Dr. Worcester had three long conversations with her prior to the operation, suggesting to her that the operation was for her good and that her physician was capable of handling the situation. With this assurance he also taught her to relax, using Scripture quotations and prayer.

A few days after the operation was performed, while still in the hospital, she sent for him. As he approached her room, her wails were clearly audible, and three frightened nurses were standing outside the door wondering what to do next because they had done all they were allowed to do as far as medication was concerned. Dr. Worcester invited them to come into the room with him because he wanted to show them what the Bible can do in such cases. He crossed to the bedside, sat down beside the patient, took her hand, and assured her that he had come to help her. In this assurance he suggested that he would recite for her four beautiful texts, and that while he was talking the pain would leave and she would sleep. The texts used were of a comforting nature dealing with rest, peace, sleep, and the watchful care of God. She became drowsy. He arose quietly, again reassuring her that she would sleep and that the pain would vanish; should it return, she was to send for him. The treatment was so effective that it was not necessary to send for him again except on the last day of her life when she wanted to thank him for making the way to death so much easier for her.

Twenty-three years after the publication of their book *Religion and Medicine,* Dr. Worcester and Dr. McComb published another volume on the Emmanuel Movement, entitled *Body, Mind and Spirit.* Dr. Worcester was looking forward to the near future when he would resign his pastorate at Emmanuel Church and devote the rest of his life to a full-time healing ministry. During these years the Emmanuel Movement spread to other cities, and this book presented their findings and the advancements that had been made in Boston. It presented many case studies of psychoneuroses, preparing the patient spiritually for surgery, cases of insomnia, analyses of dreams, psychoses of mood, suggestion, and an analysis of the healing deeds of Jesus.

Then on January 26, 1929, Dr. Worcester submitted his letter of resignation to the wardens and the vestry of Emmanuel Church after twenty-five years of service. A number of devoted friends gave him money and the church sold him the rectory as a permanent home for him and his family and purchased a new one for the in-coming rector. For many years previous to this time they had had a lay assistant, Mr. Courtney Baylor, who had been successful in the insurance business prior to his association with them. When he consulted Dr. Worcester on personal matters, he too became so interested that he decided to associate himself with the movement. Mr. Baylor was made head of the social service department, and in that capacity he made a remarkable contribution. It was his domain to correct tendencies, habits, and dispositions in men and women that make for poverty, inefficiency, and unhappiness. It seems that his greatest success was in dealing with cases of alcoholism. When Dr. Worcester submitted his resignation, Mr. Baylor came to him and said that he was also resigning and would continue to be associated with him in healing work.

He had acquired the title to 176 Marlborough Street just

five doors from the rectory, and offered it as a place to carry on their healing mission. Furthermore, he had taken the precaution to have their work incorporated under the laws of the State of Massachusetts as " The Craigie Foundation."

Now released from parochial duties, Dr. Worcester devoted more time to the training of clergymen, a phase of the work that had been neglected thus far. Classes in psychology and psychiatry were formed. Soon he was lecturing at convocations, colleges, universities. Then in 1930 he established a clinic in Grace Church, New York, and Holy Trinity, Brooklyn, at the request of the rectors, Dr. Walter Russell Bowie and Dr. Howard Melish, respectively. Through Dr. Melish, the Brooklyn Federation of Churches and the Brooklyn County Medical Association co-operated. Two qualified physicians, one a psychiatrist and the other a general practitioner, agreed to examine the patients; also many other physicians were consulted. Every week Dr. Worcester went from Boston to New York on Wednesday and returned Friday evening, to be ready for the patients in Boston on Saturday. In all this it was Dr. Worcester's purpose to return to the great principles on which Jesus, Paul, the apostles, and the early Christian teachers relied, that is, using the best scientific knowledge at his command and applying the principles of Christian living.

For financial reasons The Craigie Foundation was dissolved in 1934 but Dr. Worcester continued counseling with people in his own home at 186 Marlborough Street. In July of 1940, he died at the summer home of his daughter in Kennebunkport, Maine.[37]

Dr. McComb, who came to Emmanuel Church as the assistant minister in 1905, remained with Dr. Worcester until 1915 when he went to Baltimore, Maryland, and became the rector of the Church of the Incarnation. He came back to Boston in 1922 to deliver a series of lectures at the Episcopal Theological School in Cambridge. The next year he became the rector of the American Church in Nice, France,

returning in the summer months to be in charge of the services at the Episcopal Church in Dublin, New Hampshire.
About 1930 his health began to fail and he died in England
in 1938. At the time of his death he and Dr. Worcester were
working together on a book entitled *The Psychic Phenom-
ena of the Bible,* a book that was never published.[38]

It can be readily understood that other clergymen would
become interested enough to attempt the Emmanuel Movement in their churches. One of these was Dr. Samuel Fallows, the rector of St. Paul's Church in Chicago. He observed that thousands of people were being attracted to cults
and quackery because the Church was not making an attempt to meet their healing needs. With this in mind he
established a spiritual healing clinic in his church on the
Emmanuel plan, with the co-operation of certain physicians.
His religious therapeutics involved four principles: first,
that man is a composite being composed of mind and body;
second, that the therapeutic value of medical treatment in
organic disorders be emphatically recognized; third, that the
distinction between organic and functional disorders be considered as the domain of spiritual healing; fourth, that the
contribution of the medical profession to health and welfare
be in no way minimized.

The power of faith in the historic Christ and the efficacy
of prayer were used to bring health and happiness to the sick
who were diagnosed by a qualified neurologist and referred
to the clinic. Self-control, suggestions, latent energies in the
individual, the meaning of pain, overcoming worry and
anger, and the therapeutic value of cheerfulness were applied according to the patient's needs. Dr. Fallows wrote
special prayers to be used and a litany of health.[39]

About this same time the Emmanuel Movement spread
to Northampton, Massachusetts, a college town. Rev. Dr.
Lyman P. Powell made an analysis of the proper relationship between the minister and the doctor in the field of
healing.[40] Prior to that he made a study of Christian Science,

and wrote on that subject, as well as on faith and the art of natural sleep. Through his study of the Emmanuel Movement he came to the conclusion that it could re-energize the entire Christian Church and make it more useful to society.

Combined with his duties as rector of the parish, and without an assistant pastor, Dr. Powell established a clinic in his church. Northampton doctors were friendly and co-operated and referred patients to him when there were functional nervous disorders. Suggestion and faith, combined with scientific medicine, were employed in the healing processes. In one year he saw four hundred different people and gave systematic treatment to one hundred and five. His method of treating the patient was threefold: First, he tried to make the patient realize his oneness with God through the prescription of prayer. To accomplish this he recommended the systematic use of certain prayer and devotional books. Then he prescribed a definite reading course, with the purpose of strengthening the faith, using books on psychotherapy, *Religion and Medicine,* New Thought literature, and some of his own writings. The third phase of his treatment was the employment of autosuggestion and prescribed suggestions for the patient to say to himself.

The main weakness of the Emmanuel Movement was in the fact that none of the leaders systematically prepared other clergymen to carry on the work. Those who attempted to conduct the Emmanuel Movement in their churches were individualists, who became so engrossed in their work that they did not take the time to train others.

It is also to be mentioned that many clergymen regarded the movement with skepticism because it was unfortunately ill-timed, just when Christian Science was making inroads into the membership of the established Churches. It was regarded either as a substitute for Christian Science or as Christian Science with a clerical blessing, and the majority of the pastors wanted to have nothing to do with Christian Science. Although the originators of the movement did everything they felt they could to dispel the idea of any connection between the two, they never succeeded so far as the majority of the clergy were concerned.

The movement had the beneficial result of demonstrating that clergy and physicians can work together for the welfare of the patient in functional disorders. The articles that appeared in popular magazines and medical journals served the purpose of informing the medical profession that the two can supplement each other in the sickroom.

As far as the clergy were concerned, even those who regarded the entire movement with skepticism did read about it and were caused to think along the lines of a healing ministry. It caused many pastors to re-examine their spiritual treatment of the sick and study to make it more effective. Thus the pastoral office of the ministry was re-evaluated by many, who spent more time with their sick parishioners. In a few years pastoral counseling would evolve from this attention to the sick and pastors would study psychology, psychiatry, and psychotherapy and apply those principles in the pastoral ministry.

Another reason why the Emmanuel Movement did not meet with widespread acceptance by the clergy was because it required too much preparation on the part of the busy pastor. The average clergyman was not academically trained to undertake such a program in his congregation even though he may have possessed a personality indicating the probability of a reasonable amount of success with it. He would of necessity need to study psychiatry and kindred sciences and get the co-operation of the physicians in his locality. Either of these entails time and effort, for, aside from the study involved, the co-operation of physicians is not easily obtained in any healing venture that involves the therapeutic value of religion. In other words, the movement was too scientifically religious to gain popular favor even among the clergy.

Then, also, the average patient resented the idea of being

treated by two or more practitioners at the same time unless they all were either physicians or clergymen. He did not understand why he needed both in what he considered to be a physical ailment; either the physicians should be able to cure him or the religionists. If he turned to religion, he expected religion to do it all. That observation is witnessed by the fact that many turned to Christian Science, or the healing sects and cults that profess to do the entire job of healing. In other words the Emmanuel Movement was too complicated for popular acceptance.

But even though the movement did not meet with popular acceptance, it has special religious significance in the field of healing. The approach was scientific and also sincerely religious, and as such may be regarded as anticipating the chaplaincy program in the modern hospital, where the chaplain and the physicians co-operate for the welfare of the patient. It demonstrated the very important truth that these two professions can help each other in the treatment of the sick. As new scientific light is shed on the interrelationship of the mental, spiritual, and physical phases of man's personality, the spiritual and mental factors in organic disorders are becoming more apparent also. It can be said that the principles of the Emmanuel Movement are religiously and scientifically sound, and recent research in psychosomatic medicine, such as the work of Ray R. Grinker, M.D., and John P. Spiegel, M.D.,[41] attests that conclusion.

XIII. MEDICAL MISSIONS

Albert Schweitzer epitomizes the best in medical missions as they express the compassion of Jesus. He has made his little hospital at Lambaréné, in French Equatorial Africa, known all over the world. Dr. Schweitzer excelled first as a philosopher, then became known as one of the world's most accomplished musicians. Reaching into other fields, he has become well known as a New Testament scholar and theologian, as a medical doctor of exceptional ability, and as an authority in the field of letters, especially in the works of Goethe the great philosopher-statesman-poet of the German people. In 1949, when literary authorities were looking over the world to find just the right person to speak at the Goethe Festival in Colorado, their choice was Albert Schweitzer. Probably none of them actually believed they could lure him from his jungle hospital, but, true to his nature, this great Christian missionary surprised almost everyone concerned and came to America to deliver the lectures and then promptly returned to the work he loves.

This accomplished philosopher, teacher, musician, writer, pastor, and physician felt the call of God to go to the village hemmed in by a jungle to minister to the spiritual and the physical needs of black people. With all his talent and accomplishments he finds his greatest satisfaction in this work.

Satisfaction in the healing ministry, however, has not always been the motive behind Christian missions. It can be said that missions are as old as the Church itself. Ever since the time of Jesus his followers have felt impelled to spread the gospel, to save the heathen. The motive was definitely soul-saving. From the earliest days Christians traveled to far-away places to carry the message of Jesus. When the Romans invaded the British Isles, they found that Christians had been there before them. Even when Marco Polo returned to Venice in 1295, bringing with him wonderful tales about China, he also told about finding Christians in the interior of China who worshiped Jesus of Nazareth. It was lamented that they were heretical Nestorians, so the Roman Catholic Church forthwith sent missionaries into China to reconvert these Christians in the right way. It seems that almost everywhere travelers went they found that Christian evangelists had somehow been there ahead of them.

The reason for this diligence in evangelization was the firm conviction that the heathen were eternally lost unless a missionary got there to save them. Many believed that the return of Christ was imminent and that there was no time to be lost. With anxious hearts the missionaries went upon their journeys to save souls for eternity. Is it any wonder that the Christian faith has been carried to the far places of the earth?

In previous chapters some of these early missionaries were mentioned if they were interested in a healing ministry or practiced healing in any way. But the primary motive in early missions was to save souls for eternity, and it was not until comparatively recent years that the healing compassion of Jesus became a motivating force in missions.

For fifteen centuries Christian forces tried to invade China, and many of them got into the capital, where the ruler received them and permitted them to build a church. But it seems that they all, including the Nestorians, made no effort to develop and use Chinese teachers, doctors, or evangelists, and as a result the work died out.

Saint Francis Xavier was mentioned in a previous chapter because he healed with his evangelizing effort. He died on the threshold of China; the Dominican friar, Gaspar da Cruz, who followed in his steps, remained only a short time. It was a group of Jesuits under Matteo Ricci who penetrated the Celestial Empire; who through skill, perseverance, and tact laid the groundwork for permanent work there in 1583.

For a hundred and fifty years China was open for missionaries. Brilliant men of the Church went and associated with the court. It seems their primary interest was to influence men in places of position so the land would be open to Western civilization and the building of churches. The interest was entirely spiritual, and little was done to relieve suffering or to heal the sick until centuries later.

Now the Roman Catholic Church has medical mission stations in many lands, but they regard medical aid as a means to salvation, not as an end in itself. The primary purpose of the mission effort is to establish the Church in every land on earth.

Just as the Roman Catholic Church has healing orders in Europe and the United States that devote themselves to a ministry to the sick, it also has missionary orders, whose purpose is to minister in foreign lands. In China the Sisters of Charity, the Canossian Sisters, the Franciscan Missionaries of Mary, and the Sisters of St. Paul de Chatres do medical mission work in hospitals, in dispensaries, and in the homes of the sick.

These orders are supplemented by Catholic lay and clerical physicians. The hospitals are located in some of the larger cities of China, Japan, Korea and Indo-China. It seems the main Roman Catholic medical mission work is located in Eastern Asia.

However, the orders also do medical mission work in the Straits Settlements, Ceylon, India, the Dutch East Indies, the Philippine Islands, New Guinea, and Africa. In 1936, Pope Pius XI commended these orders, and said that the Sacred Congregation for the Propagation of the Faith would like to see new religious institutions founded for women who would dedicate themselves to health work in the missions. One of the orders that train Sisters as physicians is the Order of Medical Missions Sisters, with headquarters in Philadelphia. These go to hospitals in various foreign lands and in mission districts in the United States.

The primary aim of the medical mission enterprise of the Roman Church is conversions to Catholicism. Floyd Keeler, in *Catholic Medical Missions*,[42] says that the Church in being true to its mission of saving souls leaves no legitimate means untried to accomplish that purpose. He mentions that through the Catholic Association of the Holy Childhood twenty million pagan children have been baptized and thus sent directly to heaven.[43] Medical missions played a large part in that also.

Regarding the American Indians, the Bureau of Catholic Indian Missions has done a commendable work in the spiritual and economic fields, but not very much in offering medical and surgical care for the sick.

The Protestant Reformation did not foster missionary zeal until about two hundred years after Luther nailed the Ninety-five Theses to the church door at Wittenberg. In the intervening years the Protestants were so much concerned about establishing their Churches and securing their freedom to worship God according to the dictates of conscience that they had little thought for the heathen.

The first Protestant missionary sent out by the London Missionary Society was Robert Morrison, who was an English last- and boot-tree maker. He arrived in Canton in 1808 and spent the remaining twenty-seven years of his life in China. Morrison did the first medical missionary work in that land when he investigated the needs of the poor and opened a dispensary. Since he was not a doctor himself, he put a native practitioner at the head of the clinic, and collected about eight hundred Chinese medical books for its library.

The first American Protestant missionary society was

formed in 1810 by the General Association of Congregational Churches of Massachusetts.[44] Nothing would have been done about foreign missions even then if it had not been for four young men who appealed to the General Association of this Church to be sent as missionaries to the heathen. Then the Association had to appoint a " board " to devise ways and means to send these young men to foreign fields.

In this instance also the motive that prompted the young men was the conviction that the heathen who do not believe in Jesus are eternally lost, doomed to hell, because they do not confess Christ; the burden of this doom rested upon the hearts of the missionaries.

This was the beginning of the missionary movements of the Protestant denominations. Foreign missionary boards, or similar organizations, came into being in almost all communions. The ministers preached about the plight of the heathen and the urgency of their salvation. Missionary societies were formed in local churches, and " sewing for the heathen " became one of the main pastimes of women's organizations. Prayer bands were organized by the more pious, who studied the meager reports that came back from missionaries in India, China, Africa, and other faraway places, who were blazing the trails. A missionary came to be regarded as one of the most consecrated of all the Christian workers and held in love and awe.

When these pioneer missionaries reached many foreign lands, they found that Roman Catholics had been there before them. The Roman Catholics could make converts much faster than the Protestants because as soon as a heathen could be taught to speak the Trinity in his own language, he was eligible for baptism and another soul was saved for heaven. But the Protestant missionary, with a zeal for a confession of faith in Christ as his chief aim, could not be satisfied with less, and found his work much harder. It required painstaking effort and much patience. He had to translate the Scriptures into the native language, which he had first to learn. The consecration and patience of these Protestant missionary pioneers elicit the admiration of everyone.

Something very important happened to the missionary himself while he was about the great business of saving souls; he became keenly aware of the physical plight of the people whose souls he sought to save. He observed the needless suffering, the plight of the child wives, the unsanitary living conditions, the horrible poverty, and the fear and superstition that made life miserable. Out of pure compassion he started administering medicines to the best of his meager knowledge. In other words, he started healing the sick because compassion prompted him to do so.

When the second generation of missionaries arrived on the fields opened by the pioneers, they were concerned about saving souls, but also they were interested in saving lives. The older missionaries, when they came home on furlough, spoke in the churches about the plight of the heathen, their sickness, their diseases, their helplessness in the face of disease. All this challenged young men and young women to do something about it. It was generally the second-generation missionary who opened the dispensary and then the hospital.

At first the ministry to the sick was used as a means to an end. The missionary was in competition with the local medicine man or witch doctor. When his incantations failed and the missionary's medicine worked, the missionary could use the opportunity to talk about Christ to people who had learned to have confidence in him. In fact, the hospitals were used for that purpose. The gospel was preached and taught while the patient was healed.

There could hardly be found any better appeal than that and mission boards were quick to recognize it. " Medical missions " became a term well known in Christian circles. Young Christian physicians, surgeons, and nurses were challenged by the Church to enter the foreign mission field. Some of the finest among them accepted the challenge and were instrumental in building the hospitals and clinics and in training native men and women in the art of caring for the sick.

The primary motive with these men and women was not exclusively the salvation of souls for eternity. They felt called by God to relieve human suffering. Certainly they lost no opportunity to tell their patients about Christ. However, with them healing was no longer a means to an end but an end in itself. Motivated by compassion, certainly not by the meager salaries the Church could afford to pay them, these men and women took medical knowledge and skill to the faraway places of the earth.

In India, for example, Christian clinics and hospitals were the pioneers in medical service. Gradually, as the years passed, the Government took notice and developed a hospital system also. Through the efforts of missionary doctors and nurses, natives were trained so that today India has many well-trained native physicians and nurses. However, frequent shifting and reassignment by Government authorities, as well as political control of funds and other interferences, often hamper the work in Government hospitals. Mission hospitals are free of these difficulties, and can carry on their work in the spirit of Jesus without all this interference.

A large number of Protestant denominations have hospitals and dispensaries in India: among them are the Baptists, Lutherans, Evangelicals, Canadian Presbyterians, Church of England, Church of Scotland, Reformed Church, Evangelical and Reformed Church, Scotch United Free Church; Presbyterian Churches of Ireland, Wales, England; Presbyterian Board of Foreign Missions; Moravians, Methodists, English Baptists, Friends, and various missionary societies.

Protestant medical missionary work also has spread to Korea, China, Japan, Burma, Siam, Laos, Persia, Syria, Turkey, Arabia, Africa, the Philippines, Mexico, Central America, South America, Alaska, Puerto Rico, and Labrador. In fact, there is hardly a land on earth where Protestant medical missionaries are not working. All this may leave the impression that the Church is meeting the medical needs of the world, but nothing could be farther from the truth. There are still vast areas where medical help is not available, but the Church is doing an admirable job thus far. In many countries the missionaries are training natives in modern medical and surgical treatment so that they can be in a better position to care for themselves in the years ahead.

In a *Survey of the World Mission of the Christian Church,* published in 1938,[45] the growth of medical mission work is indicated, as well as certain trends. The available statistics on medical mission work before 1911 say nothing about the education of native physicians and nurses. The figures of that year reveal that there were 111 teaching institutions with 830 medical students. In 98 dispensaries and hospitals, 663 nursing students were being trained. By 1925, while the reported number of medical training centers had fallen to but 19, the student enrollment had risen to a total of 914. What happened was that privately organized classes, conducted in individual hospitals, often taught by a single missionary physician, were discontinued, and teachers from a larger area were brought together in teaching centers with reasonably sound curriculums. The number of nurse-training schools also declined from 98 to 72, but again, the enrollment increased to 1,085. By 1938 there were 14 medical colleges reported with 1,284 students.

While the number of training centers decreased, the number of hospitals increased considerably; from 576 in 1911 to 1,092 in 1938. As native doctors and nurses are trained, they are capable of taking over the management of these institutions, and more medical missionaries are released to begin healing institutions in new areas.

It is very difficult to get a comprehensive picture of the actual medical missionary work that is being done today. Unfortunately accurate, up-to-date information is hardly available unless all the reports of the individual denominations and societies are studied and the statistics compiled. But even that cannot be done because the reports are not uniform. Many state the needs in terms of money and personnel, others according to the country where the work is being done, but they do not give the over-all picture. Many Protestant Churches, through home or national mission boards, carry out programs of medical work in urban centers, in sparsely populated areas, and among minority nationality and language groups in the United States and its territories. Unfortunately, however, information about the over-all scope of this work is even more difficult to secure than that relating to " foreign " missions.

One of the best known of the medical missionaries is Dr. Gordon S. Seagrave, who has been in charge of the Baptist Hospital in Namkham in Burma since 1922. Through his writings he has made reading about medical missions very interesting. One of his earliest books is *Waste-Basket Surgery,* in which he tells how he succeeded in getting an audience to listen to what the missionaries had to tell about Jesus Christ. He started by building up the hospital practice, and soon patients were coming with every conceivable complaint. While he and his nurses doctored, the missionaries told the patients about Jesus.

He trained native nurses and did a remarkable piece of work there until World War II came and the Japanese invaded the land. Then he and his nurses had to flee to India with General Stillwell, where they ministered to war casualties. Then when it was all over, they found their way back again to start anew.[46] His courage and devotion is typical of modern medical missionaries.

One of the better known Christian medical associations in foreign lands today is that of India, Burma, and Ceylon, which publishes a bimonthly journal.[47] It lists an imposing array of officers; the names indicate that they are men and women physicians and nurses of many nationalities. The unique thing about this medical journal is the Christian spirit that emanates from all the articles, from the most technical discussions to the nursing news of the nurses' auxiliary of the organization.

Under the "Nursing News" the first item that catches the attention is " Aim: The Extension of the Kingdom of Christ in India."[48] Denominational differences are minimized by the promotion of a fraternal spirit among all Christian nurses. Standards of service are also recognized as being important, and the auxiliary is trying to promote the best nurse-training that is possible. Nursing is accepted as an integral part of the Christian message to India, Burma, and Ceylon.

In 1932, leading Christian laymen of seven large Protestant denominations made an intensive study of the entire mission work, which was later published under the title *Re-Thinking Missions.*[49] The study was extensive, but a chapter on the medical work of missions is of special significance in this connection. The medical work in India, Burma, China, and Japan is reviewed and certain principles are offered as a basis for activities in mission hospitals in the future. The compassion of the Lord is mentioned first, because service is to be rendered in love, in response to the need, and without inducement. The spoken word may be appropriate in the hospital, and the doctor cannot disassociate bodily from spiritual requirements, but the use of medical service as a means of making converts when the patient is at the mercy of the missionary is regarded as coercive and improper. What is needed is a clear-minded experimentation in the religious phases of hospital work, because much of the evangelistic work there is casual and perfunctory now.

From this investigation it is seen that the recommendations of the laymen's inquiry are far from the original motivation in medical missions when the primary purpose in offering assistance to the suffering was to save the soul. It may be a healthy trend and result in more sincere conversions than was the case when relief from suffering was regarded as an inducement to conversion. Only the years can decide which is the more effective approach, and the only standard for judgment will be the numbers recorded in annual reports, which, to say the least, is a faulty measure. One thing is sure: the compassion of the Lord is manifested through medical missionaries and through those who support the work financially at home.

Stories of heroism, sacrifice, and love come from many lands. Just as the early followers of the Lord were interested in the welfare of their fellow men, these Christians are motivated by the compassion of the Lord to do this in his name.

Another chapter in Christian healing zeal and devotion is in the making now in war-torn countries such as China. Conflicting reports come from that land, but it is safe to say that medical missionaries, true to their calling, will find a way to continue their work of compassion if there is any possibility at all.

Mission-minded Christians are convinced that the Church exists to continue the work Christ began. Mindful of the value that he placed on human personality, and his compassion, medical missionaries will continue to follow him in healing service and Christians at home will continue to support the work.[50]

XIV. SOME MODERN HEALERS

There are in America today a number of persons who have attracted widespread attention for their religious and healing ministries. In almost every case their life stories make an interesting study, but a full report is not possible within the scope of this volume. Therefore we shall consider in this chapter only two present-day healers of prominence, Glenn Clark and John Gayner Banks, and give attention to a few others of a different character in the next chapter.

GLENN CLARK

Glenn Clark is one of the great mystics of this age who has influenced the lives of many people. He was born in Des Moines, Iowa, on March 13, 1882, of sturdy American stock. His father was a lawyer, who with his wife established a Christian home, and the influence of Clark's early training is clearly evident in his life.

He received his higher education at Grinnell College in Iowa where he excelled in athletics as well as in his studies. His first position was that of principal of his home-town high school at Des Moines. Then, with a friend he traveled through England, Scotland, and parts of the continent of Europe. Upon his return he enrolled at Harvard, where he received his M.A. degree. In the closing days of his Harvard year he received a call to head the English department and direct athletics at William and Vashti College, Aledo, Illinois, a position he held for four years.[51]

On December 29, 1909, he married Louise Miles in her parents' home at Grinnell. She was spiritually and mentally well equipped to be his partner, although she had never participated in athletics or practiced the arts. She was of Puritan stock, with an analytical mind, the counterpart of her husband.

After four years at William and Vashti, Mr. Clark accepted a position in the English department of Macalester College at St. Paul, Minnesota, where he remained on the faculty until 1944, when he resigned to devote his entire time to the development of the spiritual life of his fellow men.

In his latest book, *A Man's Reach*, he traces the religious development of his life. The death of his brother Page when he himself was fourteen made a deep impression on his soul, and he resolved thenceforth to do the work of two men. To accomplish this, he decided to devote the next seven years to self-development. The years from twenty-one to twenty-eight would be used to mix and mingle with the world and adjust himself to people and events. From twenty-eight to thirty-five he planned to integrate the inner and outer worlds, and from thirty-five to forty-two he was to start his lifework. His vision or plans ended at forty-two, which gave him a premonition that he would die at that age.

After his marriage, the years from twenty-eight to thirty-five proved to be a winnowing out of the ego, and both he and his wife found their own souls. It was during this period that he had a premonition of his death at the age of forty-two. One night he wrestled with God in prayer until he reached the decision so to die in his physical, selfish self in the next seven years that he could actually start living in heaven here and now. Once he resigned himself wholly to the will of God, this decision became a pivotal experience of his life.

During his sabbatical leave, which followed this act of consecration, his father passed away. While he sat at the bedside, he realized that only as he gave himself to the Spirit of God and was reborn as a son of God would he bring into birth a truth of God. Then he permitted the Holy Spirit to rise within and overshadow self.

After being born again he assumed three lines of reading. The first was the teachings of Jesus, the New Testament. The second line was with the mystics, Rufus Jones, Emma Herman, Evelyn Underhill, and Brother Lawrence. The third line was in scientific literature. He especially appreciated F. L. Rawson's *Life Understood,* in which the British physicist states that he believes prayers are just as scientifically infallible as the laws of physics.

With a group of sincere people from many Churches who met in a Minneapolis hotel he learned the art of prayer. In pooling their experiences in prayer they found three essential elements: a positive faith, a sincere love, and a radiant joy. With this spiritual equipment Mr. Clark found also the healing power of prayer.

To keep himself spiritually in tune with God he observed a quiet hour each day, in which he shut out the sounds, sights, and interruptions of the outer world. He meditated upon psalm prayers and attuned his soul to the Infinite. Answers to his prayers were clearly manifested, but these external answers did not overwhelm him, because he felt that God was working in his own way and with God nothing is impossible.

Thereafter he devoted ever more time to Y.M.C.A. and Y.W.C.A. conferences, and youth camps, and this experience led him to the decision to found camps of his own. He felt that the standard camps placed too much emphasis on lectures and discussions, and regarded prayer as a routine rather than a vital, living relationship with Christ. His first venture at a Camp Farthest Out was at Lake Koronis, Minnesota, where he trained athletes of the spirit as formerly he had coached football teams in camps on the Mississippi River before the opening of school.

This first Camp Farthest Out was underwritten by twelve men of his Plymouth Bible class, and the first person to register was a Miss Sparrow, who came with the kind of spirit that was destined to distinguish those in the future who attended these camps. This was the beginning of a spiritual camp movement which soon elicited the interest of such people as Frank Laubach, Starr Daily, Alice Kraft, Claire Boyer, Glenn Harding, and others. The emphasis of the camps is on prayer, the redemptive love of Jesus, creative writing, quiet, art, and singing. But the main emphasis is on praying, not only talking about it but the actual practice of it. An all-night prayer is the climax and high point of the entire period.

Glenn Clark is included in this book because he uses prayer as a medium of healing. He feels that it is not necessary for him to be present with the person who is the subject of his prayer. In the prayers for the sick the praying person must employ the principles of faith and love and accept the will of God. In 1940 he wrote the book *How to Find Health Through Prayer*. There are seven " immersions in Jordan " [52] which serve, not as a cure for a specific disease, but as the means of cleansing the seven layers of being, heart and mind, soul and body. The first immersion is the washing of the outer skin, a thorough cleansing of the body and the teeth. The next step is the washing of the kidneys and the digestive tract with plenty of pure water. This is followed by a cleansing of the blood vessels, which is accomplished by exercise, stretching, and rhythmical calisthenics. Then the lungs are to be cleansed with fresh air, and for this he recommends walking in the fresh air. The fifth immersion is the washing of the emotions to drain their poison from the body. To accomplish this a person must have a spiritual counselor or some other friend to whom he can turn in his stress. Confession to God is also a catharsis for cleansing the emotions; they must be kept clean and sweet. The next immersion is the washing of the mind; an active, balanced mind is a

source of good health. The mind is kept clean by being oc-
cupied in wholesome thinking. Hobbies and sports also have
a cleansing effect. The seventh immersion is the washing of
the soul, and by " soul " he means the mind and heart, the
entire being by which man contacts the Infinite.[53] The
cleansing of the soul may not be accomplished in a day or
even a year, but it is worth a lifetime effort because the
wholeness of being means health to the individual. Bad
thoughts and bad emotions reflect themselves in bad health,
and wrong thinking has much to do with bringing disease
into the body. On the other hand he makes it clear that the
worst invalids are not necessarily the worst sinners. Illness
is an indication of spiritual sensitivity, and those who are
spiritually sensitive may be more inclined to the possibilities
of disease. God's messages often come in temporary illness.

In his prayers for healing he found that it is not the prayer
that creates the miracle but the condition in consciousness
that the prayer induces.[54] The healing state is the presence of
God in the individual, and God manifests himself when
prayer turns out hate, fear, and self, and, through faith, hope,
and love, enables the individual to experience the mighty
powers of God in his life.

In his books Mr. Clark gives many examples of healing in
answer to prayer. One of many such instances concerned a
dear friend[55] who had gone to a physician. He discovered
that she had a tumor on the brain and advised her to go to
the Mayo Clinic at once. She came to Mr. Clark with her
problem and asked his prayers before she left. He talked
to her and advised her to turn to God completely and put
her case entirely in his hands with the firm conviction that
he could remove the danger.

She went to the clinic, where examinations revealed the
tumor to be about the size of a hen's egg. One surgeon advised immediate surgery; another suggested that she wait
about three months and then come back. She decided to
wait, and went to the mountains, where she spent the time

in relaxation and prayer. As the days passed, she shed her fears and turned her thoughts to God and her fellow man, ridding herself of self. Then when she returned after three months the X-ray examinations revealed that the tumor was gone. This caused the physicians consternation, and one of them termed it a miracle.

The only condition Mr. Clark feels indispensable to healing by prayer is that someone around the sick person be in a state of prayer. The patient himself need not pray or even have religious faith. The key to the situation is with the one who is praying and with God. It is a complete reliance upon the power of God, with whom all things are possible through the prayer of faith.

As a matter of fact he has devised a *Correspondence Course in Spiritual Healing* [56] in which he deals with the divine law of wholeness, the healing power of light and water, washing of the soul, bathing the emotions, the mind, the lungs, the blood vessels, the skin, and the inner skin. The reader, in order to benefit from the course, is required to give co-operation, time, willingness to abandon personal habits that will retard health. Faith and confidence in the teacher are essential, and the patient must follow the suggestions and inspirations of the lessons. In addition, the reader is asked to give of his worldly possessions a just proportion to further the work of the loving God.

His quarterly magazine is *Clear Horizons,* which contains articles by leading clergymen and laymen who are interested in the health of individuals.

The number of Camps Farthest Out has grown, until in 1949, eighteen were listed in states from Texas to Michigan, California to New Hampshire. There was also a European tour from June 9 to August 9.

Glenn Clark now devotes his entire time to the use of prayer in the trying situations of life, and particularly in the healing of the sick and the prevention of illness through spiritual living.

JOHN GAYNER BANKS

Rev. John Gayner Banks, D.Litt., is the director of the Fellowship of St. Luke, a church society for the promotion of divine healing with headquarters in San Diego, California. Dr. Banks was born in England and educated at King's College, University of London, and at the University of the South, Sewanee, Tennessee. He is an ordained priest of the Episcopal Church, a graduate psychologist, and for many years was active in the Guild of Pastoral Psychology.

During his rectorship of a church, in the pastoral office, he discovered spiritual healing as a part of the gospel of Jesus as it is specifically taught in the New Testament. He feels that the healing power of the gospel has always been latent in the Church, but often obscured by ignorance, by a lack of faith, and especially by secularism. In the ministry of healing he is convinced that the Church should actively co-operate with the medical profession, with hospitals, and other healing agencies. In this phase of divine healing he differs from those who believe that healing is accomplished divinely without the aid of medicine or surgery.

The Fellowship of St. Luke is organized to quicken the spiritual life of its members and to study the influence of the spiritual life on mental and physical well-being. In this phase it pioneers in psychosomatic relationships, and also seeks to restore the apostolic practice of healing as it was taught and practiced by the Lord Christ. It believes that divine healing is still an essential part of the Christian ministry, but does not stress any one mode or technique as being the only one that can be used. All the methods, such as laying on of hands, anointing with oil, direct prayer, and silence are used by the Fellowship of St. Luke in the healing missions.

Dr. Banks not only uses these ecclesiastical methods, but also teaches that any curative agent, when it is administered in the spirit of the Great Physician, is efficacious in healing.

Prayer plays an important part in the practices of this Fellowship. Systematic intercessions are offered for the distressed in body, mind, or estate. The official booklet of the organization [57] contains numerous prayers for healing, confessions, absolutions, and a form for anointing.

The members are asked to pray daily for the healing work by using the prayer in the booklet and such other prayers as seem desirable. The prayers should be supplemented with a daily reading of the Gospels and a faithful reading of the monthly magazine of the Fellowship, *Sharing*.[58] *Sharing* contains articles on healing and the spiritual life, reviews of outstanding books, reports of healing works done, and a monthly feature on " Pastoral Psychology," as well as poems and devotional material.

Mr. Banks now devotes his life to the direction of the Fellowship and the magazine, and to healing missions that he conducts upon request in churches all over the country. In these healing missions he places emphasis upon the therapeutic value of the office of Holy Communion, and each day of the mission begins with the celebration of this sacrament.

Conversion is also regarded as a healing process because, as the soul is illuminated by the Holy Spirit and finds harmony with its Creator, it influences the physical being beneficially.

Another office of the Church that is used is that of confession, with its accompanying absolution. While " confession is good for the soul," it is also good for the body. It is mentally and spiritually cleansing and rids the consciousness of the burden of guilt. The ensuing feeling of peace contributes to the security and well-being of the individual, and these states influence the person psychosomatically toward a healthier state.

The Word of God is also used as a healing medium. It has therapeutic value either because God works through it or because the individual finds release in its promises or both.

For that reason the individual who attends the missions is urged to read the Bible daily. Instruction is also given, so that the reader can better understand the meaning. The healing mission of Jesus is studied, his technique, the use of the emotions, and such virtues as faith in God's ability to grant the healing touch to the body through the soul.

Mr. Banks says [59] that his interest in this work goes back thirty years, and observes that the most important thing he can say about his personal work is that the actual results in healing showed a higher percentage of success in his local ministry than in the itinerary work he is now doing. This observation may attest the importance of a personal acquaintance between the healer and the one to be healed. It is more likely that the parishioner who knows his pastor intimately over a longer period of time will have more confidence in him. God works in mysterious ways, and, generally speaking, confidence in his instrument (the healing pastor), as well as the personality of the pastor, is important. In his healing missions, Mr. Banks usually comes into a church situation. The resident pastor has previously inspired his people to anticipate, and with his announcements tries to establish a feeling of confidence in the one who is coming; while this is very helpful, the personal touch is necessarily lacking.

Mr. Banks realizes this situation, and for that reason encourages the local pastor to carry on the healing work of the ministry after he leaves. Numerous books and pamphlets are available in the home office of the Fellowship for the guidance of the minister. Some titles may be helpful in getting the picture of the available helps: *The Supreme Physician*, by Frank Uttley; *A Guide to Confident Living*, by Norman Vincent Peale; *Love's Healing Ministry*, by John Maillard; *The How and Why of Christian Healing*, by John Gayner Banks; *He Lives*, by Austin Pardue; *Prayer, the Mightiest Force in the World*, by Frank C. Laubach. These are only a few of the titles. There are also available healing leaflets, by Mr. Banks and others, such as: *Thoughts in the Presence; My Companion for Quiet Hours; A Message of Hope for Those Who Are Sick; A Miracle of Healing.*

The whole purpose of the healing ministry, as Mr. Banks sees it, is to build lives in harmony with God's will, so that the flood tide of his boundless life may constantly well within us. This movement is within the Church, largely the Episcopal Church, but it is not confined to any particular denomination. Its missions are sponsored by established Churches of many denominations, which invite the director for that purpose.

The Order of St. Luke the Physician grew out of this spiritual healing movement and was organized in 1947. It is for those who make spiritual therapy a regular part of their ministry — whether in the Church or in medicine, psychology, nursing, etc. The membership of the organization is growing; during the healing retreat at Bynden Wood in October, 1949, about forty candidates were inducted, including three physicians and several others who were technicians, nurses, and clergymen. The members pledge themselves to pray daily for the work, to read the Gospels daily, and to share the healing message with others.

XV. HEALING SECTS AND INDIVIDUALS

I t is estimated that ten million Americans belong to or are influenced strongly by a large number of small sects and individual religious leaders who are not identified with any group or organization. No one can say whether the estimate is correct or not, because it is almost impossible to ascertain the facts; there are so many rather permanent sects and cults, and aside from that every town, city, and village has one or more evangelists of this nature who come, stay awhile, and move on to another place. This figure is stated to help the reader to realize that the influence of sects and independent preachers and religious healers is an American religious phenomenon that needs to be considered.

Several attempts have been made to study these hundreds of groups and individuals and classify them into types, but there is such an amazing confusion among them that they defy classification. Elmer T. Clark, in his helpful treatment of the small sects, tells us that Church historians have attempted to classify them as ritualistic, experimental, and doctrinal, or as intellectual, feeling, and action types.[60] Mr. Clark divides them into more categories: pessimistic sects, perfectionist sects, charismatic sects, communistic sects, legalistic sects, egocentric sects, and esoteric sects.[61] However, neither the history nor the doctrinal teachings will be discussed in this chapter, except where these have a bearing on the healing practices. But even this restricted interest leads into a field so varied and often so confusing that the discussion will have to be very limited.

Along with the sects that claim to heal there are hundreds of individuals who set themselves up as evangelists and faith healers: some, in tabernacles, who remain in one location for a longer period of time; others, with tents, who go from city to city; and still others who are brought into localities by Holiness and Pentecostal groups to conduct revivals.

These sects and individuals range all the way from those with a mixture of Oriental-Christian beliefs to those with Pentecostal-charismatic teachings. Those that specialize in healing use anointing, laying on of hands, prayer, anointed cloths, and handkerchiefs, snakes, hysteria, hypnotism, "touching," exorcism, and other means, depending on the wishes of the healer.

It is not easy to distinguish between a Church and a sect. Often the distinction lies with the individual: if he is a member of it, it is a Church; if he is not, it is a sect. Usually there is rivalry among the sects, and between the sects and the old established Churches. In fairness it should be said that seldom do ministers of the old established denominations preach against the sects, but much of the preaching of the sects is aimed at the more orthodox Churches and clergymen. To some conservatives, the Pilgrim Holiness Church is a sect because it is an offshoot of the Methodist Church. There are about fifty such groups that were started at one time or another by dissatisfied Methodist ministers. And since the Methodist Church does not practice anointing the sick or conduct divine healing services, that was one difference that could easily become a distinguishing feature. Many ministers of these groups preach " the full gospel," pray for the salvation of the ministers of the more orthodox Churches, and practice divine healing.

There is also a large number of " unknown-tongues " sects that concentrate their religious efforts on getting the " gift of tongues." Their meetings are highly emotional; the preacher is usually self-made in the sense that he considers himself "called" and therefore needs no theological training for his position. His preaching is couched in a language that is understood by the people who attend, and his appeals are designed to affect the emotions. Sometimes while he is preaching, the choir may begin a singable tune and repeat the same stanza time and again, to the accompaniment of guitars or a piano or a brass quartet and cymbals. The members call out their praises of God while the preacher urges sinners to repentance. After a while things begin to happen: a penitent begins to jerk his head, stand up and clap his hands, and walk around shouting, " Glory to God "; then he falls prone on the ground or floor. Others may start doing the same thing. They hardly notice those who are down, step over them while they clap their hands, keep in step with the music, jerk, and shout. The preacher keeps on calling on the Holy Ghost to grant the " gift," and then a prone one arises as if in a trance and begins to babble in " tongues." Others notice him then: he has received " the gift of the Holy Ghost."

Some people are psychologically unsuited for the stress of such religious meetings and become emotionally disturbed to such an extent that they do erratic things; some become mentally ill. Others seem to thrive on them. An older man, about seventy, limping with rheumatism, came into a tent meeting one evening. As the service progressed, the minister tried to persuade those who wanted to be saved to come up to the " altar." (There was no altar.) The choir was singing and " workers " were busy in the congregation urging individuals to go up front. Two of them could be seen talking earnestly with the old man. The minister mopped his brow with his wet handkerchief and a worker escorted a woman up front. People shouted: " Praise the Lord! " " Hallelujah! " Others were urged to do likewise and a member of the choir stood up, clapped her hands, started marching back and forth on the platform in back of the preacher. A few others from the congregation followed her, singing all the time. Then the old man arose; a worker on each side took an arm and led him up front. By that time there were perhaps a half dozen kneeling there, workers with them, all praying aloud. The old man knelt also and they prayed for him. " Praise God," " Praise the Lord," came from the throats of many, and the old man joined the " dancers " on the platform. This went on past midnight until the people, exhausted, one by one or in pairs or groups, left the tent. The next evening the minister was there as usual, to conduct the same type of meeting again. Nearly all these sects practice healing through prayer or anointing or the laying on of hands.

There are other sects much more restrained than this group that practice anointing of the sick, such as the Arminian or Freewill Baptists, which dates from 1701 and is one of the oldest sects in this country. Found mainly in the South, these Baptists trace their religious ancestry to Wales. They are opposed to any worldliness, practice foot washing, immersion, and anointing the sick with oil.

Another group that claims to heal any disease by faith and prayer is the Holiness Church, a small sect in Kentucky, which was started about 1880. This is another of the fifty such groups started by erstwhile Methodist ministers. Rev. Hardin Wallace and Rev. James A. Singer started this " only true Church," which recognizes no other Church body as being authorized by Christ. The members are perfectionists and claim to be made perfect by the Holy Ghost, who can heal all diseases.

A much larger sect, the Assemblies of God, General Council, are convinced that they have discovered the original Church of Jesus. This sect started in Hot Springs, Arkansas, in 1914, and has its headquarters at Springfield, Missouri. The ministers emphasize the baptism of the Holy Ghost and fire and the miraculous divine healing of disease. Contrary to the usual practices, this sect does not oppose the use of a physician if the patient wants one.

The " snake handlers " have been featured in the news a great deal during these later years. They are found mostly in North Carolina and Tennessee. As far as is known, the practice of handling snakes was started by a preacher named Teester at Sylva, North Carolina. He wanted to prove that the Lord can heal anything, even the bite of a rattlesnake (Mark 16:18). Ever since, there have been groups playing with snakes in religious services; the practice grew until certain states found it necessary to enact laws forbidding it.

There are countless other sects that practice faith healing in one form or another. Some are absolutely opposed to any medication; others permit the employment of a physician in certain diseases; with others it doesn't seem to make much difference — a patient can be healed either way.

Along with the sects are many healing cults that do not profess to be religious, such as sun worshipers, nudists, and tree climbers. One of these healers takes a number of his patients into the woods, where they encircle a tree, holding hands. He deposits a hair from the head of each one in a crotch in the tree as an offering, and they leave believing that they will be healed. But since the discussion in this book deals with the Church and healing, the cults without religious significance are not included.

One of them should be mentioned, however, and that is the Father Divine group. It has religious significance in that the Negro leader, Father Divine, is regarded as the deity by his many followers. Those who worship him are not confined to the Negro race, since many white people are among them. Father Divine is a mysterious, pudgy Negro who has the absolute devotion of thousands, who regard him with the deepest reverence. His " heavens " are located mainly in Eastern cities and localities, but he controls property in various sections of the country. This writer was interested in a piece of property on Lake Erie about fifteen years ago until he was informed that the owner had decided to give it to Father Divine. Father Divine, it is said, owns nothing in his

own name, but seems to have an unlimited supply of resources. A visitor to one of his " heavens " related how Father Divine was received with reverent awe when he arrived
by limousine. Male " angels " acted as bodyguards. A reverent silence came over the assembly as he dramatically entered the large dining room. Before his appearance one of
the " angels " preached a sermon, and on that particular day,
this visitor said, the sermon was intelligent, full of a social
gospel with real significance. But Father Divine's speech before the meal was sketchy, contained self-coined words, was
often unintelligible until he reminded his hearers of his divinity by asking questions such as, " When the depression
was here and people were starving, there was plenty of food
on Father Divine's table, wasn't there? " The crowd, with
one voice answered, " Yes, Father." " When sugar and meat
was rationed," he continued, " you had all you wanted at
Father Divine's table, didn't you? " " Yes, Father! " After
he spoke thus for a while, he sat at the head of the great
table, and food was brought in, dish after dish, each handed
to the Father first, who blessed it as he placed a spoon or a
fork in it and passed the food on to his guests. There were
about three hundred at the table on this occasion.

Father Divine can also heal. He is " God " to his followers; he needs only to touch with his hand and the cure is
effected immediately, even a toothache or any pain. When
he touches, relief comes. The fanatic belief in his divinity
is the source of his healing power. His miraculous ability is
accepted by his followers without question; however, his
healing power is not the primary lure that attracts his disciples.

Another healer who was accepted with a similar devo-
tion on the part of her followers was Mrs. Aimee Semple
McPherson who became the founder of the International
Church of the Foursquare Gospel, with headquarters at
Angelus Temple in Los Angeles. She was converted in her
teens by a Baptist evangelist, Robert Semple, whom she

later married. She felt called by God to preach the " foursquare gospel," as she chose to call it. She practiced all the expressions of the Pentecostal, Holiness, and Fundamental sects, including speaking in tongues and divine healing. In her services she was an artist in the use of dramatic effects, publicity, costuming, lighting, and music. The fact that she was physically attractive in appearance was not a hindrance to her success. Her followers held her in such esteem that they disregarded the fact that she married three times, that there were lawsuits involving her, and that much publicity was given to some of her questionable adventures.

In this instance again, personal loyalty to a captivating personality played an important part. She used dramatics skillfully to make a deep impression on her audience, so that they regarded her every word as the pure gospel of Jesus and anticipated miracles. Today there are more than four hundred Foursquare Gospel churches, most of them very small in membership but still teaching her doctrines and practicing divine healing.

Among the hundreds of individual divine healers none has received wider publicity than a child, " Little David." He attracted immense crowds through the central part of the country as late as the beginning of 1949. Little David Walker, now about fifteen years old, had as his manager Rev. Raymond G. Hoekstra, of Indianapolis, Indiana. Mrs. Peggy Taylor, according to newspaper accounts, was his financial manager. His appearance in a city or community was usually sponsored by Holiness or Pentecostal or Independent Holiness ministers. A large hall or coliseum was rented for the revival and the healing services; people came from far and near bringing the sick of every type and description.[62]

When he conducted a service in the coliseum at Evansville, Indiana, crowds gathered early in the morning, even though he was not to appear until that evening. The large auditorium, which seats about four thousand, was filled for the occasion. Of course, many attended out of curiosity, but the majority anticipated healing. At a certain time those who wished to be healed were formed into a line and passed by him. Some were carried on chairs or cots and he laid his hands on them and prayed for their healing.

In 1949 his parents, Jack and Gertrude Walker; his manager, Hoekstra; and Attorney James Dawson were featured in the court battles for the custody of the child and his accumulated money. Hoekstra was challenged to give an accounting of the funds. Attorney Dawson said that as guardian he was given only $800 of an alleged $67,800 the boy had earned and Little David had received only $1,497.62.[63] Money received from the sale of anointed handkerchiefs was part of the income, Mr. Dawson said. Mrs. Taylor, the financial manager, denied that he sold the handkerchiefs and cloths. Finally, on May 26, 1949, the court ordered Hoekstra to turn over to Dawson all the boy's cash assets and return the money spent from the boy's fund on a house in Orlando, Florida, owned jointly by Hoekstra and Little David. A few months previously the parents had asked for the custody of the boy again, but the court denied the petition, and Mr. Dawson, who was appointed guardian in December, 1947, continues in that capacity.

With all this unfavorable publicity one wonders how Little David will fare as a spiritual healer in the future. If the attitude of one woman is an indication, it will not affect his career. Her husband was brought to a local hospital in a dying condition, obviously cancer in an advanced stage. When she registered him, she said in her anxiety that Little David had healed her husband once before and she hoped and prayed that he would live long enough for Little David to return and heal him again. But his condition was so critical that he died in the interim.

Oral Roberts, the founder and director of the Healing Waters Revival Ministry, is conducting great healing campaigns in many cities. His headquarters is at Tulsa, Oklahoma. For use in his campaigns he has an immense fireproof tent which seats about three thousand people, trucks with steel semitrailers, and other equipment which he values at $60,000.00.[64] He has ordered a larger tent to accommodate the crowds and appeals to his friends for help in defraying the expense.

Sickness is regarded by him as an oppression of the devil, and he believes the atonement of Jesus is efficacious not only in forgiveness but in healing the sick body. Human beings bear in their bodies the same oppression of Satan that Jesus took upon himself and died to deliver man from. The believer must not doubt or question that Jesus can heal all who come to him, and it is his will to heal each one. Mr. Roberts often refers to his own experience of healing. At one time he was bedfast for five months with a disease that he says the doctors could not cure.[65] Then he found healing through the "prayer of faith" of a man of God. This man commanded the sickness to leave his body in the name of Jesus Christ of Nazareth; Roberts believed and was healed. Now he conducts healing revivals to bring the same experience to others.

He uses anointing in his healing services, but advises all who want to be healed to buy a copy of his book, *If You Need Healing — Do These Things!* The book should be read and studied thoroughly before the patient joins the healing line to be anointed at the revival. Then the patient is urged to purchase a copy and present it in Jesus' name to each sick friend, so that others too may find deliverance. From May, 1947, through September, 1948, forty-three thousand copies of the book were printed.

Healing Waters Magazine is the official monthly magazine of the movement. It contains information about the meetings, where and when they will be held; advertises the Healing Waters radio broadcasts, a Healing Waters Sacred Record Album of three records, six songs sung by Oral Roberts and the Healing Waters Quartet and Trio, and healing tracts by Oral Roberts. Anointed handkerchiefs can be se-

cured by writing for them; it is suggested in the advertise-
ment that offerings make it possible to send them.

The central pages of the magazine are filled with testi-
monials from people who have been spiritually healed of
diseases such as sugar diabetes, a loose vertebra in the spine,
skin disease, pain in the left side, tuberculosis, dislocated
shoulder, heart trouble, a stiff hip, and demon possession.

These healing sects and individuals appeal to the masses
and are ingenious in reaching them. The successful ones are
masters of mass psychology and offer the people something
tangible in the way of healing. They appeal to the emotions
and prepare their patients psychologically to expect healing.
The masses are awed by the mysterious and the dramatic,
and are overwhelmed emotionally by supernatural manifestations. They expect the Lord to do something extraordinary for them and regard these spiritual healers as individuals who have special influence with him and as such the
Lord works through them. Just as at Lourdes or Sainte Anne
de Beaupré, no one will deny that some are healed. There
is a difference of opinion as to how they are healed, whether
subjectively or through the direct healing power of God.
That many imagine they are healed when they are not is also
true, as any physician can testify.

None of these sects and individuals are encouraged by the
clergy of the old established Churches, who regard them
with tolerance but are not sympathetic with their doctrines
and practices.

Part IV

LOOKING AHEAD

XVI. THE COMMISSION ON RELIGION
AND HEALTH

The Commission on Religion and Health, now operating under the direction of the Department of Pastoral Services, an organization of the Federal Council of the Churches of Christ in America, traces the origin of its eventful career to the year 1923. The Emmanuel Movement had clearly demonstrated that physicians and clergymen could cooperate in treatment for the benefit of many patients, but until this time the Federal Council, itself in a formative stage, had done nothing about it. Dr. McComb was spending most of his time in Europe, Dr. Worcester was growing older, and no other clergymen were trained to carry on. Certain influential clergymen and progressive physicians felt that some definite steps should be taken to form an organization that could explore further the possibilities and the results of a better relationship between religion and medicine.

A small selected group of leaders in medicine and the Church (on interdenominational lines) met in New York on March 8, 1923. Among those present were Dr. James Alexander Miller, of the New York Academy of Medicine; Dr. Thomas Salmon; Dr. William Darrach; Dr. Ransom Hooker; Rev. W. Russell Bowie; Rev. Henry Sloane Coffin; Dr. Harry Emerson Fosdick; and Mr. and Mrs. John Sherman Hoyt, in whose home they met. At this initial meeting it was decided to conduct research in the field of religion and medicine and to attempt to interest the medical profession in the project.

Dr. Miller, in due time, came to the Committee on Public Health Relations of the Academy of Medicine. He did such a good job of interesting these men of the medical profession that E. H. Lewinski Corwin, Ph.D., decided to investigate the various faith-healing movements and reported his findings in October of 1923 to what became known as the Joint Committee on Religion and Medicine of the Federal Council and the New York Academy of Medicine.

This report served the purpose of encouraging the Committee to engage in further research and study. For about five years this work was carried on quietly by some leading physicians and clergymen, who studied the influence of mental and spiritual states on physical illness and explored the possibilities of physicians and clergymen working together in the healing of these patients. There was little publicity about it, because the Committee did not want to speak prematurely and run the risk of adverse criticism on the part of physicians and clergymen. Enough physicians were already criticizing Dr. Richard Cabot for his participation in the Emmanuel Movement, and many of the clergy regarded this field as belonging to the cults. For these reasons the Committee proceeded cautiously, so much so that it can be criticized because there were many progressive men in both professions who were ready for some definite guidance and encouragement.

Miss Alice E. Paulsen, Ph.D., was engaged to make a survey of religious healing and reported in 1926 with a detailed account of faith healing as it was practiced in a number of sects and cults. After this report she was directed to study further: " (*a*) What is the common essential of these various practices? (*b*) How can this essence be given a form and rationale suited to scientific use? (*c*) What are the benefits, limitations, and dangers of these practices as established by a careful tryout under controlled conditions, carried on by physicians in co-operation with interested clergymen? " [66] A preliminary report which she wrote was published in the

Journal of the American Medical Association and in *Mental Hygiene.*

The next overture came from the subcommittee of the Committee on Public Health Relations of the Academy of Medicine when they invited a group of clergymen of the Federal Council to a dinner in May of 1926. The purpose of the meeting was to discuss the field of religion and health. After this there was a series of meetings, and plans were made to set up a center for the collection and dissemination of information in this field. Then, also, it was decided to continue to survey the field and study the techniques and personalities of those people who seem to be most successful in spiritual or faith healing. They also decided to promote clinics in hospitals and churches, where clergymen and physicians could work together. Informal until then, this activity led to the formation of the joint committee representing the two co-operating groups.

A detailed plan was evolved to set up a clinic in St. Bartholomew's Church in New York. But after further consideration it was decided that this move would be premature and further study of the problems should precede such an experiment.

Dr. McComb was asked by the Committee to make a study of healing centers in Europe while he was over there. Dr. Worcester, Dr. Richard C. Cabot, and Dr. Alexis Carrel were asked to address meetings of the Committee. It was decided that a joint committee, sponsored by the Federal Council and the Academy of Medicine, should be appointed. Once this was done, the Joint Committee had official status and could proceed as such. Dr. Frederick Peterson became chairman of the new subcommittee on the Academy of Medicine.

Dr. Helen Flanders Dunbar was chosen as director of the Joint Committee and given the assignment to study the whole field of emotional influence and also to offer guidance for the Council of Clinical Training of Theological Students which had just previously been started in Worcester, Massachusetts.

One of the results of all this research was the decision to establish a rest home for people who were tired in mind and body. This home was to be supported by Churches and supervised by physicians. The plan did not materialize, however, largely because of lack of funds.

The Committee received a grant of money from the Josiah Macy, Jr., Foundation, and with these resources undertook the project of compiling a bibliography of the medical literature available on emotions and bodily changes. Much had been written on the subject. Especially significant was Dr. Walter B. Cannon's contribution in that field. The findings recorded in this literature needed to be studied and organized. The result of this investigation was published in 1935 with the title, *Emotions and Bodily Changes; A Survey of Literature on Psychosomatic Interrelationships, 1910–1933,* by H. Flanders Dunbar, M.D., Ph.D. A similar survey of religious literature in that field was undertaken by Rev. John W. Suter, now dean of the Washington Cathedral. Unfortunately this study was never completed. One chapter was written and Mr. Hiltner used data from it in one of his books.[67]

Aside from these studies and investigations, the Joint Committee's greatest contribution was probably in the field of guidance offered to the Council for Clinical Training of Theological Students, Inc. Over a period of a few years many theological students were given special training in the ministry to the sick in general hospitals and hospitals for nervous disorders. Special religious techniques were developed in cooperation with physicians and psychiatrists.

The work, the contacts, and the interests of the Joint Committee grew more involved as time went on, and in 1936 it was decided that the aims could be approached more efficiently if the Academy and the Federal Council each had its own functioning committee. Under the setup there was so much consultation necessary before a step could be taken that the machinery of the organization was a handicap. On the other hand the complicated procedure may have served the very wholesome purpose of preventing any action that might later be regretted. At any rate, the Joint Committee was dissolved that year, and the Academy of Medicine appointed a new Committee on Emotions and Health with Dr. Frederick Peterson as the chairman, and the Federal Council formed a Commission on Religion and Health, with Dean Howard C. Robbins in that capacity.

The first meeting of the new Commission was held in November, 1937; a few months later Rev. Seward Hiltner was chosen to act as the executive secretary, a position that he held for more than ten years. Those present at this first meeting were Dr. Robbins and Mrs. John Sherman Hoyt, John W. Suter, Jr., Robert E. Brinkman, Edith M. Gates, Harry Bone, Robert W. Searle, Seth M. Milliken, M.D., and Samuel McCrea Cavert. Other charter members were: Reginald M. Atwater, M.D., Smiley Blanton, M.D., John Sutherland Bonnell, Russell L. Dicks, A. Philip Guiles, Edward H. Hume, M.D., Otis R. Rice, Henry P. Van Dusen, and Webb H. York, M.D.[68]

The appointment of Mr. Hiltner as executive secretary of the new Commission brought to the work a man of vision and creative ability, who guided the Commission admirably through the ensuing years. Mr. Hiltner was born in Tyrone, Pennsylvania. He graduated from Lafayette College in 1931 and from the Divinity School of the University of Chicago in 1935. During the summer months while at the seminary, he took courses in clinical pastoral training and became so interested in the ministry to the sick that after his graduation he became the first full-time executive of the Council for Clinical Training. The influence of this council will be discussed more at length in a later chapter. His ability was recognized, and the authorities of the Federal Council, in their search for just the right person to head the new

Commission, found in him the man made for the position. Mr. Hiltner now has taken up teaching responsibilities in the field of pastoral care as a member of the Federated Theological Faculty of the University of Chicago.

At this same time the religious ministry to the sick offered by Rev. Russell L. Dicks, a young chaplain at the Massachusetts General Hospital in Boston, was attracting the attention of people who were interested in this work. The year previously, 1936, with the collaboration of Dr. Richard C. Cabot, he had written *The Art of Ministering to the Sick*, which became a classic in the field of pastoral care literature. This book helped to focus the attention of the Commission on the vast field of potential service in hospitals, and one of the aims of the new Commission was to encourage capable clergymen to train themselves for religious work in hospitals.

Under the leadership of Rev. Mr. Hiltner, in 1938, the Commission adopted five aims that were to be their directives. They are stated in a pamphlet entitled *Religion and Health, Ten Years of Progress, 1937–1947.*

The first aim was to show that health of body, mind, and spirit is an essential concern of religion. To the critical reader it may seem that the concern of Christians about the health of body, mind, and soul had already been sufficiently demonstrated through the centuries, yet the Commission did make a contribution at this point by calling this concern anew to the attention of the Church leaders of various denominations.

One of the outstanding contributions of this department is the recently published book, *Older People and the Church.* Rev. Paul B. Maves and Rev. J. Lennart Cedarleaf were commissioned to investigate thoroughly the possibilities of — as well as activities in — a ministry to older people. Their research brings to light facts that are essential for any pastor. This study is quite original, and credit for it goes to the Commission as a contribution to the field of spiritual healing.

Not enough has been done in carrying out the second adopted aim: " To discover and demonstrate the distinctive function of religion in the maintenance, restoration, and improvement of health and emotional balance." Much has been done to discover the distinctive function of religion in health, but little in demonstrating it, largely because of a lack of funds for the purpose. Mr. Hiltner wrote a comprehensive study of the field, which was published in 1943 with the title *Religion and Health.* The Commission also sponsored the publication of several pamphlets or booklets to meet the devotional needs of the sick. These were written by Rev. Robert Rasche, Rev. Russell L. Dicks, and Rev. Everett B. Lesher.

The third aim of the Commission was: " To aid in revitalizing the pastor's ministry to individuals in special need and difficulty, with special reference to the normal problems of growth and development." Under this aim the Commission made a splendid contribution in the field of pastoral counseling and the ministry to the sick. A number of helpful pamphlets and booklets were written by such experts in the field of counseling as: Carl R. Rogers, John Millet, Rollo May, Russell L. Dicks, John Mixon, Seward Hiltner, and Charles Holman. The interest aroused by the Commission helped to call the attention of teachers in theological seminaries to the importance of including in the curriculum courses on pastoral counseling. The emphasis on the importance of this pastoral work also prompted other pastoral specialists to write many books on the subject, some good and others bad or indifferent. Mr. Hiltner himself wrote an excellent book on the subject, recently published under the title *Pastoral Counseling.*

The fourth aim was to promote practical co-operation between physicians and clergymen and other leaders of religious and health work. This purpose has found expression in meetings of clergymen and physicians which have been and are being held in a number of cities. While the Commission does not promote specific meetings, the impetus for them comes from the members of the Commission in many instances. These meetings contribute to better relations between the two professions, permit the exchange of ideas, and give each a better understanding of the work of the other.

The growth of the number of such meetings may be attributed to the wise move on the part of the Commission when it appointed well-chosen clergymen in strategic locations as nominal members. These men are more interested in the work of the Commission than they were before their appointment, and make more of an effort to carry out suggested procedures. They are also vitally interested in a better relationship between clergy and physicians and find that these meetings are one way to achieve that end. Some hospital authorities are receptive to the idea, and sponsor them, if for no other reason than as good public relations. Among others, the Methodist Board of Hospitals and Homes has sponsored several such meetings in connection with local Methodist hospitals. Hospital magazines occasionally carry articles on religious work in the institutions, and the *Journal of the American Medical Association* has included a number of articles on psychosomatic medicine in recent years. Several books on this subject have been written by medical authorities also. All this has helped to foster better relations, and credit for it should go to the Commission for much of the initial impetus.

The last aim mentioned in the booklet was to improve the ministry of the Churches to those in hospitals and other institutions and those suffering from chronic illnesses. The American Protestant Hospital Association decided to cooperate with the Commission to ascertain the status of religious work in its hospitals,[69] and this investigation aroused a new interest in the ministry to the sick in institutions.

It should also be mentioned that the Commission rendered a worthy religious service during the recent war. Men like Otis R. Rice, Russell D. Eitzen, John Sutherland Bonnell, and A. Philip Guiles conducted seminars on counseling with the co-operation of the General Commission on Army and Navy chaplains. More than thirty such classes were held with military chaplains. But in addition to that several hundred seminars were conducted in communities adjacent to military posts for the benefit of the local clergy, Y.M.C.A. workers, and U.S.O. personnel. Some of the leaders, like Russell L. Dicks and Charles T. Holman, gave full-time service to this cause for periods as long as six months at a time. All this helped those who dealt with the problems of the serviceman and was reflected in the personal lives of many young men and young women in the services. Excellent literature to support this program was written and widely distributed.

As the scope of influence of the Commission widened and its interests grew more varied, the more inclusive activities were grouped under the Department of Pastoral Services; and the Commision on Religion and Health then was more free to pursue its original purposes under the direction of the Department of Pastoral Services. Rev. Otis R. Rice, religious director of St. Luke's Hospital in New York City, was appointed chairman of the Department, a position he held until recently. Mr. Rice, who was educated at Harvard University, the Episcopal Theological School, and Cambridge (England) University, is devoting his life to a ministry to the sick. As this is written he is also chairman of the Executive Committee of the Council for Clinical Training, Inc., and in this dual chairmanship he is in a position to coordinate, whenever possible, the functions of these two important organizations.

Now, in 1950, the Department of Pastoral Services is undertaking a new field of study in co-operation with the Department of Christian Social Relations and the Commission on Marriage and the Home. Together they are exploring the possibilities as well as the field of the Church's activity in sex education.

Not much has been done by the Department in the field of nursing and religion. A start was made when a conference of nurses and hospital chaplains was held in New York in February, 1949. Just what will develop in this field of relationship and co-operation in the future is something to be watched with interest.

The Yale Summer School of Alcohol Studies continues with the co-operation of denominational leaders who select those who attend each year. A Western branch of the school has been opened in San Antonio, Texas. This school has been encouraged by the Commission since its inception. Dr. E. M. Jellinek, the school's director, gives Mr. Hiltner much credit for the idea which led to the launching of the school.

Plans are now being made to publish a new volume on the Church and mental health. An editorial committee has been appointed to plan the contents, and authorities in this field will be asked to contribute chapters. While valuable investigations of the influence of religion on mental states has been made, notably by Anton T. Boisen, there are vast possibilities in that sphere that need to be explored. No doubt, as funds are made available, as well as personnel competent to do it, the Department will do more in that field.

It seems that the greatest contribution the Department and Commission have made since 1923 is in the field of exploration and in writing and assembling information about the relationship of religion and health, chiefly the latter. By its very nature such a department cannot do original work but must draw upon the work of others. It shares ideas, initiates projects, collects money, and disseminates information.

It may be said that in the coming years, while exploration and investigation should never cease, the Department may make a greater contribution by putting its knowledge to work in more specific projects with the co-operation of local churches, hospitals, medical organizations, social-service agencies, schools, nursing organizations, and other groups that are interested in health.

XVII. CHAPLAINCY PROGRAMS IN HOSPITALS

PIONEERS IN THE NEW PASTORAL CARE

Just at the time when the Emmanuel Movement was being widely discussed in 1924, Rev. Anton T. Boisen started his career as a hospital chaplain when he accepted the invitation to fill such a position at the Worcester State Hospital at Worcester, Massachusetts. Mr. Boisen had studied at Indiana University (B.A.), Yale Forest School (M.F.), Union Theological Seminary (B.D.), and Harvard (M.A.). After recovering from a serious mental disturbance, he became especially interested in the spiritual welfare of patients with mental disorders. In the state institution at Worcester he found the opportunity he sought to bring a spiritual ministry to mentally ill people.

Along with his personal experience in his own recovery, he was also acquainted with the spiritual stresses that arise in various types of illness, a knowledge acquired in three pastorates in Iowa, Kansas, and Maine, respectively, where he served Congregational and union churches.

Mr. Boisen may be regarded as the father of clinical pastoral training, since in 1925 he accepted three theological students to receive training under his guidance at the hospital. The hospital administrator, William A. Bryan, M.D., was enough interested and in sympathy with the move to accept this innovation in his institution. Mr. Boisen saw to it that his students also received instruction from medical doctors and psychiatrists. He required them to make notes of their calls on the sick, so that the visits could be studied with the purpose of improving the students' technique and understanding.

Mr. Boisen served as chaplain during a period of about twenty years, first at Worcester State Hospital and then at the Elgin (Illinois) State Hospital. Through these years he was always interested in the clinical pastoral training of theological students and pastors and shared his rich experience and insight with many, not only giving his time and energy but also giving of his income to the promotion of a more effective ministry to individuals. Mr. Boisen's most influential book, *Exploration of the Inner World,* appeared in 1937. In 1946 another of his books was published, *Problems in Religion and Life.* This was a manual for pastors to use either in study groups or for personal guidance in applying the meaning of the gospel to an individual, taking into consideration the influences of the community on his life.

Two years before Mr. Boisen started his clinical training program a step was taken in that direction at Cincinnati, Ohio, when William S. Keller, M.D., a prominent layman of the Episcopal Church, suggested that the clergy should be better acquainted with the work of social agencies. He made arrangements with the dean of Bexley Hall, an Episcopal seminary, to permit several students to receive training under his guidance. These seminarians were housed and provided with food in his home while they received experience as student workers in social agencies and institutions. This was called the Cincinnati Summer School, and was supported largely by the Episcopal Church. The school continued to function until in 1944, when it was united with the Episcopal Theological School in Cambridge, Massachusetts, where the resources of Harvard University and the Institute of Pastoral Care were also available to the students. Dr. Keller's work is now continued by Dr. Joseph Fletcher, who serves on the faculty of the Episcopal Theological School as professor of pastoral theology.

While both Mr. Boisen and Dr. Keller were interested in

a better spiritual ministry to the sick, Mr. Boisen took his students into the hospital with him and gave them supervised bedside experience and guidance. One of his early students was A. Philip Guiles, Ph.D., now professor of pastoral psychology at Andover-Newton Theological School. After he received his training under Mr. Boisen, Professor Guiles became deeply interested in offering a similar opportunity for other theological students and pastors to improve their ministry to the sick.

At Worcester State Hospital he ministered primarily to the spiritual needs of mental patients. At the same time he, with others who were interested in providing better spiritual care, helped to organize the Council for Clinical Training. With Mr. Boisen and Dr. Richard Cabot, they planned and directed the early work in this hospital and in 1930 initiated the incorporation of the Council for Clinical Training. Prior to that time Dr. Guiles served as field secretary for the organization. Dr. Cabot became its first president, and H. Flanders Dunbar, M.D., its director; Dr. Guiles was chosen as the executive secretary.

From Worcester Dr. Guiles went to the Massachusetts General Hospital where he remained a short time before he became professor of pastoral psychology at the Andover-Newton school. He is the first instructor to come out of the clinical pastoral training movement to be appointed to a full-time position in a theological seminary. In 1933, due to differences of opinion among some of the leaders, Dr. Guiles disassociated himself from the Council and set up his own group with the support of the Earhardt Foundation, which continued its support for five years.

At the same time that Dr. Guiles was setting up his work independently of the Council a young minister came to the Massachusetts General Hospital who more than any other became responsible for establishing the modern chaplaincy programs in general hospitals. He was Russell L. Dicks, who was born at Stillwater, Oklahoma, and who received his education at the University of Tulsa, the University of Oklahoma (A.B.), and Union Theological Seminary, New York (B.D.). Later he received the honorary degrees of D.D. from Southwestern College, Winfield, Kansas, and Litt.D. from Adrian College, Adrian, Michigan.

In 1929, after two weeks in the seminary, Mr. Dicks was admitted to the New York Orthopedic Hospital for an operation upon an elbow, which for three years had been steadily growing worse with tuberculosis of the bone. This operation was followed by another later in the year, which necessitated the loss of a year from his studies but which laid the foundation for his later work as a hospital chaplain. While he was in the hospital, he realized quite vividly the spiritual needs of the patient. He says: " During that experience of severe suffering my religious faith was wrecked. I had the best surgical care in the world, good nursing, and dietary care, and I did not pay a hospital bill for I had no money, being taken care of by social service. The one thing I did not receive was pastoral care."

With this in mind he became associated two years later with Dr. H. Flanders Dunbar, who was serving as director of the Council for the Clinical Training of Theological Students. Later he went to Worcester State Hospital, where he spent some time studying the spiritual needs of mental patients. During this time he was associated with Dr. Carroll Wise, now professor of pastoral psychology at Garrett Biblical Institute. During this time Mr. Dicks became interested in the Council for Clinical Training which had been incorporated only a short time before. Soon after this he met Dr. Richard C. Cabot, of the Massachusetts General Hospital, who approved of his coming to that hospital as Protestant chaplain. The hospital, a private nonsectarian type of institution, had never had and still does not have an official chaplain, although the original letter which had gone out to the citizens of Boston in 1810 inviting contributions for the establishing of a hospital " for the care of idiots and other patients," was signed by a Boston clergyman at the request of two Boston physicians.

When Mr. Dicks went to the Massachusetts General Hospital, he intended to remain only three months, but this period was extended to four and a half years, during which time Dr. Cabot personally paid his salary, and later endowed the position. Professor Guiles had moved to the Andover-Newton Theological School when Mr. Dicks went to Boston.

Previously Dr. Worcester, of the Emmanuel Movement, had resigned his pastorate at Emmanuel Church, but continued to meet patients at his private clinic. Mr. Dicks learned to know him, but at that time Dr. Worcester was much interested in spiritualism, and for that reason the Emmanuel Movement did not particularly impress Mr. Dicks. But he took an active interest in the Council for Clinical Training and served for one year as its executive secretary. Later he was appointed official chaplain at the hospital for the Boston Federation of Churches, and, like Professor Guiles, disassociated himself from the Council and affiliated himself with Dr. Guiles and the so-called " New England School of Clinical Training."

There were many personality conflicts among leaders of the clinical training program in its early days. Men of such keen enthusiasm are inclined to individualism; also, the movement was experimenting and needed freedom; at the same time, the field of healing has always been fraught with dangers and differences of opinion. These differences, like the differences in the field of medicine, came sharply into focus in the clinical pastoral training movement. Interestingly, they were not theological differences so much as they were differences of opinion regarding methods and technique.

Dr. Cabot was intrigued by the approach of Mr. Dicks in dealing with patients; particularly was he struck by the latter's practice of keeping verbatim records of conversations as well as of his prayers with patients. Dr. Cabot asked him to collaborate on a book that would present a new approach to the ministry to the sick. Most of the previous literature on that subject took for granted that it was the minister's task to prepare the patient for death. The book was completed and published in 1936 with the title, *The Art of Ministering to the Sick*. It met with immediate response, and was received favorably by all religious groups as well as by many medical men. The book aroused new interest in the spiritual welfare of the sick, and caused many clergymen to re-evaluate their ministry to the suffering. At the same time it caused some of the younger clergy to become interested in the hospital chaplaincy.

Until this time the position of a hospital chaplain was generally regarded as work for an older pastor who was physically incapable of ministering to a congregation. For the most part, few hospitals other than Roman Catholic, Lutheran, Episcopalian, and a few other Church-controlled Protestant institutions had chaplains. The work consisted principally of administering the last rites and prayers for the dying. The chaplain also acted as an official greeter to as many of the patients as he had time to welcome to the hospital. Any older priest or pastor could do that type of work after retiring from an active pastorate. This was the general conception of the hospital chaplaincy — a good position in which to retire.

More than any other person, Dr. Dicks deserves the credit for instituting the modern chaplaincy program in hospitals. He was the first of the younger clergy to enter the general hospital field to do religious work, and he possessed the insight and the ability to work effectively at the bedside of the sick and dying and to bring comfort to the families of such persons.

In 1938 he accepted the call to become the chaplain of the Presbyterian Hospital in Chicago, where he remained for three years. At this time he became interested in the American Protestant Hospital Association.

Something should be said about the origin and history of this organization. In a previous chapter the founding of Protestant hospitals was described. While institutions of a given denomination were operated independently of one another, yet there was a denominational fellowship among the executives. Many of these executives had long felt the need for interdenominational fellowship for the purpose of discussing common problems. Some of the leaders held preliminary meetings, one in Cincinnati, in 1919, and another in Montreal, Canada, in 1920. Rev. Frank C. English, who was superintendent of St. Luke's Hospital, Cleveland, Ohio, took a leading interest in this movement. A tentative constitution and bylaws were prepared and when the American Hospital Association met in 1921 at West Baden, Indiana, seventy executives of Protestant hospitals met also, adopted the constitution and bylaws and named their organization " The American Protestant Hospital Association." [70]

As the years passed, many members of the A.P.H.A. became interested in a more adequate religious program in their institutions. They realized that as executives of Church-related hospitals they were not doing very much for the spiritual welfare of the patients. As a matter of fact many of these hospitals had practically no religious program at all. These executives were ready for help in that direction.

Mr. Asa Bacon, the administrator of the Presbyterian Hospital in Chicago, where Mr. Dicks went as chaplain from the Massachusetts General Hospital, was a leader in the A.P.H.A. although he never served a term as its president. He was so well impressed with the work of Mr. Dicks in his hospital that he invited the chaplain to prepare a paper to be read at the next convention of the A.P.H.A., which was held in Toronto, Canada, September 22–24, 1939.

This paper, entitled " The Work of the Chaplain in a General Hospital," can be regarded as marking the beginning of a new era in hospital chaplaincy. It was received with

enthusiasm by many of the delegates and printed in full in
the next issue of the *American Protestant Hospital Association Bulletin.*[71]

One of the results of this presentation was the appointment of a commission of the A.P.H.A. to study the field and
formulate a set of standards for the work of a chaplain in a
general hospital. *Standards for the Work of the Chaplain in
the General Hospital*[72] was worked out in detail by Dr.
Dicks, Rev. Seward Hiltner and Rev. Harold Schultz for
presentation to the commission. After due discussion it was
approved and recommended to the A.P.H.A., which adopted
it at the Boston convention in September, 1940. The adop-
tion of *Standards* marks another major step in the development of the chaplaincy program.

Standards is a comprehensive statement of a hospital chap-
lain's work and is divided into eight sections: (1) The
Chaplain Shall Be Responsible to the Administrator of the
Hospital. (2) The Chaplain Shall Co-operate with Other
Personnel of the Hospital. (3) The Chaplain Shall Have a
Rational Plan for Selecting His Patients. (4) The Chaplain
Shall Keep Records. (5) Worship in the Public Hospital.
(6) The Training of the Chaplain. (7) The Appointment of
the Chaplain. (8) Conclusion: It Is Written, " Man Shall
Not Live by Bread Alone."

This paper challenged not only the chaplains but the administrators and other hospital executives to do something
about the religious programs in their Church-related hospitals. During the years since their founding the hospitals
grew in size; many of them became large institutions; at the
same time the significance of the religious emphasis was
overlooked so that it had become hard to distinguish them
from private nonsectarian or municipally owned and operated institutions. In some instances underpaid chaplains were
kept on the premises to lend a religious air, but now the time
had come to re-examine the chaplaincy programs and employ men who were adequately trained, who possessed the

personality and the sincerity so necessary for this specialized field of the ministry.

In order to ascertain the exact status of the religious programs in these Protestant hospitals it was decided to make a survey. The commission was charged with the responsibility of making the inquiry. A questionnaire was arranged and sent to over 400 hospitals; and more than half of them replied, offering enlightening information. Out of the 214 replies from hospitals, only 18 had full-time chaplains. One half of them had some kind of part-time religious worker. Of the 18 full-time chaplains, only 3 received salaries approximating the average usually quoted for the clergy. Of the part-time religious workers, 30 per cent received less than $1,000 a year. Only 10 per cent of all the religious workers, including the full-time chaplains, received more than $2,000 a year in salary.

The statistics clearly indicated that the religious programs in the hospitals generally were carried on in a haphazard manner. The results of the survey made members of the A.P.H.A. keenly aware of the need for a more adequate program, but even at that it was not easy to convince many of the hospital executives. Of the 121 religious workers, only 3 had had supervised clinical training to prepare them for their work. It was recognized that many of the hospitals were too small to employ a full-time chaplain, but it was believed they could afford to provide the part-time worker with training that is so essential for really effective Christian work in a hospital.

After this report was made, the officials of the A.P.H.A. started an educational campaign. Nearly every ensuing issue of the official bulletin carried an article on some phase of the religious work in a modern general hospital. A new interest was awakened.

In the meantime, Dr. Dicks was teaching in four theological seminaries in Chicago, in connection with his work at the Presbyterian hospital, and lecturing in various parts of the country to clergy, nurses, and physicians. He felt that young ministers should be trained to minister to the sick just as they are carefully instructed in other phases of the ministry. He required his students to write verbatim reports of calls upon the sick, for study and criticism. The practice taught the counselor to listen to and to interpret the spiritual needs of the sick. Then, in order better to understand other functions of the pastorate, Dr. Dicks accepted the call to serve as an associate minister in a local church in Dallas, Texas, and to teach at the Southern Methodist University School of Theology, now called the Perkins School of Theology.

Then the war came. The Commission on Religion and Health of the Federal Council called upon him and others who had specialized in pastoral counseling to conduct seminars for chaplains in the armed forces, for Y.M.C.A. and U.S.O. workers, and for clergy serving in defense areas. The experience was broadening, and reaffirmed his conviction that local ministers should be more thoroughly trained to offer total pastoral care to the parishioner.

In the meantime he had continued to write, publishing a book of case studies and interpretations as a source book for ministers in their work with the sick.[73] In an attempt to help the nurse better to understand the religious stresses of the patient, he wrote *Who Is My Patient?* In 1944 he accepted the call to the position of chaplain at Wesley Memorial Hospital in Chicago, and the next four years were spent in intensive bedside work, writing in the field of pastoral care, conducting classes in clinical training at the hospital, and teaching in several theological seminaries. One of the excellent books that came from this experience is *Pastoral Work and Personal Counseling,* originally published in 1945 and revised in 1949. In 1946, *Thy Health Shall Spring Forth* was published; while to aid further the pastor in the sickroom he wrote *Comfort Ye My People,* a manual of the pastoral ministry.

THE GROWTH OF THE TRAINED CHAPLAINCY

In the meantime the Commission on Religious Work in the Hospitals had been busy. Rev. Robert D. Morris, chaplain of the Protestant Episcopal Hospital of Philadelphia, and Rev. Harold Peters Schultz, institutional missionary of St. Louis, were added to the A.P.H.A. group. An investigation was made of the clergy-physician relationships in the Protestant hospitals. The purpose was not only to investigate but to discover ways and means to foster better understanding between chaplains or clergymen and the physicians in any given hospital. This could be done by ascertaining to what degree ministers and doctors get together to discuss their common problems and propose what the hospital administration can do to promote a better and more intelligent co-operation between these two professions.

Eight strategically located hospitals were chosen for the survey, three with full-time chaplains, three with part-time chaplains, and two with none. The results of the survey were published in a booklet in 1942 [74] which was distributed throughout the A.P.H.A. membership; and through Rev. Seward Hiltner information went out to the members of the Commission on Religion and Health of the Federal Council. One of the tangible results was the creation of interest in clergy-physician meetings. The number of these gatherings is growing, and some hospitals sponsor such meetings periodically. They foster better relationships between the professions, help each become better acquainted with the other's aims, and demonstrate how they can work together for the benefit of the patient.

Four years after the Commission made its first report on the chaplain situation, the A.P.H.A. decided in 1945 to distribute another questionnaire to ascertain if any improvement had been made in the religious ministry in the Protestant hospitals. The questionnaire was sent by the executive director, Dr. Albert G. Hahn, to 376 hospitals, and 46 per cent responded. The information showed some marked improvement in the situation.

Rev. Harold P. Schultz, of St. Louis, compiled the report.[75] In four years the number of full-time chaplains had increased from 18 to 38, better than a 100 per cent increase. At least a dozen additional hospitals indicated that they had plans for securing full-time chaplains. Another significant fact brought out by the report was that an increasing number of religious workers were provided with private offices in the hospitals. This indicates an awareness of the importance of pastoral counseling as a phase of the chaplain's ministry.

Another significant fact was that still only a small proportion of the hospital chaplains had had clinical pastoral training. It seems to indicate that hospital authorities were not so concerned as they should be about adequate training for their religious workers. Even though these workers may possess pleasing personalities, that qualification cannot replace adequate training.

With this growth in the number of chaplains, the A.P.H.A., through its officers and trustees, saw the need for a chaplain's section. A preliminary committee was appointed, with Mr. Dicks as chairman, to write a constitution and by-laws, and the first meeting was held in Philadelphia, September 27, 1946, in connection with the A.P.H.A. Mr. Dicks was elected president; the other officers were Chaplain Robert D. Morris, of the Episcopal Hospital in Philadelphia; Chaplain Leicester R. Potter, Jr., of the Massachusetts Memorial Hospital; Chaplain Granger Westberg, of Augustana Hospital in Chicago; and Chaplain Carl J. Scherzer, of the Protestant Deaconess Hospital in Evansville, Indiana. When the Chaplains' Association met the next year in St. Louis, 48 were present.

The Association stresses the importance of adequate training for the hospital chaplain. It is evident that there is an increasing interest in meeting the spiritual needs of the sick.

This trend is being felt in theological seminaries also, where more instructors are being employed in the field of pastoral care. When this writer received his theological training, the course in practical theology was taught by a very likable old pastor, but the course was considered a minor. It dealt primarily with the pastor's demeanor, which is important, but very little was offered on the pastoral care of the sick. The student was taught to visit the sick faithfully, but he did not receive other instruction than to read from the Bible and offer a prayer. He was left to find his way as the Lord would direct him. The clinical pastoral training movement has had much to do with creating an interest on the part of seminary officials in better spiritual care of the sick. At present there are 14 seminaries that have full-time instructors in that field who have been drawn from the clinical training movement, and others are working to add departments of pastoral care with well-trained instructors.

Another organization that grew out of this movement is the Institute of Pastoral Care, Inc., with headquarters in Cambridge, Massachusetts. Its creation was due largely to the initiative and vision of Rev. Rollin J. Fairbanks, who is now its executive director, with the able assistance of Rev. James H. Burns, the associate director. Its board of governors is composed of representatives from the four participating theological schools, various foundations and hospitals, and the Federal Council. Schools in pastoral care are conducted at Boston State Hospital, Massachusetts General Hospital, the University Hospital at Ann Arbor, Michigan, and Worcester State Hospital. Its purpose is to organize, develop, and support an educational and research program in the entire field of pastoral care, but it places special emphasis upon the spiritual ministry to the sick.

Mr. Fairbanks has developed the " controlled interview " method in teaching, in which he assumes the role of the patient and the student's ministry to this sick person is analyzed and criticized by the instructor and other students. This method of teaching has proved very effective in the clinical pastoral training movement.

In tracing the development in this field down to the present, it is necessary to turn again to Mr. Dicks, who in 1948 relinquished his position as chaplain of Wesley Memorial Hospital to become a professor of pastoral work at the Divinity School at Duke University, where he was later appointed chaplain of Duke University Hospital. There his students receive practical guidance in ministering to the needs of the sick, and other phases of the pastoral task. Several other theological seminaries are following a similar course, and the ministers of the future who graduate from these schools will have better training and a deeper understanding of the spiritual task of the pastor in a ministry to individuals.

In 1945 a significant new development took place in one of the major theological seminaries: Dr. Wayne E. Oates, a young Baptist minister, began his work at the Southern Baptist Theological Seminary at Louisville, Kentucky. As a minister serving a rural church while he was teaching psychology and philosophy at Wake Forest College, North Carolina, he saw the need for a careful understanding of suffering people. He had been challenged by a doctor who referred a patient to him, saying: " I have done what a doctor can do for you. You should call the preacher. He can help you."

The woman sent her small son to find Dr. Oates and asked him to visit her. During his first call the woman unburdened an involved story of marital unhappiness, personal guilt, and morbid despair. Not knowing what else to do, and overwhelmed by the complexity of the woman's plight, Oates simply listened, without condemnation and without sentimentality. At the conclusion of her story, he told her he would like to think and pray about the whole thing and asked her if she would like him to pray with her. Simply listening to her story, giving her carefully selected literature, and reassuring her with prayer were the only things he knew to do. Much to his surprise, the woman who had hitherto been confined to her bed was able now to do her housework. Soon she became interested in small group meetings at her neighbor's home.

Not long after this, the doctor who had referred the woman to Oates was appointed to a state institution staff. Before he left, he said to Oates: "We are entering upon a whole new understanding of the nature of disease. I believe this will draw the minister closer to the work of the doctor. You train yourself for this. I don't know where you will get the training, but wherever you can find anybody who knows anything about it, listen to him."

Wayne Oates went to Durham, North Carolina, where he served as an assistant pastor in a city church. Then he went to Louisville as a student at the Southern Baptist Seminary. Dr. G. S. Dobbins, professor of religious education and church administration, had for years been giving such " textbook " guidance as he could to men in the field of psychology and a " person-minded ministry." He had engaged Chaplain Ralph Bonacker, of the Norton Memorial Infirmary, to teach a small group of men interested in a clinical approach to pastoral work. In the summer of 1944, Oates studied with Bonacker under the auspices of the Council for Clinical Training for a twelve-week course in general hospital work.

During the winter of 1944–1945 he served as Bonacker's assistant in teaching part-time courses in the seminary. Then, in 1945, Oates received his B.D. degree, and was appointed as an instructor in psychology of religion by the seminary administration. This was done with the understanding that he would continue his training, so in the summer of 1945 he went to the Elgin State Hospital, where he studied with Rev. William Andrews and Dr. Anton Boisen, father of the clinical pastoral training movement.

Returning to Louisville, Oates was appointed also as first

chaplain of the Kentucky Baptist Hospital. Here, in the summer of 1946, he offered his first ten-week course in clinical pastoral training to five students. In 1947 he was asked by Dr. J. A. Mendelson, superintendent of the Kentucky State Hospital at Danville, Kentucky, to bring a group of ten graduate students for a ten-week term of training. The summer following, the whole group went to the hospital and established a training program in connection with offering pastoral care and chaplaincy service to the hospital.

In 1947 he received his graduate degree, and was appointed as full-time instructor in psychology of religion and director of clinical training at the seminary. The faculty added three undergraduate courses in the field: pastoral counseling, Christianity and contemporary psychology, and an introduction to clinical pastoral training. Three other graduate students who had some training with the Council for Clinical Training, in addition to pastoral experience and Army chaplaincy service, assisted in the organization of the program. Rev. James Lyn Elder became part-time chaplain of Kentucky Baptist Hospital as successor to Oates, who was now full-time instructor at the seminary. Rev. Richard K. Young became chaplain of the North Carolina Baptist Hospital at Winston-Salem. At the same time, Rev. Aaron Rutledge became chaplain of Central State Hospital at Lakeland, Kentucky. All three of them instituted a program of training. The fourth teaching clinic was operated in 1947–1948, when Oates was asked to serve as interim pastor of one of the leading Baptist churches of Louisville. He used his students, offering them guidance in problems of church administration and group counseling. The relation of preaching to counseling was carefully studied.

The real test of the social acceptance of the whole program of clinical pastoral training at Southern Baptist Seminary came, however, in the spring of 1948. Two issues were at stake: First, a few men who had seen the results of secularized emphasis in this field while they were attending universities raised sincere resistances. Several of the students of the seminary who had attended clinics at other places " on their own " and apart from the advice of Dr. Oates and Dr. Dobbins had left the ministry. The second issue was that of recognizing the work of the clinical centers as bona fide graduate subject matter. The concept of a clinical method in education is not easy to grasp and is even more difficult to accept.

But the faculty and board of trustees of the seminary gave a vote of full confidence to the establishment of this emphasis within the undergraduate and graduate curriculums and elected Dr. Oates as assistant professor of psychology of religion and pastoral care.

At present the clinical pastoral training program is constituted of the following undergraduate courses: (1) Psychology of Religion: The Scientific Basis of Pastoral Care. (2) Pastoral Care and Personal Counseling: A Study of the Literature of Pastoral Care and the Problems of Marriage and Family Counseling. (3) An Introduction to Clinical Pastoral Care. Under the third section a group of students from the Women's Missionary Training School (operated jointly on an academic level with the seminary) are given clinical training in the care of sick people by Mrs. Lloyd Neil, a graduate nurse, a graduate of the Clinical Training School, and a member of the faculty of the Louisville General Hospital.

A group of seminary men, limited to twenty-one, work under the joint supervision of Chaplain Joseph Knowles, at Central State Hospital, and Dr. Oates.

For graduate work, clinical pastoral training is now offered at North Carolina Baptist Hospital, Inc., Winston-Salem, under Chaplain Richard K. Young; Missouri Baptist Hospital, St. Louis, Missouri, under Chaplain Everett Barnard; Central State Hospital, Lakeland, Kentucky, under Chaplain Joseph Knowles; and First Baptist Church, Richmond, Virginia, under Rev. James Lyn Elder.

In this connection it may be said also that some of the chaplains of hospitals are offering seminars on the ministry to the sick to the clergy in the area of the hospital. Such classes offer not only instruction but the exchange of ideas and experiences and help the pastor to develop a technique of counseling, interpretation, and reassurance that increases his helpfulness to his sick and troubled parishioners.

THE CHAPLAIN'S WORK

There is a definite trend in Protestant hospitals to offer a more adequate ministry to the patient. This ministry is regarded as Jesus' method of using the available medical skill and knowledge combined with the healing efficacy of the Christian religion. The use of the sacraments and rites of the Church, as well as the therapeutic value of confession and absolution, are employed. Along with that, and of vital importance, is the counseling technique that enables the patient to relieve the mind of any stress in the crisis situations that commonly arise in illness. The Word of God and prayer, as well as other wholesome religious literature, are used in this spiritual ministry.

The patients to whom the chaplain devotes most of his time are those who send for him and those whom the physicians, nurses, and relatives ask him to call upon. In each such instance his services are requested, which makes for better rapport. These requests keep him busy even in a moderate-sized hospital. Should there be time available, he may go from room to room, and when he does he will find many who need his counsel.

The modern chaplaincy program entails more than that, although it should be borne in mind that it is patient-centered. The religious training of the nurse is also important. There are a few texts [76,77] that have been written for the purpose of instructing the nurse in serving the spiritual needs of the patient.

The chaplaincy program also offers services of worship

that should be made available to all people in the institution. This presupposes a chapel, and such a suitable place for worship and meditation should be conveniently located in the hospital. The chapel may be one of the distinguishing features of a Church-related hospital. It should be designed by a capable church architect and finished in light, harmonious tones. There should be nothing depressing about it, because the Christian faith is an uplifting, edifying influence and this is what should be emphasized in an institution where there are so many depressing situations.

God will use a chaplain who is industrious, who has vision and consecration. He can be instrumental in establishing a Christian atmosphere even in a large hospital. But, more so than in any other field of religious work, a certain type of personality and temperament is essential, because he must co-operate with many department heads, and have their co-operation and love, or he may find himself frustrated on many attempted projects. His ability and sincerity will be recognized, if he has them; if he lacks these, he will not remain long in the hospital chaplaincy. Many whom he contacts in their illness will leave the hospital healed spiritually as well as physically, which should be the aim of the Church-related hospital.

The relationship between religion and health is becoming ever more apparent. As far as non-Church-related hospitals are concerned there is also an increased interest being manifested in the religious life of the patients. Some of these institutions permit chaplains to work there. In Veterans' Administration hospitals the number of chaplains increased from 9 at the close of the war to 241 almost overnight. The Veterans' Administration has drawn heavily from the clinical pastoral training movement for these men, largely through the work of Rev. Donald C. Beatty, who was one of Dr. Boisen's early students and who serves as assistant to the director of the Veterans' Administration Hospital Chaplaincy program.

The chaplain's concern is to help the patient to find his faith and the confidence that comes from peace with God. His interest is in man and God, and the aim is to help the patient to permit God to help him. In order to attain this high purpose, the chaplain must be especially trained and conditioned to deal sympathetically and understandingly with the sick. Along with understanding and training, consecration and compassion are also essential. With the growing interest in this specialized ministry, more of the younger clergy are regarding the hospital chaplaincy as a challenge, and the men who are already in that service are alert to the needs and opportunities and for the most part are eager to accept the results of research and experiment that help to make their ministry ever more effective. The trend is definitely in the direction of more adequate pastoral care in the Church-related hospitals.

XVIII. LOOKING AHEAD

No one can predict exactly what the future will bring in religion and healing, but a study of the trends of the past and the present is helpful in pointing to some definite developments that are almost certain to come. The interrelation and interaction of the various phases of the total personality of man have gone on since the Creation. Man has always been conscious of the innate oneness of his being; it is only in comparatively recent years that an attempt has been made to understand how the various phases of personality function together. This is especially true of the relationship between religion and health.

The clergy have long recognized that religion is important in life, and that it does something for the sick person, but what it does has been little understood. Recent investigations in the psychosomatic field, religious case studies, and the work of clergymen who specialize in the spiritual ministry to the sick have brought to light many facts that are of vital importance.

The therapeutic value of the Christian virtues, such as faith, confidence, courage, love, forgiveness, can now be demonstrated in case studies. The harmful effects of anxiety, guilt, loneliness, jealousy, fear, and hatred are well known. How mental and emotional states influence the functioning of the body has been investigated by physicians, psychologists, and psychiatrists. No one will deny that religion is important in health and sickness.

The problem is how to turn the resources of religion into creative channels for the average person and, while available knowledge in this field is being applied, to continue to investigate the possibilities. It may be said that while much is known about the therapeutic value of religion, the available knowledge is only the beginning of understanding. It is believed by many that the greatest discoveries in the years ahead will be in the spiritual rather than the scientific and economic phases of life. Man has always been reluctant to study the subject nearest him — himself. Science started with a study of the objects farthest away — the stars. Some of the greatest minds from Socrates to the present have attempted to understand man, but these great people were always a small minority. It is only in comparatively recent years that science has turned its light upon man himself.

Great thinkers have tried to understand God and in the attempt learned something about themselves, especially that man is something more than a functioning organism. Religious thinkers believe that he is created in the image of God and that spiritual influences have a vital effect upon his being. When man became aware of that fact, he began to study himself to see how spiritual factors influence his life and how he can use them for his benefit. This is the task of the Church, and it has engaged in that work more or less through the centuries. But the one place where the Church has been the most hesitant is in fulfilling the Lord's command to heal the sick (Matt. 10:8). Because of its hesitancy, cults and sects have to a large extent taken over spiritual healing.

Now a reawakening is manifesting itself in the Church and in Church-related institutions. The Church's ministry to the sick, the aged, the troubled, and the bereaved, is attracting more attention. Out of this revived interest the reclaiming of the pastoral office can be clearly discerned.

The religious emphasis is not on mass revivals as it was fifty or even twenty-five years ago. Personal evangelism is the prevailing mode of religious work, which expresses itself in a deep concern for the welfare of the individual. This trend does not necessarily mean that there will be less evangelistic preaching, for evangelistic preaching will always have its place in the Church; but it does mean that the pastor will devote more time to helping individuals personally. This is reclaiming the pastoral office.

The Early Church Fathers were pastors who dealt with their people individually and knew them well. In that they emulated their Lord. A study of the life of Christ as it is presented in the Scriptures, uncolored by the views of any other writers, reveals that Jesus spent most of his ministry helping individuals. Since the time of the Early Church various attempts have been made to reinstate the pastoral ministry in the Church, and there were always some clergymen who practiced the pastoral office, but in the main, during the Middle Ages, the emphasis was on the priestly and prophetic offices of the ministry.

With the Reformation came a rebirth of interest in the pastoral " cure of souls," and the clergyman came to regard himself as a physician of the spiritual nature of man. The growth of the importance of the pastoral office was augmented by the remote preparation of the parishioner through preaching and teaching, and especially through the personality of the minister. People are inclined to avail themselves of the pastor's help in the time of trouble in the measure in which he inspires confidence in his understanding of human needs and his ability to help.

This pastoral ministry entails a special preparation of the minister. The usual curriculum of the theological seminary, which includes such subjects as homiletics, ancient languages, exegesis, apologetics, and dogmatics, must be augmented by courses in psychology, psychiatry, and pastoral counseling. The trend today indicates that the minister spends about one third of his time in pastoral work, one third in study and preaching, and one third in administration and organizational planning and meetings. Since the pastoral phase of the ministry requires so much time and effort, the minister must be adequately trained to cope with the situation.

This may also indicate that the longer pastorate will prevail in the future. It requires a long time for a minister to establish rapport with his parishioners. There is a possibility of a more effective pastoral ministry when the clergyman learns to know his people well, comes close to them in their joys and sorrows, shares again and again in the stresses of the family circle in the trying situations of life. As he measures up to these situations, the people learn to love and respect him as a pastor and representative of their Lord. At the same time this intimate association helps him to interpret more effectively in his preaching the gospel's application to personal needs.

In exercising the pastoral office, the ministry to the sick and troubled will require the major portion of the pastor's time, and, to be effective, he will need to keep informed about the developments in that field. The progressive medical doctor reads his professional journals, attends refresher courses, and keeps abreast of the latest developments in medicine and surgery. Once he becomes satisfied with his knowledge and technique, he immediately begins to retrogress, because the advancements in his field pass him by. The same is true in pastoral care. There are those who are pioneering, accepting, and using the results of psychological and psychiatric research in the application of the gospel to the needs of the individual. The results of these specialized ministries are expressed in articles and books for the guidance of the pastor who wants to make his ministry more effective. Techniques are being developed and information disseminated that predict a more effective ministry to individuals in the future.

In the pastoral office the Church will continue to use its rich heritage: the sacraments, the Word of God, the rites such as the laying on of hands, anointing, confession, and absolution. Since the healing power of the Christian virtues is becoming better understood in the light of modern research, the resourceful pastor will be able to help people to understand and use them for their benefit. The therapeutic values of fellowship in worship, of quiet and meditation, and of positive assertions in prayer are fields that need to be explored further. In other words, the trends point definitely in the direction of recapturing and exercising the powers that the Lord has given his Church through the Holy Spirit.

The development of the pastoral office will bring a deeper understanding of the spiritual needs of individuals, a knowledge that is gained through personal interviews. In order to be adept at helping people, the pastor will discipline himself in counseling techniques, and on this score he can learn much from good psychiatrists. Techniques, however, can never become a substitute for understanding, and the poise and faith of the pastor will always be an important factor which will determine the measure of his ability to be helpful. There can never be a substitute for sincerity, consecration, and an undergirding love for the children of God.

The use of relics and shrines for healing purposes will continue. There is much about life and death that is still a mystery to even the most learned individual, to say nothing about the masses of people who do not have the time or the inclination to try to fathom the mysteries of life. In the face of the mysteries of life and death there will always be those who will expect God to do the miraculous in their behalf. In this connection it should be said that the expectation and anticipation of a spectacular manifestation of the power of God may have subjective values for the individual that are little understood today.

At the same time the power of God to reach into an individual's life with healing powers is well known and accepted by most Christians. The prayer of faith, by which this power is made available to man, will be used to an ever greater extent as man learns to know God better. Jesus clearly indicated that God is interested in the welfare of each individual.

Great strides are being made in the medical and surgical fields. Almost every week the news tells about another " miracle medicine " that has been discovered to combat disease. But, with all its benefits, medicine and surgery cannot heal the total man. When combined with spiritual help, they work together for the health of the total personality; God will continue to use medical and surgical skill to achieve his aims.

Since the time of Hippocrates many have felt that religion or philosophy and medicine should go their own ways, and they did as best they could, without each other, but never entirely alone. No matter how much the attempt was made to keep the two apart, it could not be done, as this study so clearly indicates. Many thinking people believe that the time is at hand when the two can work more closely together for mutual helpfulness and for the benefit of the patient. Recent research in psychosomatic states, and studies of the effect of the emotions on the endocrine glands and other organs of the body, is a beginning in the direction of understanding how wonderfully " whole " God has made man. As this new understanding of the relationship between religion and health grows, it will manifest itself in a closer co-operation between those professions that minister to the sick. Social workers who have that purpose also come into the picture, as do nurses, clinical psychologists, and others, but more particularly the greatest need in the immediate future is the interchange of experience and better co-operation between physicians and clergy.

Attitudes that make this advancement possible are formed by education and association. In this particular phase of the development the Church-related hospital will play an important part, when it becomes the common ground where the two professions can meet. The fruits of medical and spiritual research can be pooled for the benefit of the sick.

The Church-related hospital will pay more attention to religion in the future. That is its distinguishing feature — a feature that was almost lost in physical growth. The part the American Protestant Hospital Association is taking in promoting the modern chaplaincy program is an indication that its leaders are aware of the purpose of these institutions and want to see an adequate spiritual ministry offered to the patients. Every indication is in the direction of the growth of this movement, and in the future these hospitals may be an important means through which physicians, psychiatrists, nurses, medical social workers, and clergymen can work together. By offering their facilities for teaching purposes, as many are now doing, they can make a notable contribution to better pastoral care in the future.

The Department of Pastoral Services of the Federal Council has broadened its scope to take in the various phases of the work of the pastoral office. This important arm of the federated Church will be instrumental in acquiring and disseminating knowledge in the field of spiritual healing that can be used by the Church better to meet the needs of the people.

The officials of theological seminaries are becoming aware of the possibilities in the pastoral field and are moving in the direction of better training for ministerial students. Clinical pastoral schools will also grow in importance unless theological seminaries and medical schools catch the importance of this development and take over the field. Should that ever occur, it can be said that the schools in clinical pastoral training and care blazed the trail and contributed some of the finest leaders in the field of pastoral work. As this is written, already thirteen major theological seminaries have appointed instructors from the field of clinical pastoral training, and others will follow as soon as instructors are available.

The priestly and prophetic offices of the ministry will always be important in the Church; they were instituted by Jesus and are a part of the holy task of the Church. The pastoral office will take its place of equal importance with these. The trend indicates more specialized ministries in the future. Churches with large memberships which are in a position to have a number of ministers will also have those who are especially adept at pastoral work. In the future these may develop specialized ministries to the sick and older people, and also marriage counseling and youth guidance. Until that practice becomes prevalent, the minister who handles the entire spiritual work of his congregation can help himself by specialized training and reading in the field of religion and health.

Through the development of the pastoral office the Church can be most helpful to its people. Many tragedies and much unhappiness can be averted by the pastor who has the confidence of his people to such an extent that they come to him with their troubles. He can help them to make the blessings of God real in their lives and to find the peace that comes from an intimate association with Christ. Lives will be enriched and healed in the measure in which the individual applies the healing powers of God to his needs and the gospel will continue to be the " good news " Jesus intended it to be.

BIBLIOGRAPHY

BOOKS

Allen, John, *Institutes of the Christian Religion,* by John Calvin. Vols. I and II, Presbyterian Board of Education, Philadelphia, 1813.

Ayer, Joseph Cullen, Jr., *A Source Book for Ancient Church History.* Charles Scribner's Sons, New York, 1913.

Bailes, Frederick W., *Your Mind Can Heal You.* Dodd, Mead & Company, Inc., New York, 1941.

Bettenson, Henry S., *Documents of the Christian Church.* Oxford University Press, New York and London, 1947.

Blakeslee, George H., *China and the Far-East.* Thomas Y. Crowell Company, New York, 1910.

Boisen, Anton T., *Exploration of the Inner World.* Willett, Clark & Company, Chicago, 1937.

Boisen, Anton T., *Problems in Religion and Life.* Abingdon-Cokesbury Press, New York and Nashville, 1946.

Braden, Charles S., *These Also Believe.* The Macmillan Company, New York, 1949.

Brown, Charles R., *The Making of a Minister.* Century Company, New York, 1927.

Brown, N. S., *If the Minister Is to Succeed.* Wm. B. Eerdmans Publishing Co., Grand Rapids, 1937.

Bunting, Rev. John S., *A Religion of Your Own.* Church of the Ascension, St. Louis, 1943.

Bunting, Rev. John S., *The Secret of a Quiet Mind.* Hart Printing Company, St. Louis, n.d.

The Catholic Encyclopedia, by the Universal Knowledge Foundation, Inc., New York. Copyright by the Encyclopedia Press, Inc., 1913.

Cabot, Richard C., and Dicks, Russell L., *The Art of Ministering to the Sick.* The Macmillan Company, New York, 1936.

Clark, Elmer T., *The Small Sects in America.* Abingdon-Cokesbury Press, Nashville, revised edition, 1949.

Clark, Glenn, *A Man's Reach*. Harper & Brothers, New York, 1949.

Clark, Glenn, *How to Find Health Through Prayer*. Harper & Brothers, New York, 1940.

Coulton, G. G., *Life in the Middle Ages,* Vol. I. The University Press, Cambridge, 1928.

Crawford, Marie Caroline, *Romance of Old New England Rooftrees*. L. C. Page & Company, Boston, 1902.

Cushman, Mary Floyd, *Missionary Doctor*. Harper & Brothers, New York, 1944.

Dakin, Edwin Franden, *Mrs. Eddy*. Charles Scribner's Sons, New York, London, 1930.

Dearmer, Percy, *The Parson's Handbook*. Humphrey Milford, London, 1917.

Dearmer, Percy, *Body and Soul*. E. P. Dutton & Co., Inc., New York, 1909.

De Kruif, Paul, *Men Against Death*. Harcourt, Brace and Company, New York, 1932.

Dicks, Russell L., *And Ye Visited Me*. Harper & Brothers, New York, 1939.

Dicks, Russell L., *Comfort Ye My People*. The Macmillan Company, New York, 1947.

Dicks, Russell L., *My Faith Looks Up*. The Westminster Press, Philadelphia, 1949.

Dicks, Russell L., *Pastoral Work and Personal Counseling*. The Macmillan Company, New York, 1949.

Dicks, Russell L., *Thy Health Shall Spring Forth*. The Macmillan Company, New York, 1946.

Dicks, Russell L., *Who Is My Patient?* The Macmillan Company, New York, 1943.

Dodd, Edward M., *How Far to the Nearest Doctor?* Friendship Press, New York, 1933.

Douglas, Lloyd C., *The Minister's Everyday Life*. Charles Scribner's Sons, New York, 1924.

Drake, Durant, *Problems of Religion*. Houghton Mifflin Company, New York, 1916.

Eddy, Mary Baker, *Christian Healing and the People's Idea of God*. Sermons Delivered at Boston. Allison V. Stewart, Boston, 1915.

Eddy, Mary Baker, *Science and Health with Key to the Scriptures*. Allison V. Stewart, Boston, 1917.

Emerson, Ralph Waldo, *Representative Men*. Houghton Mifflin Company, New York, 1876.

Fallows, Samuel, *Health and Happiness*. A. C. McClurg & Co., Chicago, 1908.

Fox, Emmett, *Make Your Life Worth While.* Harper & Brothers, New York, 1946.
Fox, Emmett, *The Sermon on the Mount.* Harper & Brothers, New York, 1949.
Franklin, James H., *Ministers of Mercy.* Interchurch Press, New York, 1919.
Garrett, Annette, *Interviewing, Its Principles and Methods.* Family Welfare Association of America, New York, 1944.
Garrison, Winfred Ernest, *The March of Faith.* Harper & Brothers, New York, 1933.
Goodnow, Minnie, *Outlines of Nursing History.* W. B. Saunders Company, Philadelphia, 1940.
Gordon, Benjamin Lee, *The Romance of Medicine.* F. A. Davis Company, Philadelphia, 1944.
Grinker, Roy R., and Spiegel, J. P., *Men Under Stress.* The Blakiston Company, Philadelphia, 1945.
Guthrie, Douglas, *A History of Medicine.* J. B. Lippincott Company, Philadelphia, 1946.
Haggard, Howard W., *Devils, Drugs, and Doctors.* Halcyon House, New York, 1929.
Haggard, Howard W., *The Doctor in History.* Yale University Press, New Haven, 1934.
Haggard, Howard W., *Mystery, Magic, and Medicine.* Doubleday, Doran & Company, Inc., Garden City, 1933.
Harkness, Georgia, *John Calvin.* Henry Holt and Company, Inc., New York, 1931.
Hiltner, Seward, *Clinical Pastoral Training.* Commission on Religion and Health, Federal Council of the Churches of Christ in America, New York, 1945.
Hiltner, Seward, *Pastoral Counseling.* Abingdon-Cokesbury Press, New York, 1949.
Hiltner, Seward, *Religion and Health.* The Macmillan Company, New York, 1943.
Hocking, William Ernest, *Re-Thinking Missions,* A Laymen's Inquiry After One Hundred Years. Harper & Brothers, New York, 1932.
Holman, Charles T., *Getting Down to Cases.* The Macmillan Company, New York, 1942.
Hume, Edward H., *Doctors East, Doctors West.* W. W. Norton & Company, Inc., New York, 1946.
Interpretative Statistical Survey of the World Mission of the Christian Church, Summary and Detailed Statistics of Churches and Missionary Societies, Interpretative Articles and Indices. Edited

by Joseph I. Parker. International Missionary Council, New York and London, 1938.

Jamieson and Sewall, *Trends in Nursing History*. W. B. Saunders Company, Philadelphia, 1941.

Jones, Rufus M., *The Story of George Fox*. The Macmillan Company, New York, 1919.

Keeler, Floyd, *Catholic Medical Missions*. The Macmillan Company, New York, 1925.

Kemp, Charles F., *Physicians of the Soul*. The Macmillan Company, New York, 1947.

Kleist, James A., Editor and Translator, *Ancient Christian Writers*. Newman Press, Westminster, Maryland, 1948.

Latourette, Kenneth Scott, *Missions Tomorrow*. Harper & Brothers, New York, 1936.

Lee, Umphrey, *John Wesley and Modern Religion*. Abingdon-Cokesbury Press, Nashville, 1936.

Maclaren, Ian, *The Cure of Souls*. George H. Doran, New York, 1896.

Major, Ralph H., *Faiths That Healed*. D. Appleton-Century Company, Inc., New York, 1940.

Marr, George S., *Christianity and the Cure of Disease*. H. R. Allenson, Ltd., London.

Maves, Paul B., and Cedarleaf, J. L., *Older People and the Church*. Abingdon-Cokesbury Press, Nashville, 1949.

McConnell, Francis J., *John Wesley*. Abingdon Press, New York, 1939.

McGiffert, Arthur Cushman, *Protestant Thought Before Kant*. Charles Scribner's Sons, New York, 1922.

McHugh, J. A., and Callan, Charles J., *Catechism of the Council of Trent for Parish Priests*. Joseph F. Wagner, Inc., New York, 1934.

McKown, Edgar M., and Scherzer, Carl J., *Understanding Christianity,* Ronald Press, New York, 1949.

McNeill, John T., *Christian Hope for World Society*. Willett, Clark & Company, Chicago, New York, 1937.

Mergner, Sister Julie, *The Deaconess and Her Work*. Translated by Mrs. Adolph Spaeth. General Council Publication House, Philadelphia, 1915.

Meyer, Frederick, *Deaconesses and Their Calling*. Translated by Emma A. Endlich. George Brumder, Milwaukee, 1878.

Mode, Peter G., *The Frontier Spirit in American Christianity*. The Macmillan Company, New York, 1936.

Nutting, M. Adelaide, and Dock, Lavina L., *A History of Nursing*.

G. P. Putnam's Sons, New York, 1935.

Oliver, Edmund H., *The Social Achievements of the Christian Church*. Board of Evangelism and Social Service of the United Church of Canada, Toronto, 1930.

Paetow, Louis J., *The Crusaders and Other Historical Essays*. F. S. Crofts & Co., New York, 1928.

Palmer, Albert W., *How Religion Helps*. The Macmillan Company, New York, 1949.

Parker, Percy Livingston, *The Heart of John Wesley's Journal*. Fleming H. Revell Company, London and Edinburgh, n.d.

Penrose, Valeria Fullerton, *Opportunities in the Path of the Great Physician*. The Westminster Press, Philadelphia, 1902.

Petry, Ray C., *No Uncertain Sound*. The Westminster Press, Philadelphia, 1948.

Powell, Lyman P., *The Emmanuel Movement in a New England Town*. G. P. Putnam's Sons, New York and London, 1909.

Roberts, Rev. Alexander, and Donaldson, James, *Clementine and Apostolic Constitutions*. T. and T. Clark, Edinburgh, 1870.

Roberts, Rev. Alexander, and Donaldson, James, *The Writings of Irenaeus*. T. and T. Clark, Edinburgh, 1868.

Roberts, Rev. Alexander, and Donaldson, James, *The Writings of Origen*. T. and T. Clark, Edinburgh, 1869.

Roberts, Oral, *If You Need Healing — Do These Things!* Standard Printing Company, Tulsa, 1948.

Schaefer, Theodor, *Im Dienste der Liebe*. Gütersloh, Germany, 1896.

Schaefer, Theodor, *Zur Erinnerung an die Diakonissen-Einsegnung,* Gütersloh, Germany, 1904.

Schaff, Philip, and Wace, Henry, *The Nicene and Post-Nicene Fathers*, Vols. III and VIII. The Christian Literature Company, Oxford and London, 1892.

The New Schaff Herzog Encyclopedia of Religious Knowledge. Funk & Wagnalls Company, New York, 1908.

Scherzer, Carl J., *Meditations for the Sick*. Abingdon-Cokesbury Press, New York, 1945.

Schweitzer, Albert, *African Notebook*. Henry Holt and Company, Inc., New York, 1939.

Seabrook, W. B., *The Magic Island*. The Literary Guild of America, New York, 1929.

Seagrave, Gordon S., *Burma Surgeon Returns*. W. W. Norton & Company, Inc., New York, 1946.

Seagrave, Gordon S., *Waste-Basket Surgery*. The Judson Press, Philadelphia, 1930.

Silver Anniversary Program, American Protestant Hospital Association, Herman L. Fritschel. 1946.

Simpson, Henry Jerome, *Pastoral Care of Nervous People.* More-house-Gorham Company, Inc., New York, 1945.

Smith, Roy L., *The Revolution in Christian Missions.* Abingdon-Cokesbury Press, New York and Nashville, 1941.

Spalding, John Howard, *The Kingdom of Heaven, as Seen by Swedenborg.* E. P. Dutton & Co., Inc., New York, 1916.

Stetson, Augusta E., *Reminiscences, Sermons and Correspondence.* Proving Adherence to the Principle of Christian Science as Taught by Mary Baker Eddy. G. P. Putnam's Sons, New York and London, 1913.

Stolz, Karl Ruf, *The Church and Psychotherapy.* Abingdon-Cokesbury Press, New York, 1943.

Taylor, Henry Osborn, *The Mediaeval Mind,* Vols. I and II. The Macmillan Company, New York, 1919.

Taylor, John M., *The Witchcraft Delusion in Colonial Connecticut.* The Grafton Press, New York, 1908.

Thomas, Henry and Dana Lee, *Living Biographies of Religious Leaders.* The Garden City Publishing Co., Inc., Garden City, 1942.

They Caught the Torch. Published by Will Ross, Inc., Milwaukee.

Uhlhorn, Gerhard, *Christian Charity in the Ancient Church.* Charles Scribner's Sons, New York, 1883.

Uhlhorn, Gerhard, *The Conflict of Christianity with Heathenism.* Translated by Egbert C. Smyth and C. J. H. Ropes. Charles Scribner's Sons. New York, 1888.

Uhlhorn, G., *Die Christliche Liebesthätigheit.* Verlag von D. Gundert, Stuttgart, 1895.

Umberg, Johannes Bapt., S. J., *Denzinger, Enchiridion Symbolorum, Definitionum et Declarationum de Rebus Fidei et Morum.* Editio 21–23 Friburgi Brisgoviae, Herder and Co., Typographi Editores Pontificii, 1937.

Walker, Williston, *The History of the Christian Church.* Charles Scribner's Sons, New York, 1920.

Walker, Williston, *Great Men of the Christian Church.* The University of Chicago Press, 1928.

Walker, Williston, *John Calvin.* G. P. Putnam Sons, New York and London, 1909.

Wilbur, Sibyl, *The Life of Mary Baker Eddy.* Concord Publishing Company, New York, 1908.

Wise, Carroll A., *Religion in Illness and Health.* Harper & Brothers, New York, 1942.

Worcester, Elwood, and McComb, Samuel, *Body, Mind, and Spirit.* Marshall Jones Co., Boston, 1931.

Worcester, Elwood, *Life's Adventure*. Charles Scribner's Sons, New York, 1932.

Worcester, McComb, and Coriat, *Religion and Medicine*. Moffatt, Yard and Co., New York, 1908.

World Mission of the Church, Findings and Recommendations of the International Missionary Council, Tamboram, Madras, 1938.

Wright, F. A., *Fathers of the Church*. George Routledge and Sons, Ltd., London, 1928.

Wright, F. A., *Select Letters of Jerome*. Translated. G. P. Putnam's Sons, New York, 1937.

PAMPHLETS

Administrators Reference Book, Rev. Harold Peters Schultz and Mr. E. I. Erickson. American Protestant Hospital Association, 1945.

American Protestant Hospital Association Bulletin, Albert G. Hahn, editor. Vol. IV, No. 7. Evansville, Indiana. January, 1940.

Annual directory number of *Hospital Progress*. Vol. XXIX, No. 10A. St. Louis, Missouri.

Camps Farthest Out, The. Macalester Park Publishing Company, St. Paul, 1949.

Christian Eschatology and Social Thought, Ray C. Petry. Reprinted from *Theology Today*, July, 1948.

Clear Horizons, Glenn Clark, editor. St. Paul.

Committee on Religion and Medicine of the Federal Council of Churches of Christ in America and the New York Academy of Medicine, The History of the, Helen Van Voast and Ethel P. S. Hoyt. 1923–1936.

Counseling Viewpoint, A, Carl R. Rogers. Commission on Religion and Health, Federal Council of the Churches of Christ in America, New York, May, 1945.

Divine Mission of Joseph Smith, The, John A. Widsoe. Zions Printing and Publishing Company, Independence, Missouri.

Drift of the Times, The. Gospel Missionary Union, East Seventh Street, Kansas City.

Ecclesiastical Review, The. August, 1927, Vol. LXXVII, Nos. 2, 3, and 4. The Dolphin Press, Philadelphia.

Federal Council Bulletin, The, Paul B. Maves. New York, May, 1949.

Federal Council of the Churches of Christ in America, Committee of Religion and Health, The. New York, 1939.

Healing, Keith L. Brooks. American Prophetic League, Inc., Box 13B, Eagle Rock Stations, Los Angeles.

Healing Waters, Oral Roberts. Tampa, Florida, issue, 1949.

His Protecting Spirit. Unity School of Christianity, Kansas City.

If Bereavement Comes, Charles T. Holman. Federal Council of Churches and United Council of Church Women, New York, September, 1945.

Information Service, Benson Y. Landis. Department of Research and Education, Federal Council of Churches, New York, 1944.

Journal of Pastoral Care, The. The Institute of Pastoral Care, Cambridge, Massachusetts.

Medical Mission Sisters. Philadelphia.

Methodist Hospitals and Homes, Eighth Annual Report of the Board of Hospitals and Homes of the Methodist Church, Karl P. Meister. Chicago, 1949.

Modern Tongues Movement, Louis S. Baumann. Long Beach, California, 1930.

Non-Medical Missionary, The, Sister Alma Julia, S.C.M.M., Ph.G., M.T. Reprinted from *The Medical Missionary,* 1937.

Nursing by Religious Orders in the United States, Part I, Ann Doyle, R.N. Reprinted from *The American Journal of Nursing,* Vol. XXIX, No. 7, July, 1929.

Nursing by Religious Orders in the United States, Part II, 1841–1870, Ann Doyle, R.N. Reprinted from *The American Journal of Nursing,* Vol. XXIX, No. 8, August, 1929.

Nursing by Religious Orders in the United States, Part III, 1871–1928, Ann Doyle, R.N. Reprinted from *The American Journal of Nursing,* Vol. XXIX, No. 9, September, 1929.

Nursing by Religious Orders in the United States, Part V, Deaconesses, 1855–1928, Ann Doyle, R.N. Reprinted from *The American Journal of Nursing,* Vol. XXIX, No. 11, November, 1929.

Nursing by Religious Orders in the United States, Part VI, Episcopal Sisterhoods, 1845–1928, Ann Doyle, R.N. Reprinted from *The American Journal of Nursing,* Vol. XXIX, No. 12, December, 1929.

Reading in Religion and Health, Seward Hiltner. Federal Council of Churches, New York, April, 1945.

Religion and Health, 1937–1947, Commission on Religion and Health, Federal Council of Churches, New York.

Religion and Health, Seward Hiltner. Federal Council of Churches, New York, Summer, 1946. Reprinted from *The American Scholar.*

Religion and Health, Ethel P. S. Hoyt. Commission on Religion and Health, Federal Council of Churches, New York, 1942.

Report on the Clergy-Physician Relationship in Protestant Hospitals. American Protestant Hospital Association, 1942.

Report of the Religious Work in the Protestant Hospitals. American

Protestant Hospital Association, 1941.

Sisterhoods of Southern Indiana. Marianist Vocation Service, Dayton, Ohio.

Sisters of Charity of St. Vincent de Paul, The. Marillac Seminary, Normandy, Missouri.

So-called "Unity" Movement, The. Gospel Union Publishing Company, East Seventh Street, Kansas City.

Spirit of Truth and the Spirit of Error, The, Keith L. Brooks. The Christian Fundamentals League, Los Angeles.

Spirit Manifestations and "The Gift of Tongues," Sir Robert Anderson, K.C.B., LL.D. Publication Office *Our Hope,* New York, 1921.

Strength in Our Sickness, Everett B. Lesher. Federal Council of Churches, New York, March, 1947.

Why a Mission Sister?, Rev. M. D. Forrest, M.S.C. Radio Replies Press, 1946.

NOTES

[1] Jamieson and Sewall, *Trends in Nursing History*, pp. 105–107. W. B. Saunders Company, Philadelphia, 1941.

[2] *Select Letters of Jerome,* translated by F. A. Wright, p. 309. G. P. Putnam's Sons, New York, 1937.

[3] Adapted from Bede, *Ecclesiastical History of England,* J. A. Giles, editor. London, 1847.

[4] Taylor, Henry Osborn, *The Mediaeval Mind,* Vol. I, p. 559. The Macmillan Company, New York, 1919.

[5] Adapted from V. L. von Seckendorff, *Ausführliche Historie des Lutherthums.* Leipzig, 1882.

[6] From Luther's *Tisch-Reden,* Chapter 14, freely translated by the author.

[7] From Luther's *Haus Postil,* freely translated by the author.

[8] Adapted from P. J. Bacci, *Life of St. Philip Neri,* tr. by F. Antrobus.

[9] Adapted from St. Francis de Xavier, by Jos. Marie Cros.

[10] Major, Ralph H., M.D., *Faiths That Healed,* pp. 234, 235. D. Appleton-Century Company, Inc., New York, 1940.

[11] From *The Deaconess and Her Work,* tr. by Mrs. Adolph Spaeth, p. 25. General Council Publication House, Philadelphia, 1915.

[12] Goodnow, Minnie, R.N., *Outlines of Nursing History,* p. 67. W. B. Saunders Company, Philadelphia, 1940.

[13] Parker, Percy Livingston, editor, *The Heart of John Wesley's Journal,* p. 43. Fleming H. Revell Company, London and Edinburgh, n.d.

[14] *Ibid.,* p. 75.

[15] *Ibid.,* p. 126.

[16] *Ibid.,* p. 146.

[17] Meyer, Frederick, *Deaconesses and Their Calling,* tr. by Emma A. Endlich. George Brumder, Milwaukee, 1878.

[18] From Rev. Granger Westberg, chaplain of Augustana Hospital, Chicago, Illinois.

[19] Meister, Karl P., *Annual Report,* 1949, Board of Hospitals and Homes of the Methodist Church, Chicago.

[20] *1949 Year Book, Evangelical and Reformed Church,* p. 50.

[21] From the *Second Annual Report of the Presbyterian Hospital in the City of New York,* 1870, p. 28. Supplied by Dr. William Barrow Pugh.

[22] From the Presbyterian Hospital in Philadelphia, *History, Charter, and By-Laws,* 1871, pp. 9, 10, 13, 14. Supplied by Dr. William Barrow Pugh.

[23] From the *Nineteenth Annual Report of the Presbyterian Hospital of Pittsburgh, 1914.* Supplied by Dr. William Barrow Pugh.

[24] From personal correspondence with Chaplain Richard K. Young, of the North Carolina Baptist Hospital, Inc., Winston-Salem.

[25] This statistical information supplied by Dr. Albert G. Hahn, executive director of the American Protestant Hospital Association.

[26] Annual Directory Number of *Hospital Progress,* A Journal of Hospital Science and Nursing Education, Vol. XXIX, No. 10A, p. 2. Catholic Hospital Association of the United States and Canada.

[27] *The Ecclesiastical Review,* Vol. LXXVII, No. 4, October, 1927, p. 369. Published by American Ecclesiastical Review, The Dolphin Press, Lancaster, Pennsylvania.

[28] Mode, Peter G., *The Frontier Spirit in American Christianity,* p. 79. The Macmillan Company, New York, 1923.

[29] *The Literary Digest,* August 6, 1932.

[30] Wilbur, Sibyl, *Life of Mary Baker Eddy,* p. 87. Concord Publishing Company, New York, 1908.

[31] Eddy, Mary Baker, *Science and Health with Key to the Scriptures,* p. 107. Allison V. Stewart, Boston, 1917.

[32] Bach, Marcus, *They Have Found a Faith,* pp. 222–253. The Bobbs-Merrill Company, Indianapolis and New York, 1946.

[33] *Metaphysical Bible Dictionary.* Unity School of Christianity, Kansas City, 1944.

[34] *Good Business,* a Unity publication, pp. 24, 25. Silent Unity, Kansas City, January, 1943.

[35] Worcester, McComb, and Coriat, *Religion and Medicine,* p. 13. Moffatt, Yard and Company, New York, 1908.

[36] Worcester and McComb, *Body, Mind and Spirit,* p. 109. Marshall Jones Company, Boston, 1931.

[37] From information supplied by Rev. Robert G. Metters, rector of Emmanuel Church, Boston.

[38] *Ibid.*

[39] Fallows, Samuel, *Health and Happiness,* pp. 241–274. A. C. McClurg & Co., Chicago, 1908.

[40] Powell, Lyman P., *The Emmanuel Movement in a New England Town*. G. P. Putnam's Sons, New York, 1909.

[41] Grinker, Ray R., and Spiegel, John P., *Men Under Stress*. The Blakiston Company, Philadelphia, 1945.

[42] Keeler, Floyd, *Catholic Medical Missions*, p. 17. The Macmillan Company, New York, 1925.

[43] *Ibid.*, p. 97.

[44] Smith, Roy L., *The Revolution in Christian Missions*. Abingdon-Cokesbury Press, New York and Nashville, 1941.

[45] *Interpretive Statistical Survey of the World Mission of the Christian Church,* Summary and Detailed Statistics of Churches and Missionary Societies, Interpretive Articles and Indices. Edited by Joseph I. Parker, pp. 255, 256. International Missionary Council, New York and London, 1938.

[46] Seagrave, Gordon S., *Burma Surgeon Returns*. W. W. Norton & Company, Inc., New York, 1946.

[47] *The Journal of the Christian Medical Association of India, Burma and Ceylon*. May and Baker, Ltd., India, 1947.

[48] *Ibid.*, Vol. XXII, July–September, 1947, No. 45, p. 199.

[49] Hocking, William Ernest, Chairman, *Re-Thinking Missions,* A Laymen's Inquiry After One Hundred Years. Harper & Brothers, New York, 1932.

[50] *The World Mission of the Church,* Findings and Recommendations of the International Missionary Council, p. 79. Tamboram, Madras, 1938.

[51] Clark, Glenn, *A Man's Reach*. Harper & Brothers, New York, 1949.

[52] Clark, Glenn, *How to Find Health Through Prayer*, p. 9. Harper & Brothers, New York, 1940.

[53] *Ibid.*, p. 17.

[54] *Ibid.*, p. 79.

[55] *Ibid.*, p. 106.

[56] Clark, Glenn, *Correspondence Course in Spiritual Healing*. Macalester Park Publishing Company, St. Paul, Minnesota.

[57] *Fellowship of St. Luke,* John Gayner Banks. San Diego, California.

[58] *Sharing,* A Journal of Christian Healing, John Gayner Banks. San Diego, California.

[59] From personal correspondence with the author.

[60] Clark, Elmer T., *The Small Sects in America*, p. 25. Abingdon-Cokesbury Press, Nashville, 1937.

[61] *Ibid.*, pp. 26–29.

[62] *Evansville Press,* March 18, 1949.

[63] *Ibid.*

[64] Roberts, Oral, *If You Need Healing — Do These Things!*, p. 8. Standard Printing Company, Tulsa, 1948.

[65] *Ibid.*, p. 28.

[66] *The History of the Committee on Religion and Medicine of the Federal Council of the Churches of Christ in America and the New York Academy of Medicine, 1923–1936*, p. 4, Helen Van Voast and Ethel P. S. Hoyt.

[67] From correspondence with Dean John W. Suter, Washington Cathedral, Mount Saint Alban, Washington, D. C.

[68] *Religion and Health, Ten Years of Progress, 1937–1947*, p. 13. Federal Council of the Churches of Christ in America, New York.

[69] See Chapter XVII.

[70] Fritschel, Herman L., *American Protestant Hospital Association, Silver Anniversary Program*, A Retrospect Over Twenty-five Years. 1946.

[71] Hahn, Albert G., editor, *American Protestant Hospital Association Bulletin*, Vol. IV, No. 7, January, 1940.

[72] Dicks, Russell L., *Standards for the Work of the Chaplain in the General Hospital*. Reprinted from *Hospital*, November, 1940.

[73] Dicks, Russell L., *And Ye Visited Me*. Harper & Brothers, New York, 1939.

[74] *Report of the Clergy-Physician Relationship in Protestant Hospitals*. American Protestant Hospital Association, 1942.

[75] *Religious Work in Protestant Hospitals*, compiled by Harold P. Schultz and Albert G. Hahn. Evansville, Indiana, 1945.

[76] Dicks, Russell L., *Who Is My Patient?* The Macmillan Company, New York, 1943.

[77] McKown, Edgar M., and Scherzer, Carl J., *Understanding Christianity*. The Ronald Press, New York, 1949.

INDEX

Aesculapius, 23, 31, 35
American Hospital Assn., 235
American Medical Assn., 146
American Prot. Hosp. Assn., 131, 226, 235 ff., 255
Anne, Queen, 90 f.
Anointing, 35 ff., 84, 202, 207, 213, 214
Apostolic Constitutions, 36, 40
Ascetics, 34, 43

Banks, John Gayner, 202
Barbers, 49, 65 f.
Beaupré, St. Anne de, 141
Bezoar stone, 75
Black Death, 63 f.
Blumhardt, Pastor, 142 f.
Boisen, Anton T., 229 ff., 243
Bracelli, Virginia, 110 f.
Bread, 36, 45
Burns, James H., 241

Cabot, Richard C., 171, 174, 220, 231, 234 f.
Calvin, John, 63, 70 ff.
Catholic Hospital Assn., 134
Celibacy, 34
Chaplains' Association, 236, 240
Children of the Light, 92
Church
    Anglican, 88, 90, 175, 191
    Assemblies of God, 209
    Baptist, 91, 131, 191, 244
    Christian Science, Ch. X, 164, 169, 175, 182
    Congregational, 189

English Lutheran, 121
Episcopal, 87 f., 125 f., 205
Evangelical, 120, 127, 191
Evangelical and Reformed, 127, 191
Foursquare Gospel, 211 f.
Freewill Baptist, 209
Friends, 94, 120, 191
Holiness, 207, 209, 212
Lutheran, 102, 120, 123 ff., 142, 191
    Augustana Synod, 124
    Iowa Synod, 122
Mennonite, 117, 128
Methodist, 106, 120, 126 f., 191, 207, 226
Moravian, 105, 191
New Thought, 160 ff., 165
Orthodox, 84
Pentecostal, 207, 212
Presbyterian, 129, 191
Puritan, 91
Reformed, 102, 105, 191
Salvation Army, 131
Seventh Day Adventist, 131
Shakers, 144 f.
Swedenborgian, 161
Ciudad, Juan, 109 f.
Clark, Glenn, 196 ff.
Clinical pastoral training, 229 ff.
Confession, 57 f., 68, 71 f., 85, 203
Conversion, 203
Coriat, Isador, 169, 171, 175
Council for Clinical Training, 223, 233
Crusades, 49, 52 ff.

Dancing mania, 64 f.
David, Father, 132
David, Little, 212 f.
Deaconesses, 29, 40 ff., 70, 71, 102, 105, 118, 126
Demons, 26, 28, 37, 64, 67, 88, 96
Dentistry, 74
Department of Pastoral Services, 219, 255
Diaconate, 28 f., 70, 101, 115
Dicks, Russell L., 224, 231–236
Divine, Father, 210 f.
Dresser, Julius, 153, 161
Dunbar, Helen Flanders, 221, 222, 231, 232

Evans, Warren F., 153, 161
Extreme unction, 85 f.

Fabiola, 43 f.
Fairbanks, Rollin J., 241
Fallows, Samuel, 181
Federal Council of Churches, 219, 239
Fellowship of St. Luke, 202 ff.
Fillmore, Mr. and Mrs. Charles, 164 ff.
Fliedner, Pastor Theodor, 117 f.
Fox, George, 91 ff.
French Academy of Science, 146

Galen, 32 f., 48, 66, 80
Greatrakes, 90
Guiles, A. Philip, 227

Handkerchiefs, 39, 213
Harvey, William, 33, 97
Herbs, 32, 33, 48
Hiltner, Seward, 223–228
Hippocrates, 25, 31, 254
Holy Communion, 37 f., 43, 70, 203
Holy Ghost, 37
Hospitals, 45, 49, Ch. VIII
Hôtel-Dieu, 73, 75, 83
Huguenots, 73
Hygieia, 23

Incubation, 51
Institute of Pastoral Care, Inc., 241
Irenaeus, 35

James, King, 96, 97
Jenner, 146

Kaiserswerth institutions, 116, 125
King's Evil, 88 ff.

Lambert le Begue, 56
Lankenau, John D., 123
Laying on of hands, 202, 213
Lazarus, 54, 82
Lee, Ann, 144
Liége, Council of, 58
Lister, 146
London Missionary Society, 188
Lourdes, 135
Loyola, 80
Luther, Martin, 63, 67 ff., 101, 188

Macrina, 45
Martyr, Justin, 35
Materia Medica, 32
McComb, Samuel, 169 ff., 219
McPherson, Aimee Semple, 211 f.
Medicine, 32, 38, 72, 109, 145 f., 178, 210
Mementos, 51
Mental hygiene, 157, 249
Miracles, 26, 28, 51, 172
Monasteries, 48, 49, 101 f.

New York Academy of Medicine, 220
Nightingale, Florence, 118, 132, 146
Nurses, 45 f., 104 f., 190 f.
Nurses' education, 120, 146, 193, 194

Oates, Wayne E., 242 ff.
Oil, 35, 84, 202
Orders (male), 49, 54, 56, 57, 77 f., 80, 110, 205
Origen, 57, 84 f.

Panakeia, 23
Paracelsus, 63, 66

Paré, Ambroise, 72 ff.
Passavant, W. A., 121 f.
Pasteur, 146
Pastoral office, 68, 72, 103, 106, 225, 250 ff., 255 f.
Paula, 44 f.
Penance, 57 f.
Peter the Hermit, 53
Physicians, 25, 45, 46, 64, 72, 74, 143, 157, 171, 190
Pliny, 32
Pope, 49, 59, 78, 95, 110, 187
Powell, Lyman P., 181 f.
Pratt, Joseph H., 173
Private confession, 57 f.

Quimby, Phineas P., 148 f., 153, 160 f.

Relics, 38 f., 51, 53, 72, 84, 253
Roberts, Oral, 213 f.
Roman Catholic missionaries, 81, 186

Sacraments, 36, 38, 43, 69
Saint
  Andrew, 166
  Anne, 141
  Anthony, 56
  Basil, 45 f., 57
  Bede, 85
  Benedict of Nursia, 56
  Catherine of Siena, 51
  Ephraem, 46
  Francis Xavier, 80 f., 186
  James, 35 f., 166
  Jerome, 44
  John of Beverly, 49 ff.
  John of God, 109
  Louis, 53

Luke, 25 f., 205
Mark, 35
Martin of Tours, 36
Mary, 55
Michael, 50
Paul, 26, 34, 37 f.
Peter, 28, 34, 166
Philip Neri, 77 ff.
Theodore, 37
Timothy, 29
Vincent de Paul, 82, 132
Vitus, 65
Saliva, 26
Schweitzer, Albert, 185
Seagrave, Gordon S., 193
Seton, Mother Elizabeth Ann, 132
Shrines, 39, 52, 70, 72, 84, 88, 253
Sieveking, Miss Amalie, 116
Sisterhoods, 57, 73, 82, 110, 120, 132, 187
Surgery, 22, 33, 38, 46, 49, 65, 72, 79, 157, 176, 200

Tertullian, 36
Trent, Council of, 85 f.

Vesalius, 63, 79 f.
Veterans' Administration, 247
Virgin, 41, 43

Water, 36, 50, 72
Wesley, John, 106 ff.
Widows, 41, 42
Witches, 65, 94 ff.
Witches Hammer, The, 96
Worcester, Elwood, 169, 219, 233

Xenodochium, 45

Zwingli, 63, 69 f.

DATE DUE